History Of The Corporation Of Birmingham: With A Sketch Of The Earlier Government Of The Town...

John Thackray Bunce, Charles Anthony Vince

Nabu Public Domain Reprints:

You are holding a reproduction of an original work published before 1923 that is in the public domain in the United States of America, and possibly other countries. You may freely copy and distribute this work as no entity (individual or corporate) has a copyright on the body of the work. This book may contain prior copyright references, and library stamps (as most of these works were scanned from library copies). These have been scanned and retained as part of the historical artifact.

This book may have occasional imperfections such as missing or blurred pages, poor pictures, errant marks, etc. that were either part of the original artifact, or were introduced by the scanning process. We believe this work is culturally important, and despite the imperfections, have elected to bring it back into print as part of our continuing commitment to the preservation of printed works worldwide. We appreciate your understanding of the imperfections in the preservation process, and hope you enjoy this valuable book.

CO
(Birmingham
Bynce

HISTORY

OF THE

CORPORATION OF BIRMINGHAM;

WITH

A SKETCH OF THE EARLIER GOVERNMENT OF
THE TOWN.

BY

JOHN THACKRAY BUNCE, F.S.S.,

AUTHOR OF A
"*History of The Birmingham General Hospital and the Musical Festivals.*"

VOL. I.

PUBLISHED FOR THE CORPORATION,
BY CORNISH BROTHERS, 37, NEW STREET, BIRMINGHAM.
1878.

[*All rights reserved.*]

INTRODUCTORY NOTE.

The origin and intention of this volume are explained by the following Minute of the Town Council of Birmingham, passed at a Council Meeting held on the 11th of January, 1876, Joseph Chamberlain, Esq., Mayor, in the chair—"That the General Purposes Committee be instructed to prepare and publish a History of the Proceedings of the Corporation of this Borough, from the grant of the Charter of Incorporation, in 1838, to the present time, to be continued annually; and that the said Committee be authorised to retain and employ such assistance for that purpose as they may deem necessary or advisable."

At a meeting of the General Purposes Committee, held on the 24th January, 1876, Mr. Alderman Lloyd in the chair, it was resolved—"That the Mayor and Chairman be requested to invite Mr. J. T. Bunce to undertake to edit the proposed History of the Proceedings of the Corporation authorised to be prepared by Council Minute 10,212."

At a meeting of the General Purposes Committee, held December 11th, 1877, Mr. Alderman Kenrick

(Mayor of Birmingham), Mr. Alderman Baker (Deputy Mayor), and Mr. Alderman Chamberlain, M.P., were appointed a Sub-Committee to supervise the publication of the History of the Corporation.

It has been thought desirable to expand in some degree the original plan of the Work, and to include an account of the earlier local government of Birmingham, previously to the establishment of the Corporation. This change of arrangement, and the consequent research required, has necessarily delayed the publication; and has rendered it advisable to issue it in two volumes. The first volume, now published, contains an Introductory Sketch of the History of our Local Government from the earliest known period, and a fuller account of the history and proceedings of the Corporation to the close of the year 1851, when the various governing authorities within the Borough were finally consolidated, and when their powers were transferred to the Corporation, which thenceforward became the sole governing authority of the Borough. The second volume will continue the general history of the proceedings of the Corporation from the beginning of 1852 to the close of 1878, and will also contain a more detailed account of the work of the Corporation in its several departments. To that volume an index to the complete Work will be appended; and, if it is found possible, illustrative Maps and Plans will be included.

The Writer of the History has now to express a hope that his Work may not be found unsatisfactory to those by whom it was commissioned, or unacceptable to the town. He has endeavoured to the extent of his ability to fulfil the honourable trust reposed in him, and with this desire he has spared neither time nor labour. In extenuation of omissions or errors that may be discovered—and he cannot but anticipate that such will be observed—he must plead the complexity of the work, and the difficulty of arranging and reducing to order the vast mass of materials which the nature of his task required him to examine. He has but to add that he will regard as an obligation any communication that may enable him to correct or to supply, in the second volume, whatever errors or defects may be discovered in the portion of the Work now issued.

J. T. B.

BIRMINGHAM,
    May 18th, 1878.

TABLE OF CONTENTS.

CHAPTER I.

Early Government of Birmingham.

Antiquity of the Town—Saxon Origin—Domesday Book—General Development of Local Government in England—Early Government in Birmingham—Justices—Court Leet—Churchwardens—Powers and Officers of the Leet—Charge to the Leet Jury—Duties of Officers—Extracts from Court Rolls—Hutton's Account of the Leet—Bailiff's Feast—Party Contests in the Leet—Legal Proceedings on Elections of Bailiffs and Summoning of Jury—Trials in 1722 and 1792—Resistance to Usurpations of the Lord of the Manor—pp. 1—20.

CHAPTER II.

Gild of the Holy Cross.

Origin and Character of Gilds—Religious Gilds—Craft Gilds—Town Gilds or Gilds Merchant—The Birmingham Gild peculiar in its Constitution—Mr. Toulmin Smith's Account of it—Founders of the Gild—Members—Purposes—Endowments—Grant of Charter to the Gild—The Gild a Town Association—Its Common Seal—Officers and Gild Hall—Report of King's Commissioners on the Gild (Henry VIII.)—Their Explanation of the Gild Work—Its Income and Outlay—Church Plate belonging to it—Pensioners—Repair of Roads and Bridges—Establishment of Grammar School upon the Ruins of the Gild—Lench's Trust an Offshoot from the Gild—pp. 21—31.

CHAPTER III.

FIRST PROPOSAL OF INCORPORATION.

Hutton's Account of Local Government—Petition to George the First for a Charter (1716)—Failure of the Petition—Hutton's Comments upon it—His Estimates of Population, and Calculations of its probable Growth—Hutton's fanciful Conjectures and actual Errors—His just View of the Disadvantages of a Charter—Birmingham a Free Town—Restrictions imposed by then existing Charters — Advantages to Birmingham of thorough Freedom from Restrictions—Hutton's generous Testimony to Birmingham—State of the Town in 1716—Riots—Consequent Desire for a stronger Local Government—Final Acquiescence in then existing Institutions—No further Movement for Half a Century—pp. 32—38.

CHAPTER IV.

BIRMINGHAM IN THE EIGHTEENTH CENTURY.

Bradford's Plan of the Town, the first published (1751)—Westley's "Prospect" (1731)—Description of Bradford's Plan—Names of then existing Streets—Number of Houses and Inhabitants in each Street—Bradford's Account of Birmingham—Arrangement and Extent of the Town — Character of the Buildings — Hutton's Description of the Streets—Neglect of the Local Authorities—Encroachments of the Lord of the Manor—State of the Town in 1768—Increase of Population—Sanitary Defects—State of the Roads—the Carriers; their Complaints—The Postal Service—Banks and Library—Social Conditions and Life of the Town—Advertisements of Houses—Mode of Life amongst the Manufacturers—Dr. Alexander Carlyle's Visit to Birmingham (1760)—His Account of Mr. Samuel Garbett—His Visit to Baskerville—Baskerville's "First Kitchen"—His Folio Bible—Sketchley and Adams's Directory (1770)—Trades of the Town—Notes on Particular Trades—Rating and Rentals (1782-1787)—Overseers' Assessments—Examples of Rating—Hutton's Objections to the Rating of Small

CHAPTER V.

ESTABLISHMENT OF STREET COMMISSIONERS—FIRST REGULAR LOCAL GOVERNMENT.

Hutton on the Humility of Birmingham Institutions—Proposed Application to Parliament for Local Governing Powers (1765)—Movement Postponed—Renewed in 1768—Hutton's Opposition to it—His Confession of a Self-interested Motive—His Subsequent Conversion, also on the Ground of Self-interest—General Opposition to the Proposed Act—Arguments for and against it—Assertion that Street Lamps promote Robberies—Proposal to Build more Churches instead of Rating the Town for Sanitary Purposes—The Street Act passed (1769)—State of the Town described in the Preamble—Names of the First Commissioners—Powers of the Act—The Second Act (1773)—Names of Additional Commissioners—Provisions of the Act—The Third Act (1801)—Names of Commissioners appointed by it—New Borrowing and Rating Powers—Fourth Act (1812)—Extended Powers—Purchase of Markets and Fairs from the Lord of the Manor—Removal of Cattle Market from Dale End—Provision of Smithfield Cattle Market—Fifth Act (1828)—Appointment of Police—Powers over New Streets—Authority to Build a Town Hall, by Special Rate—Town Hall to be used for Musical Festivals—Rights for this Purpose reserved to the General Hospital—Acts for the Government of Deritend and Bordesley—Duddeston and Nechells Governing Acts—pp. 67—95.

CHAPTER VI.

PETITION FOR CHARTER OF INCORPORATION.

Influence of Reform Act of 1832—The Political Union—Birmingham a Parliamentary Borough—Anomalies of Local Government—General Description of Unreformed Municipal Corporations—Report of Royal Commissioners on Corporations—Government Bill to Incorporate Birmingham (1833)—Bill withdrawn—Municipal Corporations Bill

Resistance of the Tory Party in Parliament—Proposals to give Town Councils Power over Public-house Licenses—Hostility of the Peers to the Bill — Meeting and Protest in Birmingham — Compromise Effected — The Municipal Corporations Act passed — Inaction in Birmingham—Causes of it—Ultimate Movement to Obtain a Charter of Incorporation (1837) — Appointment of a Committee—Refusal of the Conservatives to Concur—Discussions in the Town—Arguments for and against a Charter—Description of the then existing Local Government—Town's Meeting to Petition for Charter—Account of the Meeting — Speeches at the Meeting — Resolutions passed— pp. 96—117.

CHAPTER VII.

Opposition to Grant of Charter.

Petition presented (December, 1837)—Private Meeting of Conservatives—Their Counter Proposals—Opposing Principles in the Contest — Public Meeting of Conservatives — Description of the Meeting—The Speeches and Arguments—Attitude and Motives of the Conflicting Parties—General Feeling of the Town—The Government and the Birmingham Radicals—Whig Dislike of Birmingham—Evidence from the " Greville Memoirs"—Lord Grey and the Political Union: "Haydon's Journals"—The Charter opposed by the Conservatives— Government Enquiry—Examination of Petitions—Deputations and Memorials to the Privy Council—Newspaper Comments—Opposition Debate in the House of Lords—Resolution of the Privy Council to recommend Grant of Charter.—pp. 118—141.

CHAPTER VIII.

Grant of the Charter.

Announcement of the Grant (October, 1838)—Division of the Borough into Wards—Public Reading of the Charter in the Town Hall—Speeches at the Meeting—Vote of Thanks to the Queen— Preparations for the Election of Councillors—Political Choice advised— Revision of the First Burgess List—Numerous Conservative Objections— A Test Question—Failure of the Objections—pp. 142—152.

CHAPTER IX.

Election and Proceedings of the First Council.

Election (December 26, 1838)—Both Political Parties contest each Ward—Lists of the Candidates—Number of Votes given to each—Orderly Proceedings at the Election—Difficulties as to the Oaths of Office: Mr. Joseph Sturge's Objections — Election of Aldermen—Mr. W. Scholefield elected first Mayor of Birmingham—Election of Officers—Further Objections to Oath of Office—Admission of a Jewish Member without the Oath—Discussion as to Consideration of Political Subjects by the Council—Deputation against the Corn Laws received—Dinner to celebrate Grant of the Charter—Description of the Town Hall—Nomination of Borough Justices—Commission of the Peace granted to the Borough—Appointment of Magistrates—Lord John Russell's Explanation of Principle of Selection—Designs for the Corporate Seal—Grant of Quarter Sessions applied for—Grant of Quarter Sessions conferred by the Crown—Election of Coroner and Clerk of the Peace—Estimated Expenditure of Corporation—Returns of Rateable Value of the Borough—Borough Rate ordered—Difficulties as to its Collection—pp. 153—183.

CHAPTER X.

The Birmingham Police Act.

Police Arrangements previous to the Charter—Riots of 1839—The London Police applied for by the Magistrates—Discussion as to Appointing a Borough Force—Corporation Financial Difficulties—Debate in the House of Lords on the State of Birmingham—Proposed Government Loan to the Borough—Bill introduced—Measure approved in Birmingham—Local Conservative Opposition—Petition to Annul the Charter—Conservative Action against the Police Bill—Sir Robert Peel proposes a Government Police for Birmingham—Attack of Sir Robert Peel on the Town Council—Protest by the Members for Birmingham—Lord John Russell adopts Sir Robert Peel's Proposal—The first Bill withdrawn—Second Bill, creating a Government Police, introduced—

Resentment in Birmingham—Petition against the Bill—Speeches in the Town Council—Birmingham supported by the Corporation of London—Strange Conduct of the Government—Second Reading of the Police Bill carried—Further Debate in the House of Commons—Deputation from the Council to Lord Brougham—He opposes the Bill in the House of Lords—Opposition unavailing—The Bill passed—Indignation in Birmingham—Formal Protest by the Town Council—pp. 184—220.

CHAPTER XI.

VALIDITY OF THE CHARTER OF INCORPORATION DISPUTED.

Defects of the Municipal Corporations Act — Its imperfect Definitions—Consequent Opportunity to challenge Validity of Charters on Technical Points—The Manchester Case—Political Opposition in Manchester and Birmingham—Distinctions between the two Places—Manchester Conservatives consistently oppose Charter—Birmingham Conservatives first accept and afterwards resist it—Opening Act of Opposition—Overseers refuse to levy a Borough Rate—Technical Grounds of Refusal—Opinions of Sir W. Follett and Sir F. Pollock—Difference between a Statutory Charter and a Common Law Charter—Proposed Method of Testing the Question—Hesitation of the Town Council—Appeal to the Government for Assistance—Grant of Money for Quarter Sessions asked for—A small Grant made by way of Loan—Legal Opinions taken by the Council on the Validity of the Charter—The Appointment of Coroner challenged—A Writ of *Quo Warranto* applied for—The Case of " Rutter *v.* Chapman "—Difficulties with the Justices for Warwickshire—Pecuniary Troubles of the Corporation—Validity of the Quarter Sessions questioned—The Recorder's Opinion — Position of the Borough in 1840 — New Difficulties—Party and Personal Bitterness—A Conservative Denunciation—Summary of Difficulties—Misconduct of the Government—Resignation of the first Town Clerk—Election of Mr. S. Bray—A Gleam of Hope — A New Disappointment—The Quarter Sessions suspended—The Magistrates practically superseded—The Government interposes—Debates in Parliament—Government Proposals rejected—The *Times* on Birmingham—Fresh Difficulties with the County Justices—Birmingham Convictions quashed by the County Quarter Sessions—Disputes on Appointment of Overseers—pp. 221—267.

CHAPTER XII.

The Charter Enforced and Confirmed.

Resolution to Enforce the Charter—Divisions in the Council—A Borough Rate made—Legal Opinion taken by the Overseers—They are advised to obey the Mayor's Precept—New Efforts of the Government to remove Difficulties—Local Opposition—Resistance in the House of Lords—Lord Lyndhurst attacks the Corporation—His estimate of a Radical Council—The Government Proposals defeated—Complaints of Birmingham Liberals—Proposed Salary to the Mayor—New Aggressions by the County Justices—Their Proposal to levy a County Rate in Birmingham—Serious Distress in the Town—A Tenth of the Houses vacant—Meat an unknown Luxury amongst the Poor—Conservatives attribute Distress to the Corporation—Mr. R. H. Muntz's Defence of the Council—The County Justices make their Rate—Litigation in the Queen's Bench—The Rate declared illegal—New Claims by the Justices—Dispute on the Coronership—The Beginning of the End—Corporation Difficulties draw to a Close—Negotiations on the Police Act—Government Bill to restore the Police to the Corporation—Bill to confirm the Charter of Incorporation—Compensation to County Officers—The Charter Bill and the Police Bill passed—Lord Brougham supports the Conservative Opposition—Neglects his Clients and makes a Fiasco—Royal Assent to the Bills—Liberal Rejoicings—The *Journal in Excelsis*—Watch Committee appointed—Review of the Conflict—Estimate of Party Feeling—The Whig and Conservative Governments contrasted in their Treatment of Birmingham—The Town indebted to Sir Robert Peel and Sir James Graham—The Local Founders of Representative Government—pp. 268—289.

CHAPTER XIII.

Union of Governing Bodies in the Borough.

Limited Powers of the Corporation—Statement of the several and conflicting Governing Bodies—Business transacted and Subjects discussed by the Council—Growing Opinion in favour of United Government—Evil Effects of Divided Authority—Progress delayed by various Causes—Political Dissensions—Apathy of Burgesses—Movements towards Union—Appeals by the *Journal*—Commissioners' Bill rejected by Town's Meeting—Action by the Town Council—Conciliatory Proposals ineffectual—The Public Health Act—Petition for Amendment of it successful—The Town Council proposes to adopt the Act, and thus to unite Governing Powers of the Borough—Government Enquiry undertaken—Report of Mr. Rawlinson, the Inspector—[Geological Situation of Birmingham—Rainfall—Climate and Manufactures—Extent of Town—Health—Variety and Number of Trades—Distribution of Wealth — Steam Power — Public Houses — Social Habits — Clubs — Wages—Women in Factories—Allotment Gardens—Rent of Land—Gas and Water Supply—Impurities of Well Water—Overcrowded Graveyards—Governing Bodies in the Borough—Conflicting Powers—Difficulties of Drainage—Excessive Number of Public Officers—Irritating Mode of Collecting Rates—Amount of Rating in 1849—Comparison with 1878—Sanitary Defects of the Town—Specimen Courts—Evidence of Mr. Hodgson and Mr. Russell, Corporation Medical Officers—State of the Rivers—Shameful Sanitary Condition of Edgbaston—Open Drains in the Hagley and Bristol Roads—State of the Town Courts—General Nuisances—Neglected Condition of Deritend and Bordesley—Summary of the Enquiry—The Inspector's Conclusions and Recommendations]—Discussion on Mr. Rawlinson's Report—Disputes of Local Bodies—The Commissioners prepare an Amalgamation Bill—Resistance by the Town Council—The Council petition for Provisional Order under the Public Health Act—Parliamentary Contest—Both Parties defeated—Council promote an Improvement Bill, providing for Union of Powers under the Corporation — Virtual Concurrence of the Commissioners — The Bill introduced and passed—United Local Government finally established on the Representative Principle—Causes of Success—Opposition by Duddeston Commissioners — A Model Surveyor — Taking Levels by "Crow-sticks"—General Sketch of the Improvement Act of 1851—Final Transfer of Powers—New Arrangements by the Corporation—Appointment of Committees and Officers—pp. 290—345.

CHAPTER XIV.

Summary and Review.

Early Objections to the Representative Principle—The Municipal Reform Act—General Conflict of Opposing Principles—Difficulties of New Corporations—Special Causes of Resistance in Birmingham—Religious and Political Differences—Opposition to the Charter—Local Government supported by Leading Citizens—Members of Parliament and Magistrates who have been Members of the Council—Contrast of Present Time with Fifty Years ago—Three Periods of Corporation History—Comparison of 1838 with 1878—The Progress Achieved—The Spirit in which it has been undertaken—Influence of Municipal Institutions—Conclusion—pp. 346—356.

CHAPTER I.

EARLY GOVERNMENT OF BIRMINGHAM: THE COURT LEET, ETC.

Purpose of the Book.

The purpose of this Book is to give an account of the Municipal Corporation of Birmingham, which is derived by grant of a Royal Charter, under the authority of the Municipal Corporations Act, passed in 1835; and the narrative consequently relates mainly to events and incidents within living or recent memory. In order to show how the desire for municipal and representative government came about, it is necessary, however, to present a sketch of the previous forms of local administration, and thus to indicate the growth of the town, and to exhibit the disposition which its people have always manifested towards freedom and self-control.

Antiquity of Birmingham.

Birmingham, though commonly supposed to be a modern town, is one of the oldest communities in the kingdom. It existed in Saxon times—possibly, indeed, still earlier—and at the Conquest, according to the description in Domesday Book, it was a place of some importance, having four hides of land and half a mile of woods, and a market—at least, in a suit brought by the lord of the manor in 1309 he defended his right by contending that his predecessors levied customary tolls before the date of the Norman invasion. The ancient records of the place, however, are lost: the records of courts leet and courts baron, parochial records, and all others that might serve to throw light upon the earlier history of the community. We are consequently driven to conjecture the rudimentary forms of government existing in the town, and to trace their character and development by examples derived from other places and from general custom. Those who desire to acquaint themselves with these matters in detail, may do so by consulting Professor Stubbs's Constitutional History.* Here it will be sufficient to make a brief general statement. Settlements in England began with the family; then followed the tribe, or association of kindred families; then the mark, or boundary which separated one community of free and kindred cultivators from others; next the township, the members of which held land partly in personal ownership, and partly in common; next the parish, or district assigned to a church or priest, and often including more townships than one. With these later developments there grew up the lordship or manor, rudimentary before the Conquest, and fully developed after it, under which the lord, holding under grant from a superior lord or from the King, had control over the inferior landholders, and held his court baron for manorial rights, and his court leet, or King's court, a division of the sheriff's court which exercised a wider jurisdiction

---

* The Constitutional History of England, in its Origin and Development. By William Stubbs, M.A., Regius Professor of Modern History. Oxford: Clarendon Press. 1875.

for the hundred or the shire. In the court baron, by-laws for local government were made, and other local business was transacted; in the court leet certain judicial powers were exercised—stewards were appointed to look to the lord's interests and to collect his dues, bailiffs were elected to oversee the fairs and markets, constables were appointed to maintain order and to apprehend criminals.

CHAP. I.

From this condition some towns advanced to the completer self-government of boroughs or cities, with rights conferred by Royal Charter. Birmingham was not one of these. From Saxon times down to the middle of the seventeenth century it remained subject to the simpler forms of government above indicated, with such variations as had been introduced in the course of centuries—namely, justices of the peace to exercise criminal jurisdiction in their petty sessions; churchwardens and overseers to administer the affairs of the ecclesiastical parish and to manage the relief of the poor; and surveyors of highways, chosen at parish meetings, to look to the condition of the roads. All this time, however, the ancient courts of the manor, the court baron and court leet, continued to be held; and though now in abeyance, they are still existing, for such rights as have not been sold by the lords of the manor to the representatives of the town: the markets and fairs being the chief of the rights transferred.

Government in Birmingham.

There were thus three sets of authorities, broadly stated—1, the Justices, to keep the peace and to punish crime; 2, the Leet, to look to markets, nuisances, and other matters belonging to the lord of the manor, or interfering with his rights; 3, the Churchwardens, who transacted the Church and parish business, called vestry meetings for town purposes generally, and for the election of surveyors. Of these authorities the Leet was the most ancient, and in some senses the freest and most popular—originally, indeed, the common assembly and court of justice of the township; itself exercising authority by the jury at its annual meeting, and continuing to exercise it by the steward, bailiffs, and constables, throughout the year. No meeting of the Leet has been held since 1854, the last year in which bailiffs were elected; but, as has been observed, the court may still be summoned, and it might be worth while for the Corporation to complete the transfer of powers by purchasing the remaining rights of the lord of the manor, and thus acquiring the power to hold or to disuse the Leet at its own pleasure.

It is much to be regretted that the Court Rolls of the Manor of Birmingham go no further back than the year 1779—all the previous records having been destroyed or lost by the neglect of previous stewards. The duties of the Leet may, however, be gathered from an account given in a Tract now extremely rare (a copy of which exists in the Corporation Reference Library), drawn up and printed by Mr. Thomas Lee, Solicitor, steward of the Manor in 1789, and entitled "The Duty of the Respective Officers appointed by the Court Leet in the Manor of Birmingham." These duties are defined and put on record as follows:—

CHAP. I.
Powers and Officers of the Leet, 1789.

THE DUTY OF THE RESPECTIVE OFFICERS APPOINTED BY THE COURT LEET, IN THE MANOR OF BIRMINGHAM.—BIRMINGHAM: PRINTED BY E. PIERCY, NO. 96, BULL-STREET. M,DCC,LXXXIX.

Manor of Birmingham.—The Court Leet, or View of Frank Pledge, with the Court Baron of the Right Honourable SARAH LADY ARCHER, *Lady of the said Manor, holden in the Chamber over the Old Cross, in Birmingham, on Wednesday the Twentieth Day of October, in the Year of our Lord, 1779.*

Before THOMAS LEE, Gentleman, Steward.

The Jury, as well for the King as the Lady of the Manor.
JOHN TAYLOR, Esq.

John Kettle, Esq., Mess. Joseph Wilkinson, William Scott, John Ryland, Timothy Smith, Michael Lakin, John Richards, John Francis, John Rickards, Benjamin May, George Humphrys, William Humphrys, Claud Johnson, William Ryland, Samuel Ryland, Joseph Webster, Joseph Cotterell, William Dallaway, *Sworn.*

The Steward having given it in Charge to the Jury, to make a Presentment of the Duty of the respective Officers, elected and appointed by this Court; the Jurors made the following Presentment thereof accordingly, viz.

The Office of High Bailiff.

I. The Jury find and present, that this Officer is annually elected by the Jury; and that it is his Duty to see that the Fairs be duly proclaimed, and that due Order be preserved in the Fairs and Markets; and if he see any Persons in such

Fairs or Markets, using Unlawful Games, to the Injury of Ignorant Persons, and thoughtless Youths, he may seize them and commit them to Custody, to be taken before a proper Magistrate.

II. That it is his Duty, to see that all Persons exposing any Wares to Sale in the Fairs or Markets, or as Shopkeepers within the Manor, have legal Weights and Measures.

III. That it is his Duty, to see that the Town has a Common Ballance with Common Weights, sealed according to the Standard of the Exchequer, at the Costs of the Town, at which Ballance all the Inhabitants may weigh gratis, but Strangers are to pay for every Draught within 40lb., a Farthing, and for every Draught betwixt 40lb. and 100lb. one Half-penny, from 100lb. to 1000lb. a Penny.

IV. That it is his Duty, to examine all Measures, and see that they be duly Gauged by the Standard, which he shall have out of the Exchequer, for which he is to be paid for Sealing a Bushel one Penny, for a Peck or half Peck one Half-penny, and for a Gallon or any less Measure, one Farthing; and any Person using any other Weight or Measure, is to forfeit Five Shillings, to be recovered before one Justice, or the Offender may be presented by the High Bailiff in the Lord's Leet, and be amerced by the Jury.

V. That it is his Duty, twice in the year at least, to examine all Weights and Measures within the Manor, and such as he shall find defective, he is to cause to be broke or burnt, and the Offender is to pay Six Shillings and Eight-pence for the first Offence, Thirteen Shillings and Fourpence for the second, Twenty Shillings for the third Offence; and two Justices may determine these Offences.

VI. That it is his Duty, by the Custom of the Manor, to Seize for the Use of the Poor, all Butter and other Articles made up into Pounds, or any other certain Weight, ready for Sale, which on Examination he shall find deficient; and any Offenders in these Articles he may present at the next Court, to be amerced by the Jury.

<small>CHAP. I.
Powers and Officers of the Leet, 1789.</small>

The Office of Low Bailiff.

The Jury find and present, that this Officer is annually elected by the Jury, and that his Office is in the Nature of Sheriff of the Manor, that to him all the Process of the Court is to be directed, and that it is his Right and Duty to return and summon all Juries at this Court. And the Low Bailiff at each Fair is entitled to one Penny for each Stall or Standing pitched in the said Fairs.

The Office of Constable.

The Jury find and present, that these Officers are annually elected by the Jury; and their Duty is to suppress all Riots and Affrays within the Manor, to arrest all Felons, Night Walkers and suspicious Persons, which they may do of their own Authority: and they may charge and command any Person, to assist them in the Execution of their Office, if needs require, and they are to be attendant upon the Justices of the Peace, and to execute their Warrants: and they have a power, by virtue of their Office, of Billetting the Officers and Soldiers, which they are to do fairly and impartially.

The Office of Headborough.

The Jury find and present, that this Officer is annually elected by the Jury, and is a Secondary Constable, and in the Absence or on the Death of the Constable, it is his Business, to do and execute the Duties of the Constable, and when required, he is personally to assist the Constable in preserving the Public Peace.

The Office of Ale Conners, otherwise High Tasters.

The Jury find and present, that these Officers are annually elected by the Jury; and their Duty is to see that all Publick

CHAP. I.

Powers and Officers of the Leet, 1739.

Brewers and Ale Sellers within the Manor, do Brew good and wholesome Drink, and that they do not Use in Ale or Beer any Guinea Pepper, Coculus, Judiac, or any other unwholesome or intoxicating Ingredients: and for the purposes of these Assays, the Officers may at seasonable Times, demand of each Publick Brewer or Ale Seller, a reasonable Quantity of his Ale or Beer, and which the Jury Estimate at half a Pint Ale Measure. And these Officers are to present all Publick Brewers and all Ale Sellers, selling or exposing to Sale bad and unwholesome Drink; and all common Tiplers and Drinkers, and all Alehouse-keepers permitting unlawful Tipling or Gaming in their Houses by Apprentices or others.

The Office of Flesh Conners, otherwise Low Tasters.

The Jury find and present, that these Officers are annually elected by the Jury; and their Duty is to see that all Butchers, Fishmongers, Poulterers, Bakers and others, Sellers of Victuals, do not sell or expose to Sale within this Manor, any unwholesome, corrupt, or contagious Flesh, Fish, or other Victuals: and in case any such be exposed to Sale, we find that the said Officers by the ancient Custom of the Manor, may seize burn or destroy the same, or otherwise present the offenders at the next Court Leet to be holden for this Manor.

The Office of Searchers, and Sealers of Leather.

The Jury find and present, that these Officers are annually elected by the Jury; and that the Office is instituted by Act of Parliament, 1st. James 1st. Chap. 22: and their Duty is to search and view all Tanned Leather brought to Market, whether it is thoroughly tanned and dryed; and if it is, they are to Seal the same; and they ought to be honest Men, and skilful in their Business, and they are to Search as often as they shall think good, or need shall be, and are to Seal what they find sufficient. And if they find any Leather offered to be Sold, or brought to be Sealed, which shall be insufficiently Tanned or Curried, or any Boots, Shoes, Bridles, or other Things made of Tanned or Curried Leather insufficiently tanned, curried or wrought, they may seize the same, and keep it till it can be tryed by the Tryers, to be appointed as the Act directs. And they are to have a Seal of Office, and are to take no more than the old and accustomed Fee for sealing any Leather.

<small>CHAP. I.

Powers and Officers of the Leet, 1789.</small>

At the same time Mr. Lee drew up a Charge to the jury of the Leet, according to his view of their duties, founded upon enquiry into precedents and analogous jurisdictions. This document is too lengthy for insertion here, and can scarcely be considered as of historical value; but the subjoined charge, in use in the adjoining manor of King's Norton, and which is of more ancient date, may be cited as illustrating the duties of Courts Leet, which, with occasional local variations, were everywhere substantially the same:—

<small>Charge to the Jury of the Leet.</small>

CHARGE TO THE JURY OF THE COURT LEET.

To the following purport:—

That it is the Steward's province to remind the Jury that the Court Leet (frequently called a law day) is a court of record of great antiquity, and accounted the King's court, to which all persons resident within the jurisdiction of it, of the age of twelve years or upwards, with the exception of peers and prelates, and tenants in ancient demesne, owe suit and service, and that it is their duty to present and amerce such as make default.

That they are to present the names of such proper officers as, either by the common law or by the particular usage of the Manor, &c., for which the Court is held, are generally chosen and sworn at the Leet, such as constables, tithing men, ale conners, &c., and to enquire of and present any neglect

CHAP. I.
———
Charge to the Jury of the Leet.

in the duties of the several public officers within the precincts of the Leet.

That if any offence was presented at the last court by way of admonition, and the party has not obeyed the terms which were enjoined, it is their duty to certify the default to the court, in order that the amercement set for it may be levied; but that the jurisdiction of the Leet Jury, like that of the Grand Jury, is confined to things done or neglected to be done since the last Court, and to things happening immediately before their being sworn, and during their sitting.

That it is their province to inquire of and present all acts of petty treason, and the crimes of murder, and manslaughter (as felony), rape, arson, burglary, larceny, accessaries, voluntary escape, and every other description of felony, and negligent escape, in order that such offences (though not punishable in Leet) may be certified to the King's Justices according to the rules prescribed by law, and that they are likewise to inquire what lands and tenements, goods and chattels any felon had at the time the felony was committed.

That it is also their province to inquire of and present all assaults and batteries with bloodshed; all railers, common scolds, evesdroppers and sowers of discord: all conspiracies and combinations of victuallers, labourers and artificers; the several offences of exacting excessive tolls; neglecting to pursue hue and cry lawfully raised; of vagrancy and noctigavancy; and the receivers of any such characters; of buying and selling by false weights and measures; and violating any assize; of forestallers, ingrossers, and regraters; and of all offences directed to be inquired of in Leets by particular Acts of Parliament, as, for instance, the Act of 1 Eliz. c. 17, intituled, "An Act for preservation of Spawn and Fry of Fish."

And lastly, that it is the duty of the Jury to inquire of and present all obstructions of public bridges, ways and paths, the stoppage of all public watercourses, the removal or destruction of landmarks, and any pound breaches, the neglect of cleansing pools or of enclosing stone, marl, and other the like pits, or of the reparation of bridges and causeways, the laying of dung, soil or other offensive thing in any public highway; and also every other act which may tend to the injury or nuisance of any of the King's liege subjects.

<small>Charge to the Jury of the Leet.</small>

The names of the officers mentioned in the foregoing presentment are for the most part self-explaining. The Steward was the peculiar representative of the lord of the manor. The High Bailiff controlled the markets and fairs, and by custom became the chief officer and representative of the town; indeed in 1552, Richard Smalbroke is described in a legal document as "now Bailiff of the Town," he being obviously then High Bailiff of the Manor. The Low Bailiff, who came afterwards to have an almost equal prescriptive dignity with his colleague, had for his province to summon the jury by whom the year's officers were appointed. The two Constables, usually persons of good rank in the town, were empowered to suppress riots, to arrest felons, to execute justice, to billet soldiers, &c. The Headborough was an assistant or deputy constable. The High Tasters examined the quality of ale sold in the public houses; the Low Tasters examined the meat sold in the markets and at the butchers' shops. The Leather Sealers stamped the leather made in the town, this being once so considerable a trade here that the leather makers had a meeting place—the Leather Hall—a room erected over the gateway which formerly blocked the entrance into New Street, and which

<small>Officers of the Leet.</small>

was sometimes used for town meetings. The Affeirer was an officer who received the rents and fines belonging to the lord of the manor. Two courts were held annually, within a month of Easter and Michaelmas respectively; and if their records were still in existence much light of an interesting character would be thrown upon the history of the town. But unhappily all the records previous to 1779 have disappeared. From the date of the downfall of the Birmingham family, by the attainder of Edward Birmingham in 1553, the lord was non-resident, the officers practically irresponsible, the bailiff was probably often changed; and so the records of the Court were neglected or destroyed. Tradition charges much of the loss upon a Mr. Brooke who was steward in 1791. The Court Rolls which remain, and are now in possession of Mr. Arnold, the present steward of the Manor, afford little that is worth recital. A few examples of the entries will be sufficient for the reader:

1779. Thomas Bellamy, presented by Jury for interrupting and insulting Joseph Green, the High Bailiff, in regulating the market and "establishing the Farmers frequenting the market in the enjoyment of their standings on the Cornhill, according to their ancient usage." Amerced £5. [The Cornhill is now the Bull Ring, opposite the chancel end of St. Martin's; it was sometimes called the Cross Cheaping.]

1786. George Swaine, Coal Dealer, and Thomas Burton, Coal Carrier, presented by Jury for selling coals by false weights, "in contempt of the law, and to the manifest oppression of the poor." Swaine amerced 40s.

1787. John Cox, of Birmingham, Butcher, presented by

Jury for exposing to public sale bad and unwholesome meat, noways fit for sale. Amerced £5 5s.

Thomas Sanders, of Tamworth, Butcher, presented for like offence. Amerced £5 5s.

William Ashley, of Birmingham, Coal Dealer, for selling coals by false weights, amerced 6s. 8d.

1792. John Kiddey, presented for setting up a stall in the street or highway called High Street, between the Hen and Chickens Inn and the Castle Inn, whereby the same is much straitened and obstructed, to the injury and common nuisance to the King's people having occasion to go pass and repass. Amerced 2s. 6d.

Thomas Halfpenny, for a like offence. Amerced 2s. 6d.

1793. Samuel Taylor, of Edgbaston, presented for laying down potatoes and garden stuff in Dale End. Amerced 2s. 6d.

1796. John Flint, presented for keeping a stall for selling butcher meat in the street or highway called the Little Bull Ring. Amerced 21s.

Hutton, writing in 1794,* says "these manorial servants instituted by ancient charter, chiefly possess a name without an office. Thus order seems assisted by industry; and thus a numerous body of inhabitants are governed without a governor."

"Exclusive of the choice of officers (he proceeds) the jury impanelled by the Low Bailiff have the presentation of all encroachments upon the lord's waste, which has long been neglected. The duties of office are little known, except

---

* History of Birmingham, 3rd edition, p. 143.

Chap. I.

Bailiff's Feast, 1794.

that of taking a generous dinner, which is punctually observed. It is too early to begin business till the table is well stored with bottles; and too late afterwards. During the existence of the House of Birmingham, the Court Leet was held at the Moat [now the site of Smithfield Market], in what we should now think a large and shabby room, conducted under the eye of the Low Bailiff, at the expense of the lord. The jury, twice a year, were witnesses that the famous dish of roast beef, ancient as the family who gave it, demanded the head of the table. The Court was afterwards held at the Leather Hall [at the lower end of New Street], and the expense, which was trifling, borne by the Bailiff. The jury in the beginning of the present century were impanelled in the Old Cross [in High Street, above St Martin's Church], then newly erected, from whence they adjourned to the house of the Bailiff, and were feasted at the growing charge of two or three pounds. This practice continued until about the year 1735, when the Company, grown too bulky for a private house, assembled at the tavern, and the Bailiff enjoyed the singular privilege of consuming the sum of ten pounds upon his guests. It is easier to advance in expenses than to retreat. In 1760 they had increased to forty pounds, and in the next edition of this work we may expect to see the word *hundred*. The lord was anciently founder of the feast, and treated his Bailiff; but now that custom is inverted, and the Bailiff treats his lord. The proclamation of our two fairs is performed by the High Bailiff, in the name of the Lord of the Manor; this was done a century ago, without the least expense. But the strength of his liquor, a silver tankard, and the pride of showing it, perhaps induced him, in process of time, to treat his attendants. His ale, without a miracle was, in a few years, converted into wine, and that of various sorts, to which was added a small collation; and now his friends are complimented with a card, to meet him at the Hotel, where he incurs an expense of thirty pounds. While the spirit of the people refines by intercourse, industry, and the singular jurisdiction among us, this insignificant principle on our head of government, swells into a wen. Habits approved are soon acquired: a third entertainment has of late years sprung up, termed the Constables' feast; with this difference, it is charged to the public. We may consider it a wart on the political body, which merits the caustic."

<small>CHAP. I.</small>

Long after Hutton's time—indeed until the Court Leet ceased to be held, through the government of the town being wholly vested in the Corporation —the Bailiffs' feasts continued, and grew in magnitude and cost: the old Manorial officers having become in effect the heads of the town, and being chosen from amongst the leading citizens. By an unwritten but unbroken rule, the High Bailiff was a Churchman, and the Low Bailiff a Nonconformist, and frequently also there was a political distinction between the two officers. This division of office between political and ecclesiastical opponents began, however, long before our time. In 1722 there was a trial in the King's Bench, to oust one Robert Fulwood from the office of Low Bailiff, on the ground of illegal appointment. At that time two parties, the Churchmen and the Presbyterians, contended for supremacy in Birmingham: a contest which had continued in one form or another from the beginning of the Civil War, when Birmingham was a Nonconformist stronghold, and took sides vigorously with the Parliament against the King. The Presbyterians had for some time previously to 1722 held possession of the office of Low Bailiff, by the successive nomination of one of their number. As the Low Bailiff summoned and selected the jury of the Court Leet, and as the jury elected the officers of the Manor—and thus practically of the town—

<small>Party Contests in the Leet Court, 1722.</small>

<small>Churchmen and Presbyterians.</small>

the Presbyterians were masters of the Leet, and had the entire choice of its officers. They allowed the Churchmen to keep the High Bailiffship—the more dignified but less powerful appointment—but this did not satisfy the Church party, and they made an effort to secure for themselves the office of Low Bailiff also, and thus to transfer the management of town affairs from Nonconformist hands. Power was retained by taking care to summon a jury of the Presbyterian colour; and if the opposite party could, for a single year, get possession of the jury, the authority would, as a matter of course, be transferred to them, for they would take care to summon jurors of their own way of thinking, and would thus control the elections. The Low Bailiff for 1721-22 was one Joseph Worrall, a glover, and to him was delivered the lord's precept to summon a jury of twenty-four inhabitants, on the 23rd of October, 1722, to elect new officers. The Steward, an attorney named Hare, informed him that although 24 was the proper number, he need summon only 13, the customary number. Hare, who was in ill health, deputed his clerk, Thomas Perks, to attend the Court as his deputy. When the Court opened, at nine o'clock in the morning, only six of the 13 jurors summoned answered to their names, and Perks, in the interests of the Church party, demanded a full pannel of 24, to be made up of the persons present in Court—his partisans, who seem to have been there by arrangement. The Low Bailiff protested, and went away to get together the remainder of his jurymen, which he succeeded in doing, but meanwhile Perks, acting on behalf of the Steward, had impannelled his jury, and had elected the officers: the Nonconformists present, according to affidavits afterwards put in, having refused to serve "with such a pack of rascalls," and thereupon they "behaved themselves very rudely, and went away in great haste and passion." It is plain that there was a considerable disturbance, and that while one party was lawless, the other was indignant. Another question, however, arose besides that of conflicting political or religious interests. The custom of the manor assigned to the Low Bailiff, the elected officer of the Leet, the right of summoning the jury. This had now been usurped by the Steward, the nominee of the Lord of the Manor; and thus the right of free and popular election was taken away. The Presbyterians constituted themselves the defenders of the common right against the pretensions of the lord. They raised a subscription to take legal proceedings to test the validity of the election. William Kettle and Samuel Harvey were appointed treasurers of the fund, and the object of it, as stated in the paper drawn up by the subscribers, was "in order to regaine the choice of the offices of High Bayliff, Low Bayliff, Constables, &c., in the Towne of Birmingham, which was Violently and Tumultuously Wrested out of our hands." The amount of the subscriptions ranged from £5 to 10s. 6d.; there were 37 subscribers, and the sum raised was between £80 and £90. Amongst the subscribers are names which are still represented in Birmingham—such as Payton, Harding, Archer, Hadley, Baker (to whose name is added a note, "the baker"),

CHAP. I.
1723.
Legal Proceedings.

Webster, &c. The first proceedings were taken in the Court of King's Bench in 1723, in the nature of a *quo warranto* against Perks, to show by what authority he (for the Steward) claimed the right to nominate the jury, and against Fulwood, to show by what authority he claimed to exercise the duties of Low Bailiff. The defendants pleaded that they had acted in accordance with the custom of the manor, and on this affidavits were filed to show that the custom had been for the Low Bailiff, and not the Steward, to summon the jury. The case was tried at Warwick Assizes in 1723, and a verdict was returned "that the persons admitted and sworn on the jury, who ought to nominate the constables, should be summoned, returned, and nominated by the Low Bailiff; and that a sufficient number of those returned by Worrall did appear and offer to serve."

Popular Right Vindicated.

Thereupon judgment was given by the Court for the appellants, and £90 costs was awarded to them; and thus the right of free election, as against the lord of the manor, was established by the vigorous action of the Presbyterians.

1792.
Renewed Contest.

The same question was revived and again tried in 1792, and again with the same result. Hutton, who seems to have known nothing of the earlier contest, thus quaintly describes the later one:—"Power is the idol of man. It appears that the choice of our slender corps of officers has, for seven hundred years, been in the breast of the Low Bailiff. But in 1792 the Steward of the Manor dying, his successor wisely concluded that it was vested in himself; therefore proceeded in methodical error, till a Court of Law declared, at the expense of £600, that prescriptive right could not be overthrown."

The case referred to by Hutton was almost identical with that above described. Mr. Brooke, the steward of the Manor in 1792, was a strong partisan, a Churchman and a Tory. The jury of the Leet, nominated by the Low Bailiff, had been chiefly Liberal and Nonconformist. The Church and King riots of 1791 left behind them a violent state of feeling on both sides; and the Steward and his party thought they might use this as a means of seizing the government of the town, so far as the Leet jury could give it to them. Accordingly, instead of sending the usual precept to the Low Bailiff, the Steward summoned a meeting, read to it a letter from Mr. Christopher Musgrave (then one of the lords of the Manor), directing him to see that the composition of the jury should be changed—it had for some years consisted mainly of the same persons—and thereupon he nominated a jury of his own choice, and this jury appointed the officers of the Court. The opposite party, headed by Mr. John Taylor, of Moseley Hall, an eminent member of the Unitarian body, and a chief sufferer by the late riots, contested the legality of these proceedings. Their case was conducted by Mr. Thomas Lee, solicitor, and the son of a former steward of the Manor; and the proceedings ended in the establishment of the right of the Low Bailiff to summon the jury—thus maintaining the popular franchise against the encroachment of the Lord and his nominated officer.

We have thus seen that in their past history Birmingham men were justly tenacious of their privileges, and were zealous in the maintenance of the freedom of self-government, and the right of free election of local officers. We have now to revert to a still earlier period, and to recall an example of local government established so far back as the end of the 14th century. This is recorded in the history of the Gild of the Holy Cross, upon the ruins of which our present Grammar School was founded by King Edward the Sixth.

CHAPTER II.

GILD OF THE HOLY CROSS.

The foundation of the Gild of the Holy Cross must be regarded as a most interesting and important endeavour to develop, by the union of all classes, a kind of local government; and in some respects, as will be presently seen, the character of the gild was peculiar to Birmingham. It is not necessary to enter upon a consideration of the history and constitution of gilds. Those who desire to master the subject will find ample materials in the volume of Statutes and Ordinances of English Gilds, prepared by the late Mr. Toulmin Smith for the Early English Text Society, and in the elaborate essay on "The History and Development of Gilds," by Dr. Brentano, included in the same volume. It is sufficient to say generally that gilds were (1) of a religious or social character, the members of which were bound to certain defined religious exercises, to the maintenance of chaplains to say Mass for the souls of brothers and sisters departed, and to the assistance of the brotherhood in various ways, personal and pecuniary; (2) craft gilds, which were composed of members of several trades, or of a particular trade, and which dealt with trade laws, customs, and

Chap. II.
A.D. 1392.

General Character of Gilds.

Divisions of Gilds.

usages; and (3) town gilds or gilds merchant, which in some instances—such as Winchester and Worcester—included the whole community, and had powers of local goverment, and of undertaking trading enterprises for the benefit of the brotherhood.

The Birmingham Gild was not a craft gild, nor a gild merchant, for it neither engaged in trade, nor did it concern itself with the customs or laws of labour. It was not a town gild in the strict sense of that name, for while it undertook specified public duties for the benefit of the community, it did not exercise any general authority in local government. It was to some extent a religious association, since it maintained a chantry in the parish church of St. Martin, not specially for the purpose of having Mass said for the souls of deceased members, but for the ministration of the sacraments and services to them while living. It was also a social and friendly gild, for its members had their feasts and common meetings, and certain services were rendered to them at the gild cost. In a word, the Gild of the Holy Cross was an association very characteristic of Birmingham, as it is painted for us in such local history as we have, and as we know it now—united in purpose, practical in object, taking from any source the arrangements thought to be most helpful, and putting aside customary observances and methods not manifestly suitable to the desires or the needs of the town. On this point Mr. Toulmin Smith makes a just observation in his notes on the Gild: "The records (he says) from which the story of the foundation of this gild is learned, illustrate in a striking manner the true and practical constitutional principles which, long ages ago, found their home in England: of which the fundamental basis was that in a sound political society the men who make it up must be trusted, and that the men of every neighbourhood must best understand their own affairs, and ought to be held bound to fulfil their duties to their neighbours."

CHAP. II.
1392.

The earliest record of the Gild of the Holy Cross is found in a writ issued by Richard the Second on the 10th of July, 1392. The writ recites that in the sixth year of the King license was granted to Thomas Sheldone (since dead), John Colleshulle, John Goldsmythe, and William atte Stowe, "burgesses of Bermyngeham," to assign lands, houses, and rents, in Birmingham and Edgbaston (then spelt Egebaston), valued at 20 marks a year, to two chaplains, for the celebration of Divine service "in the church of Saint Martin of Bermyngeham, to the honour of God, the blessed Mary his Mother, the Holy Cross, Saint Thomas the Martyr, and Saint Katherine." "And now (the writ proceeds) the Bailiffs and Commonalty of Bermyngeham have prayed us that, instead of those letters patent, which have never, they say, taken effect, we will, for us and for our heirs, grant license that they may make and found, in honour of the Holy Cross, a Gild and lasting brotherhood of bretheren and sisteren among themselves in the said town, to which shall belong as well the men and women of the said town of Bermyngeham, as men and women of other towns and of the neighbourhood who are well disposed towards them. And that they may

Founders of Gild.

Members of Gild.

make and ordain a Master and Wardens of the said Gild and brotherhood, who shall have rule and governance over the same: And that they may make and found there a chantry, with chaplains to celebrate Divine service in the Church of St. Martin of Bermyngeham: And that they may do and find there other works of charity, for our welfare and that of the Queen, and for the bretheren and sisteren of the said Gild and brotherhood, and for all good-doers to them, and for their souls' sake and for those of all Christians, according as the ordering and will of the said Bailiffs and Commonalty shall appoint in that behalf: And moreover that we will, for us and our heirs, grant license unto the said John Colleshulle, John Goldsmythe, and William atte Stowe, that they may give and assign to the said Master and Wardens, eighteen messuages, three tofts, six acres of land, and forty shillings of rents, with the appurtenances in Bermyngeham and Egebaston, to have and to hold to the said Master and Wardens, and their successors, Masters and Wardens of the said Gild and brotherhood, to enable them to find two chaplains to celebrate Divine service in the church aforesaid, and to find other works of charity for ever, according to the ordering and will aforesaid." On this writ an enquiry was ordered to be made by a jury to ascertain how much the lands, &c., were worth, of whom and by what tenure and service they were held, whether the rights of the King would be injured by the grant, and whether after the gift the donors would still have sufficient property left to fulfil the customs and services which were bound to be rendered in respect of the lands proposed to be given, and the lands still kept by the donors, and "also to meet all other burdens which it belongs to the holders thereof to bear—such as suits, views of frank-pledge, aids, tollages, watches, fines, redemptions, amerciaments, contributions, and all other charges whatsoever incident thereto: And whether the aforesaid John, John, and William will still be liable to be put on assizes, juries, and all other recognisances whatsoever, the same as their ancestors have heretofore been, so that through the proposed gift, and in default of the givers, the neighbourhood may not become charged or burdened more than has been wont."

In obedience to the King's writ a jury enquired into these matters, and gave answer that the establishment of the gild "will not bring harm or danger to any one," and that the donors of the land would still be able to meet all their obligations. Thereupon letters patent and a license in mortmain were granted by the King on the 7th of August, 1392, for the establishment of the Gild of the Holy Cross, for the purposes recited in the petition of the Bailiffs and Commonalty of Birmingham, the consideration being "fifty pounds which they have paid to us"—that is, to the King—a sum equivalent to at least £1,000 in the present value of money.

For the purpose of this work it is not necessary to enter at length into the history of the Gild of the Holy Cross, or its ordinances and works; the present object being only to show that it constituted a real and important part of the Government of the town. As has been seen, the foundation of it was the business of all the townsfolk. The original intention of the donors of the land was to establish a religious foundation alone; but, as we have seen, the grant for this purpose was never carried into effect. Mr. Toulmin Smith conjectures, and it may be assumed not without reason, that the Birmingham people had been influenced by the teaching of Wiclif, who from his Lutterworth vicarage, would be known in the midland district, and that works such as the Vision of Piers Ploughman, and other attacks upon the superstition, ignorance, and corruption of the priesthood, had operated in the same direction, and that, as a consequence, the merely religious foundation offered no attractions to the townsfolk. It may be, also, that being of a practical turn of mind—as Englishmen are and have been used to be—the townspeople, while not under-valuing the religious part of the matter, desired likewise to get some temporal advantage out of the liberality of the founders of the Gild. However this may be, it is certain that the petition to King Richard for an alteration of the foundation was an act of common consent and local government, the result of meetings of the communitas, or the town, and that the necessary steps were taken by the Bailiffs of the Court Leet, the body which then represented the community, and performed within the manor various functions now assigned to municipal councils. The communal spirit manifested at the outset characterised the general proceedings of the Gild. The association had a common seal, bearing the image of Christ upon the cross, with the Virgin and St. John standing on either side, and having round it the legend "Sigill: comune: gylde: sancte: crucis: de: bermyngeham"— that is, "The common seal of the Gild of the Holy Cross of Birmingham." The government of the body was obviously vested in meetings of the Master and Wardens, and brethren and sisters, the consent of the whole being required to business of importance, as is evident from the terms of leases granted of the Gild lands—thus, in one granted in 1426—"William Rydware, master of the Gild of the Holy Cross of Bermyngeham, and the brothers and sisters of the same Gild, with unanimous assent and consent," &c. As to its work, the Gild built a hall for its members, called indifferently the Gild Hall and the Town Hall. It maintained two priest chaplains at St. Martin's, to minister to the members; but, curiously enough, there is no trace of any direction that these priests should pray for the souls of the founders. It also maintained a bellman, a midwife, and an organist, and the rest of its funds were laid out in alms-houses, gifts to the poor, and reparation of roads and bridges. These works are set forth in the report made by the Commissioners of 37 Henry VIII., when the possessions of the Gild, like those of all other bodies partaking of a religious character, were seized upon by the King. In this document the yearly income is set down at £26 2s. 10d., and the out-goings at £19 1s. 8d. In order to bring the Gild within the purview of the Commissioners, the report treats it, incorrectly, as a purely religious and charitable foundation. The terms are as follow :—"The seyd Gylde was ffounded by Thomas Sheldone and other, in the xvjth yere of Kyng Edwarde the seconde [a wrong date] to ffynd

CHAP. II.
1892.

The Gild Hall and Officers.

1546.
Report of King's Commissioners: Henry VIII.

CHAP. II.
1546.
Report on Gild.

certaine prestes to syng dyvyne seruyce in the par(i)she Church aforseyde for euer; And to pray ffor the soules of the same ffounders. [Again a wrong statement, there being no such provision.] And in the same towne of Byrmyngham there be $\frac{1}{M}$ $\frac{1}{M}$ [2,000] houselyng peaple. And, at Ester tyme, all the prestes of the same Gilde, wt dyuers other, be not sufficient to mynyster the sacramentes and sacramentalles vnto the seyde peaple. Also there be dyuers pore peaple ffounde, ayded, and suckared, of the seyde Gylde, as in money, Breade, Drynke, Coles; and whene any of them dye, thay be buryed very honestlye at the costes and charges of the same Gilde, wt dyrge and messe, according to the constitucyons of the same Gilde."

1547.
Report of King's Commissioners: Edward VI.

A further account of the Gild and its works is given in the report of the Commissioners appointed in the first year of Edward the Sixth, when a project was on foot to restore, for the purpose of providing schools, the lands seized by Henry the Eighth. This report runs as follows:—

Income and Outlay of Gild.

"The Guilde of Brimincham was ffounded by one Thomas Sheldon & other, in the xvjth yere of King Henrye the Seconde [again a wrong date] and incorporate, by the name of Mr. & Brethern of the Guilde of tholye Crosse in brymyncham, ffor the maintenaunce of certein priestes; whereunto belong landes and possessions to the yerelye value of xxxij. *li.* xij. *s.* v. *d.* prima facie: wch to dedes of charyte *and to the common-welth there*, as hereafter shall appere—xxxij. *li.* xij. *s.* v. *d.*

CHAP. II.
1547.

" Whereof,—

" In Rentes Resolute, as well to therle [the Earl] of Warwick as to diuers other, going oute of the premisses, lv. *s.* x. *d. ob. qr.*; In stipendes of priestes & other ministers of the churche, xx. *li.* vj. *s.* viij. *d.* ; In ffes and annuytes, lx. *s.*; ffor bread & wyne ffor the churche, xx. *s.* ; ffor keeping the Clocke and the Chyme, xiij. *s.* iiij. *d* ; And in allowance ffor Reparacions of the same possessions, consisting moste parte in tenementes, communibus annis, iiij. *li.* In all xxxj. *li.* xv. *s.* x. *d. ob qr.*

Payments from Gild Funds.

" So Remains ... ... xvi. *s.* vi. *d. qr.*

" Plate & Jewells to the same guilde belonging; viz., three chalices of silver, waying xxiiij. *oz.*, and a nutte [another?] wth a cover— waying iiij. *oz:*, in all ... ... } xxviiij. *oz.*

Church Plate, &c., of Gild.

" Whereof ij. chalices waying xvj. *oz.* are left for Adminis . . . .

" Goods, Ornamentes, & howshold stuffe, are praysed at ... } xlj. *s.* viij. *d.*

" Theare be relieved and mainteigned uppon the same possessions of the same guilde, and the good provision of the Mr. and bretherne thereof xii poore persones, who have their howses Rent free, and alle other kinde of sustenaunce, as well ffoode and apparelle as alle other

Pensioners of Gild

Chap. II.
1547.
Repair of Roads and Bridges.

"Also theare be mainteigned, wt parte of the premisses, and kept in good Reparaciouns, two greate stone bridges, and diuers ffoule and daungerous high wayes; the charge whereof the towne of hitsellfe ys not hable to mainteign; So that that [*so in original*] the Lacke thereof wilbe a greate noysaunce to the Kinges ma^ties Subjectes passing to and ffrom the marches of wales, and an vtter Ruyne to the same towne—being one of the fayrest and moste profittubble towne[s] to the Kinges highness in all the Shyre.

Grammar School.

"The said Towne of Brymyncham ys a verey mete place, and yt is verey mete and necessarye that theare be a ffree Schoole erect theare, to bring vppe the youthe, being boathe in the same towne and nigh theareaboute."

And so by gift of Edward the Sixth, the lands of the Gild of the Holy Cross were restored to the town for the maintenance of the Free Grammar School, for which purpose they are used until this day.

1525.
Lench's Trust.

It may be well to record the fact that another foundation, still existing, was a direct offshoot of the Gild of the Holy Cross. This was William Lench's Trust, founded by deed of feoffment in 1525, the trustees being directed, after the death of the founder's wife, to do the same sort of works of charity as the Gild of the Holy Cross, "according as the ordering and will of the Bailiffs and Commonalty shall appoint;" and the Master of the Gild being one of these trustees. By giving his wife a life interest in the trust, and by making it a separate trust instead of merging it in the Gild, William Lench saved his foundation from seizure by Henry the Eighth. This trust was distinctly connected with the government of the town, by two provisions—namely, (1) that the funds of it should be used "ffor the repairing the ruinous waies and bridges in and about the same towne of Birmingham, where it shall want; and for default of such uses to the poor liveing within the Towne aforesaid, where then shall be most need;" and (2) by the provision that the "two said [managing?] ffeoffees shall, vppon the Tuesday in Easter weeke, make their iust accompts, before the rest of the said ffeoffees, and other the enhabitaunts of the said Towne of Birmingham; . . . . and that vppon Tuesday in Easterweeke, yearely, in the afternoone, vppon the tolling of a bell, such meeting, for the purpose aforesaid shalbe had, and the like accompte shalbe made and taken, & two new officers chosen."

Chap. II.

1547.

The Foundation a Town's Trust.

CHAPTER III.

FIRST PROPOSAL OF INCORPORATION.

<small>CHAP. III.
1716.
Hutton's Statement of Motive.</small>

The desire to obtain a Charter of Incorporation seems to have been manifested in Birmingham more than a century before a charter was actually granted. The authority for this statement—the only one producible—is to be found in Hutton's "History of Birmingham."[*] The chapter—it is but a brief one—is worthy of transcription in its more important passages: "Riches and power are often seen to go hand in hand. Industry produces property; which, when a little matured, looks out for command; thus the inhabitants of Birmingham, who have generally something upon the anvil besides iron, eighty years ago having derived wealth from diligence, wished to derive power from charter; therefore petitioned the Crown that Birmingham might be created into a Corporation. Tickled with the title of alderman, dazzled with the splendour of a silver mace, a furred gown, and a magisterial chair, they could not see the interest of the place; had they succeeded, that amazing growth would have been crippled which has since astonished the world, and those trades would have

---

[*] History of Birmingham. By W. Hutton, F.A.S.S. The Third Edition, 1795. Page 373.

been fettered which have proved the greatest benefit. When a man loudly pleads for public good, we shrewdly suspect a private emolument lurking beneath. There is nothing more detrimental to good government than men in power, where power is unnecessary; free as the air we breathe, we subsist by our freedom: no command is exercised among us, but that of the laws, to which every discreet citizen pays attention—the magistrate who distributes justice, tinctured with mercy, merits the thanks of society. A train of attendants, a white wand, and a few fiddles, are only the fringe, lace, and trappings of charteral office. Birmingham, exclusive of her market, ranks among the very lowest order of townships; every petty village claims the honour of being a constablewick—we are no more. Our immunities are only the trifling privileges anciently granted to the lords; and two-thirds of these are lost. But, notwithstanding this seemingly forlorn state, perhaps there is not a place in the British dominions where so many people are governed by so few officers; pride, therefore, must have dictated the humble petition before us.

"I have seen a copy of this petition, signed by eighty-four of the inhabitants: and though without a date, [it] seems to have been addressed to King George the First, about 1716; it alledges, 'That Birmingham is, of late years, become very populous, from its great increase of trade; is much superior to any town in the county, and but little inferior to any inland town in the kingdom; that it is governed only by a constable, and enjoys no

CHAP. III.
1716.

more privileges than a village; that there is no justice of the peace in the town, nor any in the neighbourhood, who dares act with vigour; that the county abounds with rioters who, knowing the place to be void of magistrates, assemble in it, pull down the meeting houses, defy the King, openly avow the Pretender, threaten the inhabitants, and oblige them to keep watch in their own houses, that the trade decays, and will stagnate, if not relieved. To remedy these evils, they beseech his Majesty to incorporate the town, and grant such privileges as will enable them to support their trade, the King's interest, and destroy the villanous attempts of the Jacobites. In consideration of the requested charter, they make the usual offer of lives and fortunes.'

Hutton's Comments and Objections.

Failure of the Petition.

"A petition and the petitioner, like Janus with his two faces, looks different ways; it is often treated as if it said one thing and meant another; or as if it said anything but truth. Its use, in some places, is to lie on the table. Our humble petition, by some means, met with the fate it deserved. We may remark, a town without a charter is a town without a shackle. If there was then a necessity to erect a corporation, because the town was large, there is none now, though larger; the place was governed a thousand years ago, when only a twentieth of its present magnitude; it may also be governed as well a thousand years hence, if it should swell to ten times its size. The pride of our ancestors was hurt by a petty constable; the interest of us, their successors, would be hurt by a mayor; a more simple government cannot be instituted, or one more efficacious; that of some places is designed for parade, ours for use; and both answer their end. A town governed by a multitude of governors, is the most likely to be ill governed." Hutton's estimates of early population are fanciful; as much so as his preference for primitive forms of local government. His notion that the same system which suited Birmingham before the Conquest suited it at his own day, and would suit it a thousand years hence, may be dismissed as entirely as his idea that the population of the town a thousand years before his time was a twentieth part of its population in 1791—he puts the number of inhabitants in in 1066 at 3,500!—and he is wrong even as to his estimate of population in 1791, which he gives as 73,650, living in 12,681 houses, whereas the first census—that of 1801—returns the number of houses at 15,630 and the population at 73,670. It is curious, however, to note that his conjectured estimate of a population ten times as large in another thousand years, is not far from being realised in less than seventy years, for the population in 1791 was probably not actually more than 60,000, while the census of 1871 gave us within the borough a population of 343,000; and the Registrar-General's estimate, at the middle of 1877, puts it at 375,000. If to this number we add the residents in the suburban districts, all of whom really belong to Birmingham, we do not fall far short of half a million; and thus we are well advanced towards the fulfilment of Hutton's dream of a ten-fold increase, though we have nearly accomplished it in less than a tenth of the period which he conjecturally assigned for the process.

CHAP. III.
1716.

Objections to an early Charter.

Birmingham a Free Town.

Advantages of Local Freedom.

But if the venerable historian of Birmingham was inaccurate in his figures and his predictions, he was not so wrong in his conclusion that the grant of a Corporation to Birmingham in 1716 would have been a misfortune to the town. Any charter granted at that period would have been clogged with restrictions as to the number and powers of the electing body, and probably also as to the regulations affecting trade. Of the Corporations then existing some were self-elected—literally close Corporations, which had degenerated into political or family cliques—while the rest were chosen by small bodies of freemen, who, as a rule, were endowed with exclusive governing and trading privileges. The great glory of Birmingham, the source of its strength, and the cause of its rapid advance in prosperity and population, was that it was a free town. Neither personal nor corporate hindrances existed in it: whoever chose to come was free to settle in the place, and to make his way according to his chances and capacity. It is to this absolute freedom that Hutton refers when he says that "a town without a charter is a town without a shackle;" and there can be no doubt that if Birmingham had been incorporated then, it would have been shackled, for it could not have received with freedom the vast number of immigrants who came to it from all parts of the country. Of how it received them, and how deeply it grew into their affections, Hutton himself affords a notable illustration. He came to Birmingham in 1750, poor and friendless. In 1781, when he published the first edition of his History, he was wealthy, respected, and influential. He owed it to its simplicity and sincerity, he acknowledges the obligation: "Were I to enter upon dedication, I should certainly address myself 'To the Inhabitants of Birmingham.' For to them I not only owe much, but all; and I think among that congregated mass there is not one person to whom I wish ill. I have the pleasure of calling many of those inhabitants friends, and some of them share my warm affections equally with myself. Birmingham, a compassionate nurse, not only draws our persons, but our esteem from the places of our nativity, and fixes it upon herself: I might add 'I was hungry, and she fed me; thirsty, and she gave me drink; a stranger, and she took me in.' I approached her with reluctance, because I did not know her; I shall leave her with reluctance, because I do." Many others, since Hutton's day, might justly bear this witness as their own; and while they have had cause for thankfulness in the choice or chance which led them to the town, Birmingham has reason to rejoice in the services rendered to her by those who are proud to have renounced their own birth-places to become her sons by adoption.

It is probable, however, that at the date mentioned by Hutton—1716—there was a real desire for a charter, and no doubt that there was actual necessity for a better form of government than was then existing: government, if it could be so called, by the officers of the manorial court, so far as regarded the markets and fairs; by one or two county magistrates for the irregular administration of justice; and by occasional meetings of the inhabitants in

of parochial improvement. The allegation in the petition above quoted that disorders occurred in the town, was not without foundation. A previous visit of the notorious Dr. Sacheverel had left its traces in the development of an intolerant spirit, and the petition itself may be taken as evidence that the prevalent dislike of the House of Hanover existed in Birmingham. In 1714 there were riots in the town itself, and in the following year these were renewed in the district, and especially in Staffordshire, where the Nonconformist meeting houses were roughly handled. Dread of a recurrence of these troubles doubtless prompted the desire for a stronger and settled local government. With the defeat of the Pretender, and the general acceptance of the Hanoverian dynasty, the town, however, settled down into a prosperous condition of advancing wealth and continually increasing population and industry; and in the presence of these material advantages, the desire for improved government seems to have passed away. For more than fifty years longer Birmingham, if not content, was at least submissive to the antiquated rule of high and low bailiffs, constables, magistrates, and vestry. It was not until 1768 that a real effort was made to institute, at least for sanitary purposes, a mode of public administration better suited to the importance and the necessities of the place.

CHAPTER IV.

BIRMINGHAM IN THE EIGHTEENTH CENTURY.

It will be interesting to go back for something more than a century, and to try to realise the character of the town at the date of the institution of regular local government by means of the first Act constituting the Street Commissioners. In order to obtain a clear view of it we must begin with a somewhat earlier period—namely 1751. This is the date of the first map or plan of Birmingham now known to be in existence. There was published in 1731, by Westley, a "Prospect" of Birmingham—a bird's eye view, showing the general disposition of the houses, and distinguishing the principal buildings. Copies of this work are well known; but Bradford's map or plan, published in 1751, the earliest which shows the street lines, and marks the boundaries of the town, is now extremely rare. Fortunately, a copy of it is included in the valuable collection of Birmingham maps and views deposited in the Corporation Free Library, and Mr. Samuel Timmins is the possessor of another copy. The map is handsomely engraved on copper, and is enriched with views of St. Martin's and St. Philip's Churches, which are balanced, on the opposite side, by figures of a couple of

Chap. IV.
1751.
Sketch of Birmingham.

Bradford's Plan: the first published.

stalwart Birmingham artificers, working at an anvil, in front of an ornamental tablet, bearing this inscription: "A Plan of Birmingham, surveyed in MDCCL., by Samuel Bradford, and engraved by Thomas Jefferys, Geographer to his Royal Highness the Prince of Wales;" and the name of Thomas Jefferys, "at the corner of St. Martin's Lane, Charing Cross, London," is given as that of the publisher, with the date April 29, 1751. On one side of the Plan is given a list of the streets in the town, with the number of houses and inhabitants in each. As a measure of the progress which Birmingham has since made, this list is worthy of being copied. It is as follows:—

Names of Streets, and number of Houses and Inhabitants.	Name.	Houses.	Inhab.	Name.	Houses.	Inhab.
	Aston Street and Upper Gosty Green	54	294	Cherry Street and Crooked Lane	28	190
	Bell Street	39	179	Coleshill Street	37	199
	Bewdley Street	14	53	Colemore Row	36	268
	Bordesley	83	405	Colemore Street	58	359
	Buckle Row	5	19	Cooper's Mill Lane	7	25
	Bull Street	140	819	Corbett's Alley	4	19
	Bull Lane	14	80	Corn Cheaping	29	162
	Bullin Alley	4	18	Cross Street	1	4
	Butts Lane	1	3	Dale End	181	932
	Cannon Street and Needless Alley	64	568	Deretend	198	1,096
				Digbeth	303	1,646
	Carr's Lane	36	207	Dock Alley	13	51
	Castle Street	25	162	Duddeston		
	Chappel Row	7	33			
	Chappel Street					

Name.	Houses.	Inhab.	Name.	Houses.	Inhab.
Farmer Street	7	27	Pitt Street	—	—
Freeman Street	16	137	Porter Street	—	—
Froggary	25	147	Queen's Alley	10	45
St. Bartholomew's Street	—	—	Sand Street	1	4
Handes Square	26	140	Shutt Lane and Well Court	7	55
Harlow Street	—	—	Slainey Street	60	302
High Town	247	1,565	Smallbrook Street	101	795
Hill Street	3	16	Snow Hill	84	471
Hinkleys	37	275	Spicer Street	41	249
Jenning Street	1	5	Square	16	129
John Street	59	348	Stafford Street and Ditch	85	408
King Street	36	217	Steelhouse Lane	122	645
Leek Street	—	—	Swinford Street	5	19
Lease Lane	23	148	Temple Alley	3	19
Litchfield Street	104	841	Temple Row	17	129
Livery Street	—	—	Temple Street	53	316
Lower Minories	11	58	Thomas Street	52	316
Lower Priory	17	90	Tonke Street	13	57
St. Martin's Lane	11	49	Upper Minories	4	4
Mass House Lane	16	77	Upper Priory	23	155
Mill Lane	16	114	Walmer Lane	2	9
Moor Street	195	1,076	Weaman Street	78	486
Moat Lane	43	252	Westley Street	68	402
New Street	105	649	Wood Street	35	204
New Meeting Street	21	149	Worcester Street	66	349
Newport Street	1	—	Houses Inhabited	4,058	23,688
Newton Street	54	312	Houses not Inhabited	112	
Old Meeting Street	34	231	Total Houses	4,170	
Park Street	156	944			
Peck Lane	35	187			
Philip Street	38	213			

Names of Streets, and number of Houses and Inhabitants.

CHAP. IV.
1751.
Description of Birmingham.

Appended to this table is a short sketch of Birmingham, ending with the following passage:—"This Place has been for a long series of Years increasing in its buildings, and is superior to most Towns in ye Kingdom, for its elegance and regularity, as well as Number and Wealth of its Inhabitants. Its prosperity is owing greatly to ye Industry of ye People, who have for many years carried on an extensive Trade in Iron and other Wares, especially in the Toy Business, which has gained the Place a name and great esteem all over Europe."

Arrangement and extent of the Town.

Looking at the map, we note a mass of houses in what is now the middle of the town, broken by three or four broad and continuous street lines, and hemmed in on all sides by fields or gardens, or by land just beginning to be laid out for building. From the top of Bordesley up to the top of Digbeth there is a fringe of houses on each side, the fields lying close behind them: Bradford Street, Cheapside, and Moseley Street—now great lines of traffic —have no existence; nor is there any trace of Bromsgrove Street, while towards the Bristol Road the houses come to a full stop at the upper end of Smallbrook Street, which itself backs close up to the fields, Ladywell and its "cold bath" lying well out in a perfectly rural district, below St. Martin's Parsonage, embowered in trees, and almost entirely surrounded by a broad moat. Behind Digbeth, on the present site of Smithfield Market, we have the Moat House, the site of the ancient manor house of the lords of Birmingham, and from this—completely surrounded by a broad moat—the present Moat Lane leads into St. Martin's

Lane, at the back of the Church, and so on to Edgbaston Street in one direction, and to Corn Cheaping and the Corn Market in the other: these places occupying the space between Moor Street and Park Street, and the area in front of St. Martin's—the present name of the Bull Ring being of later date. St. Martin's Church itself is on three sides completely shut in by houses, fronting to Spiceal Street (then called Spicer Street) and to the Corn Market and Corn Cheaping; and there are also houses built close up to the Church-yard wall in St. Martin's Lane: flights of steps leading down between them. In front of the Church, beside the Corn Market, are large blocks of building, and above these, filling up the middle of the present open space in High Street, are the Shambles. Opposite Philip Street is the Old Cross, a sort of Town Hall, raised on arches, with a meeting room over them. From this point, past the corner of New Street, and as far as the corner of Bull Street, the street is called the High Town; and at the intersection of Bull Street and Dale End stands the Welsh Cross, another building on arches, with a meeting room over, and topped with a cross. Between the High Town and Dale End and the corner line of Park Street southward, there is a dense mass of building; and northward we have the same as far as Colmore Row and Steelhouse Lane, but most of the houses have gardens behind them, and Park Street, scarcely built upon on the lower side, forms the field boundary, St. Bartholomew's Chapel, then newly erected, being bounded by fields on three sides. At the end of Coleshill Street, just beyond Chapel Street, "Turner's Brass House" closes the line of buildings on that side of the town; but a little beyond, Aston Street, with three or four houses in it, is just begun. Turning up Lichfield Street from Aston Street, we come to the Workhouse, a large building occupying three sides of a square, with the chapel in the centre, and a detached infirmary, and with the open fields behind it. Higher up we have "The Square," shut in with four gates, and bordered by trees. Almost side by side with it, filling up the space between the Upper Priory and Bull Street, is the Quakers' Meeting, with its extensive grounds and grave-yard. The now densely-crowded St. Mary's district is only slightly sprinkled with houses; Bull Street is flanked on each side with pleasant-looking gardens behind the shops; at the corner of Snow Hill and Bull Lane (now Monmouth Street) is a weighing machine; Snow Hill is built upon only on the right-hand side, and that thinly; and half way up Constitution Hill, then called the Wolverhampton Road, "Tew's Bowling Green," at the sign of the Salutation, brings the town to an end—the rest, over the present St. George's, Hampton, All Saints', and Hockley districts, each now a great town in itself, being nothing but fields. Returning towards the centre, by way of Colmore Row, we find St. Philip's Church (then and long afterwards known as the New Church), bordered with a double row of trees all round the Church-yard, while there are ample gardens behind the Colmore Row and Temple Row houses. Behind the former there is nothing in the way of building; from Livery Street westward there is a street line laid out, labelled Hill Street, Charles Street, and Harlow Street, (now Little Charles Street and Edmund Street), but there are no buildings in them. The line of Newhall Street, also wholly unbuilt upon, is here called Newport Street: it leads to the stately old mansion of New Hall (the house of the Colmore family), long since cleared away, with its extensive gardens and its avenue of fir trees. What is now Ann Street is called Bewdley Street; there are a dozen houses on the upper side of it. On the opposite side, where Christ Church and Waterloo Street now exist, there is a fine old house, standing in a well-timbered park, extending in the rear to St. Philip's Church-yard, and in front having a long wall—with seemingly a lodge—at the top of New Street, then called Swinford Street; for New Street proper did not begin until below Temple Street, and ended in the Swine Market, at its junction with the High Town, to which it had access by a narrow passage or gateway, hardly large enough for a horse and cart to get through. Temple Street, it is worthy of note, is bordered by trees on one side for its whole length; and there are trees along New Street, on one side, from Temple Street to the Swine Market, with another row on the opposite side, in front of the then Free Grammar School, a quadrangular building with a clock tower in the centre of the front. At the top of Swinford Street the buildings cease—there is only a turnpike road, marked "To Stourbridge and Bewdley," leading to "Meredith's Bowling Green," and to Baskerville's house at Easy Hill. The character of the town, as regards its streets and buildings, can be gathered only from scattered notices. It seems, however, that there was no particular rule observed, either in laying out the streets or in erecting the buildings: indeed the first Act of the Street Commissioners was largely directed against irregularities in these respects. Hutton compendiously describes them—"The inhabitants of Birmingham may justly be styled masters of invention: the Arts are obedient to their will. But if Genius displays herself in the shops, she is seldom seen in the streets; though we have a long time practised the art of making streets, we have an art to learn; there is not a street in the whole town but might have been better constructed. When land is appropriated for a street, the builders are under no control; every lessee proceeds according to his interest or fancy; there is no man to preserve order, or prescribe bounds; hence arise evils without a cure: such as a narrowness which scarcely admits light, cleanliness, pleasure, health, or use; unnecessary hills, like that in Bull Street; sudden falls, owing to the floor of one house being laid three feet lower than the next, as in Coleshill Street; one side of a street, like the deck of a ship, 'gunnel to,' several feet higher than the other, as in Snow Hill, New Street, Friday Street, Paradise Row, Lionel Street, Suffolk Street, Brick-kiln Lane, and Great Charles Street. Hence also that crowd of enormous bulk sashes; steps projecting from the houses and the cellars; buildings which, like men at a dog fight, seem rudely to crowd before each other; penthouses, rails, palisades, &c., which have long called for redress. Till the year 1769, when the Lamp Act was obtained, there were only two powers able to correct these evils; the Lord of the Manor and the freeholders—neither of which were exerted. The Lord was so far from preserving the rights of the public, that he himself became the chief trespasser. He connived at small encroachments in others to countenance his own. Others trespassed like little rogues, but he like a lord. In 1728 he seized a public building, the Leather Hall, and converted it to his private use. George Davis, the constable, summoned the inhabitants to vindicate their right; but none appearing, the Lord smiled at their supineness, and kept the property. In about 1745 he took possession of the Bull Ring, their little market place, and began to build it up; but although the people did not bring their action, they did not sleep as before, for they undid in the night what he did in the day. In 1758, when the houses at No. 3 were erected in that extreme narrow part of Bull Street, near the Welch Cross, the proprietor, emboldened by repeated neglects, chose to project half a yard beyond his bounds. But a private inhabitant [in Mr. Hamper's copy of Hutton, the name of Wheeler is here inserted in writing] who was an attorney, a bully, and a freeholder, with his own hands, and a few hearty curses, demolished the building, and reduced the builder to order. But though the freeholders have power over all encroachments within memory, yet this is the only instance upon record of the exertion of that power."

In another part of his "History," when treating of the governing body created under the Commissioners' Act, Hutton speaks with vigour of the condition of the town at the date of that Act and for a considerable time afterwards —especially the narrowness, dirt, and irregularity of the streets:—"The buildings in some of the ancient streets had encroached upon the path four or five feet on each side,

CHAP. IV.
1768.
Condition of
the Town.

which caused an irregular line; and their confined width rendered the passage dangerous to children, women, and feeble age, particularly on the market day and Saturday evening. Narrow streets (he adds) with modern buildings are generally dirty for want of the natural helps of the light, the sun, and the air—as Digbeth, St. Martin's Lane, Swan Alley, Carr's Lane, &c. The narrower the street, the less it can be influenced by the sun and the wind, consequently the more dirt will abound; and by experimental observations upon stagnate water in the street, it is found extremely prejudicial to health."

Increase of Population.

There was, indeed, great need of some organised governing power when the first local Act was obtained in 1769, for between 1751 and 1769 the population had increased to over 30,000, and the houses to 6,025, without any progress having been made in sanitary affairs. The streets, as we have seen, were narrow and irregular; the pavements were wretchedly imperfect; there was no drainage—even the rainwater plashed off the house roofs into the roads and lay there, with the house refuse, until it dried up. The removal of refuse was unprovided for by any public organisation; the streets and roads were unswept, excepting by volunteers, for there were no scavengers; at

Sanitary Defects.

night all was pitch dark, save for the light of the moon or the rays of a friendly lantern, for there were no lamps. Right in centre of the town, New Street, one of the

houses, and other offensive buildings. The parish church was literally hidden by obstructions of the same character. The state of the roads may be inferred from a notice issued in 1763, announcing that the carriers from Birmingham to London intended to raise their prices because "they cannot carry so much by one third of the weight as they aforetime have done, on account of the badness of the roads." How important the carrying trade was at this period may be inferred from the fact that, according to a list appended to a Directory of the period, Birmingham had communication by means of carriers' carts with one hundred and sixty-eight other towns, so wide apart as to include York northward and Bristol southward, Welshpool westward, and Lincoln eastward—the whole of the intervening country being thoroughly covered by this means of conveyance. The carriers could venture upon this advance, as they had a monopoly of the trade, the first canal (Brindley's canal)—that connecting Birmingham with Staffordshire—not being authorised by Parliament until 1768, when the bells of the churches were set ringing to commemorate the important event. Postal accommodation was as deficient as the arrangements for the conveyance of goods. It was not until 1767 that daily communication by post was established with places so close at hand as Dudley, Hales Owen, Stourbridge, Kidderminster, and Bewdley. A Post Office notice issued at the same time informs the public that letters " from Worcester and places beyond it, in the

CHAP. IV.
1769.
Postal Service.

"such letters as are to be sent to that county" are to be posted at the Birmingham office "before ten o'clock on those nights." In the next year there was a further advance. Notice was given by the Post Office that "for the further improvement of correspondence" a post has been established "six times a week, instead of three as at present, between England and Ireland, by way of Holyhead," and that "letters hitherto sent through London will be circulated directly through the bye or cross roads." But while this improvement was effected for long-distance letters, the communication between Birmingham and other places in the midland district was still extremely imperfect. Even in 1770 the post between Birmingham and Derby was limited to four days a week each way—namely, Sunday, Wednesday, Thursday, and Friday. In this dearth of the means of communication, tradesmen and others seem to have employed whatever agencies happened to present themselves, for a Post Office notice shortly forbids, on pain of prosecution, the carriage and private delivery of letters by "carriers, coachmen, watermen, dispensers of country newspapers, &c."

Banks and Library.

A few other notes may be added to indicate the social and business condition of the town at the time when regular local government was first established. Thus, the first bank—Taylor, Lloyd, and Co.'s—was not opened until 1765; the first circulating library (afterwards well known as Evans's in Colmore Row) was opened in 1763, and in 1769 it is reported—with a touch of pride in its progress—to possess 3,000 volumes. Fish supplies at the latter date are advertised as being arranged "by special stage from the North, twice a week."

The modern system of manufacturers and tradesmen living in the suburbs of the town, away from their places of business, had not then been introduced. With rare exceptions, they lived where they worked. The warehouse was side by side with the dwelling house; the workshop or factory was behind it, in the yard. Numerous advertisements in the newspaper of the day *(Aris's Gazette)* afford evidence of this custom. One or two quotations will suffice as illustrations. Thus, in 1769, we read that in Park Street, there is to be let a house, " of four stories, four rooms on a floor, four cellars, one arched, with a cold-bath therein constantly filled by springs of water, and continually discharging itself from the top, through gutters or sewers, into the fields." There is also "a large garden, walled round, planted with fruit trees, and a summer house therein, two stories high, adjoining to the fields." In Aston Street there is to be let " a good genteel substantial dwelling house, with shopping in which 200 pair of hands may be employed," with a " good warehouse adjoining," a four-stall stable, and "a large garden" planted with all sorts of wall and standard fruit trees, with a summer house at the top of the garden, all walled in and entire." In Edgbaston Street, there is advertised a "handsome large commodious house, consisting of a large warehouse, with a counting house behind it, two good parlours, a hall, two staircases, a china pantry, three large chambers, each having light and dark closet, each of them large enough

CHAP. IV.
1769.
Town Houses.

to hold a bed; a spacious dining room, wainscotted; six good upper chambers with closets, a kitchen, pantry, four large cellars, in one of which there is an oven and a pump to bake bread; a good stable with large loft over it, a coach-house, a large garden, with a canal, and other conveniences thereto belonging." Another example, from Digbeth. This is a house, with "three rooms on a floor, and four large ware-rooms adjoining, over a broad gateway, with trap-doors to let down goods into a cart; very convenient for a factor—the ware-rooms having a communication with the house; entire court-yard, and a pleasant garden, adjoining the fields. Likewise shopping for twenty pair of hands in the toy way."

Social Life, 1760.
Carlyle's Autobiography.

While the conditions of business life were thus limited by locality of work and residence, the mode of life was unostentatious and homely. An illustration of it is given in the Autobiography of Dr. Alexander Carlyle, of Inveresk—"Jupiter Carlyle" as he was called—an eminent Scotch minister, who had friends in Birmingham. He visited the town on his way back from London to Scotland (about 1760) in company with Robertson the historian, and Home, the author of "Douglas." Their host was Mr. Samuel Garbett, one of the leading manufacturers and most respectable residents in Birmingham; a gentleman who, as will be seen presently, was included in the first body of Street Commissioners. Carlyle describes the visit and his host, and his way of living, in a narrative which—preserv-

been an ordinary worker in brass at Birmingham, and had no education further than writing and accounts; but he was a man of great acuteness of genius and extent of understanding. He had been at first distinguished from the common workmen by inventing some stamp for shortening labour. He was soon taken notice of by a Mr. Hollis, a great merchant in London, who employed him as his agent for purchasing Birmingham goods. This brought him into notice and rank among his townsmen; and the more he was known, the more he was esteemed. Let me observe once for all, that I have known no person but one more of such strong and lively feelings, of such a fair, candid, and honourable heart, and of such quick and ardent conceptions, who still retained the power of cost and deliberate judgment before execution. He received us with open hospitality, and we were soon convinced we were welcome by the cordiality of his wife and daughter, who lodged the whole company but me, who, being their oldest acquaintance, they took the liberty to send to a friend's house. Hitherto they had lived in a very moderate style, but for his Scotch friends Garbett had provided very good claret, and for the time we stayed his table was excellent, though at that time they had only one maid and a blind lad as servants. This last was a wonder, for he did all the work of a man, and even brewed the ale, but that of serving at table; and for this Garbett provided according to the custom of the place, where no man was then ashamed of frugality. He made Patrick Downy, who was then an apprentice, stand at our backs. Patrick afterwards married

CHAP. IV.
1760.
Social Life:
Samuel
Garbett.

Homely Mode of Living.

to Prestonpans [where Mr. Garbett, in conjunction with Dr. Roebuck, had some vitriol works], and was at last taken in as a partner; such was the primitive state of Birmingham and other manufacturing towns, and such encouragement did they then give to industry." It is a pleasant and honourable study, this of the well-to-do manufacturer, not ashamed of his business or of his prudent economy; nor ashamed either, to take his wife's cousin as a servant, or to reward his faithful apprentice alike with a wife and a share in his business. These were the men who made Birmingham. Another sketch shows us almost equal simplicity in regard to the mode of living at the house of a greater celebrity—Baskerville the printer. "We passed the next day after our arrival in visiting the manufactures at Birmingham, though it was with difficulty I could persuade our poet [Home] to stay, by suggesting to him how uncivil his sudden departure would appear to our kind landlord. I got him, however, to go through the tedious detail, till at last he said 'that it seemed there as if God had created man only for making buttons!'" Next day, Mr. Home insisted on leaving Birmingham, and went to Hagley. The others paid a visit to Baskerville, the printer, who lived at Easy Hill, now the lower end of Broad Street. "We saw (Mr. Carlyle writes) the Baskerville press, and Baskerville himself, who was a great curiosity. His house was a quarter of a mile from the town, and in its way handsome and elegant. What struck us most was his first kitchen, which was most completely furnished with everything that could be wanted, kept as clear and bright as if it had come straight from the shop, for it was used, and the fineness of the kitchen was a great point in the family; for there they received their company, and there were we entertained with coffee and chocolate. Baskerville was on hands with his folio Bible at this time, and Garbett insisted upon being allowed to subscribe for Home and Robertson. Home's absence afflicted him, for he had seen and heard of the tragedy of 'Douglas.' Robertson hitherto had no name, and the printer said bluntly that he would rather have one subscription to his work of a man like Mr. Home, than an hundred ordinary men. He dined with us that day, and acquitted himself so well that Robertson pronounced him a man of genius, while James Adam and I thought him but a prating pedant."

These examples will suffice to show the simplicity of Birmingham life at that period. Garbett, a leading and wealthy manufacturer, with his maid servant, and the apprentice converted into a footman for the day; and Baskerville, the great artist printer, receiving visitors in his first kitchen, with all the kitchen utensils about him! Further illustrations of the character of the town are afforded by the records contained in the first Directory of Birmingham, published in 1770 by Sketchley and Adams, two local booksellers, and entitled the "Tradesman's True Guide or Universal Directory"—a somewhat pretentious description, seeing that the book is a thin volume of 122 pages, and that within these narrow limits it contains not only a directory of Birmingham, but of Wolverhampton, Walsall, Dudley, "and the manufacturing villages in the neighbourhood of Birmingham," "the

CHAP. IV.
1770.
Trades of the Town.

whole," as the publishers add, "being a compleat view of the Trade and Commerce of this large and populous Country." The Directory opens with a list of "Professors of the Polite Arts and Sciences." These are only 39 in number, and are very various in occupation. There are three physicians amongst them—Dr. Small, Dr. Ash (the founder of the General Hospital), and Dr. Heseltine. The rest consist of 21 schoolmasters (including the masters at the Grammar School), an oculist, accountants and writing masters, organists, dancing masters, a carver and gilder, and the secretary to the General Hospital. The surgeons, of whom there were twenty—Mr. Edmund Hector, the friend and host of Dr. Johnson, being amongst them—are not considered worthy to rank with the "professors of the polite arts and sciences:" they stand in a class apart, under the head of "apothecaries and surgeons," some of them having the additional designation of "man midwife." The other trades classified in the lists are worthy of quotation, as furnishing a picture in little of the industries of the town a century ago. They are as follow :—

	No.		No.
Anvil, Augur, and Awl-blade Makers	9	Booksellers, including Hutton, the historian, and Aris, publisher of the first Birmingham newspaper	7
Attornies	21		
Bakers	56		
Bellows Makers ...	5		
Black, White, and Jobbing Smiths	32	Brush Makers	10
		Buckle Makers	44
Box Iron Makers ...	3	Butchers	42
Brassfounders ...	33	Button Makers	83
Braziers	10	Cabinet Makers	19

	No.
Candlestick Makers	7
Carpenters	12
Chaffing Dish Makers	2
Chape Makers and Filers and Forgers	14
Clock Makers and Founders	8
Cock Founders	5
Comb Makers	2
Compass Makers	4
Coopers	11
Cork Cutters	2
Cork Screw Makers	4
Curriers	8
Curry Comb Makers	2
Cutlers	16
Die Sinkers	6
Druggists	11
Edge Tool Makers	7
Enamel Manufacturers	3
Engravers and Chasers	22
Excise Officers	13
Factors and Chapmen (among whom Boulton and Fothergill, Snow Hill, are included)	24
File Cutters	11
Fork Forgers	2
Gardeners	13
Gimblet Makers	12
Glass Pinchers	6
Grocers	36
Gun and Pistol Makers	38
Gun Barrel Makers	5
Gun Lock Makers	6
Hammer Makers	3
Hard-wood Turners	13
Hatters	11
Hinge Makers	10
Ironmongers	18
Jack Makers	7
Japanners (including Baskerville, and Clay, the first maker of papier maché goods)	13
Jewellers	23
Joiners	22
Lapidaries	6
Linen and Woollen Drapers	25
Lock Smiths	18
Malt Mill Makers	6
Maltsters	32
Masons and Bricklayers	23
Merchants (including Boulton and Fothergill, Garbett, Sampson Lloyd and Son, Richards, Salt, Abraham Spooner, Taylor, and Galton)	43
Milliners	10
Nut Crack Makers	2
Painters (with whom Artists are included)	18
Peruke Makers	56
Plane Makers	5
Platers (including Ryland, Dudley, Sargant, Colmore, Barker, Winfield, and Yates)	45
Printers (including Aris, Baskerville, Warren, and "Robert Martin, with Mr. Baskerville's types")	9
Publicans	285

58 BIRMINGHAM IN THE EIGHTEENTH CENTURY.

CHAP. IV.
1770.
Trades of the Town.

Trade	No.		Trade	No.
Rule Makers	4		Thread Makers	10
Sadlers' Tool Makers	4		* Toy Makers	
Sadlers	7		Trap Makers (one of them described as making traps for "rat, fitchew, fox, and man")	6
Saw Makers	7			
Stampers	7			
Stay Makers	13			
Shoe Makers	59		Upholsterers	5
Steel Snuffer Makers	9		Watch Chain Makers	13
Steel Spur Makers	3		Watch Key Makers	5
Stilliard (Steel-yard) Makers	5		Watch Makers	6
Stirrup Makers	8		Wire Drawers (including Pidduck, the founder of Pidduck's Charity, Ryland, and Webster)	8
Sword Cutlers	4			
Taylors	67			
Thimble Makers	4		Miscellaneous, about	300

The "miscellaneous" list includes several trades which have died out, amongst them being—buckle cutter, silver caster and bluer, fire-shovel bit maker, heckle maker, paste moulder, harrateen (?) maker, ink-horn maker, steel convertor (Kettle, John, New Street), wool-comber, bag weaver, sacking weaver, flax dealer, &c. It includes also staple trades not classified in the lists, such as split-ring makers, screw makers, rope makers, &c.

---

* Some of the introductory notes to the Directory are curious: Thus of the Toy Makers we read:—"These Artists are divided into several branches, as the Gold and Silver Toy Makers, who make trinkets, seals, tweezers, tooth-pick cases, smelling bottles, snuff boxes, and philigree work, such as toilets, tea-chests, inkstands, &c. The Tortoise Toy Maker makes a beautiful variety of the above and other Articles; as does also the Steel, who make cork-screws, buckles, draw and other boxes, snuffers, watch chains, stay hooks, sugar nippers, &c.; and almost all these are likewise made in various metals, and for cheapness, beauty, and elegance, no place in the world can vie with them."

At the end of the Directory is a list of Public Offices, &c. These are The Bank, 7, Dale End; Excise Office, 89, Dale End; Navigation Office, 30, New Hall Street; Lamp Office, 28, Spiceal Street; Court of Requests Office, 39, New Street; and "The Court of Conscience held at the Old Cross every Friday." A Street List is also appended, giving the number of houses and inhabitants (male and female) in each street. The summary is—6,025 houses; 15,363 male inhabitants, 15,441 female—total 30,804.

The Brassfounders are described as "these ingenious artists (who) make an infinite variety of articles, as sconces, cabinet handles, escutcheons, hinges, cloak pins, &c.; and this is the only place for Merchants and others to be provided upon the best terms." The Buckle Makers produce "an infinite variety, both in white, yellow, Bath metal, pinchbeck, silver, tuetinage, and soft white, also of copper and steel." Button Making is described as a "very extensive branch, distinguished under the following heads, viz., gilt, plated, silvered, lacquered, and pinchbeck; the beautiful new manufacture, platina; inlaid glass, horn, ivory, and pearl; metal buttons, such as Bath, hard and soft white, &c." Of the Candlestick Makers we read that "these mechanic artists are divided into two branches, one makes brass, the other iron and steel; their variety of patterns are very numerous, and in both branches they make from a very low price to 30s. and upwards per pair; there is also made here silver [candlesticks], silvered, plated, japanned, and enamelled, but these are generally made by

1770.
Trades of the Town.

the gilt toy makers, enamellers, japanners, &c." Of the Edge Tool Makers we read that "they are the makers of axes, chisels, plane-irons, adzes, hooks, bills, &c., great quantities of which are exported to North America and various other parts." The Enamel Manufacturers are described as "ingenious artists who make candlesticks, ink-cases, tweezers, tooth-pick cases, quadrille pooles, smelling bottles, clock and watch faces, and all sorts of small trinkets for ladies' watches." The Glass Pinchers are "artists who prepare the glasses for the common glass link-buttons; they are also makers of glass buttons." The Lapidaries "are those that cut and polish large stones for snuff boxes, knife handles, cabinets, seals, rings, buttons, &c." On the Platers there is a note stating that they "make buckles, spurs, bridle-bits, and stirrups, not inferior to those made of solid silver."

1782—1787.
Rating and Rental.

Another and valuable illustration of the condition of the town is furnished by the rating and rental value of the dwelling houses and the other properties. We have no record of these particulars for the precise date under consideration; but a few years later, in 1782, the Overseers of the Poor of Birmingham parish published a complete rate book, giving the names of all the inhabitants, alike those who were and who were not rated. This volume is now very rare, and is especially worth referring to as indicating the vast number of exemptions then allowed, and the enormous difference between that period

streets of the town. The return was issued in parts or divisions, classed as follows—1, Edgbaston Street Quarter; 2, Bull Street Quarter; 3, Middle Town Quarter; 4, Dale End Quarter. These parts contain only the entries of persons actually rated; but there was also issued, in one volume of 77 pages, "A Copy of the Grand Levy Book; or an Account of all the Inhabitants who pay and those who do not pay, the Poor's Rates, in Birmingham. Printed by Pearson and Rollason, 1787." The Preface explains the object of the publication: "The various objections made respecting the great inequality of the Poor's Rates have determined the Overseers to lay before the Town the whole account of them; that every inhabitant may know how far such complaints are founded in truth or error; and from that result, either to silence complaint, or to lead to a New General Assessment. Together with those who do pay, are the names and residence of that very numerous body of people who contribute nothing to these payments—many of these, doubtless, ought as equally to bear a proportion, as numbers of those who do it already. The Collectors, since their appointment, have rated upwards of two hundred old houses, but there are many people capable of paying who elude their enquiry, as well as the vigilance of former Overseers; and it is hoped that in consequence of the publicity of this Catalogue, many such persons will be obliged to pay their just proportion." The list thus published contains the entries of 12,000

Chap. IV.
1787.
Large Exemptions.

500	above £9	and under	£10
500	„ 8	„	9
2,000	„ 7	„	8
3,000	„ 6	„	7
2,000	„ 5	„	6
1,000	under 5		

Unequal Rating.

The rating seems, indeed, to have been strangely unequal. While there were 6,000 houses of above £6 yearly value, altogether unassessed to the rate, there were many rated of the values of £5, £4, and even so low as £2 yearly. All the values assessed were, however, very low. In Spiceal Street, for example, the highest assessment—or rental, as the Overseers put it—was £18; in Edgbaston Street the house and warehouse of Mr. Abraham Spooner, a leading merchant, £34; in Smallbrook Street, £12, excepting the Riding House—then occupied by the Rev. Mr. Curtis, which was rated at £35, the land attached to it being rated at the same amount. In the Bull Ring the highest rental was £30; in Suffolk Street, £13; in the Old Hinkleys several houses were rated at £1. In New Street the ratals were strangely low. The highest—the Play House (Theatre Royal)—stood at £50; Kettle's house and steel-house works, £26; and other houses and warehouses at from £8 to £15. In Peck Lane we have an "Elabatory" (Laboratory), rated at £3. In Temple Row, then one of the best residential streets, the highest ratal is £40, paid by Dadley and Palmer; Dr. Ash, the physician, for his house and stables, is rated at £16. In Colmore Row

Examples of Rating.

£20. In Newhall Street, Dr. Male, whose house formerly stood on the site of the Union Club, is rated at £16; Clay, the papier maché maker, at £14; Samuel Garbett, a leading brassfounder, at £16; William Chance, the merchant, at £10;—these are the highest amounts. In Paradise Row (now Paradise Street) there is nothing higher than £14, excepting the Navigation Office (Old Wharf), which stands at £42. Park Street and the neighbouring smaller streets are almost blank: everybody escapes rating. In Digbeth the ratals run generally from about £3 to about £24—the bulk being under £10, with one conspicuous exception, "Sampson Lloyd and Co., mill and meadow," £44. In Worcester Street the rents range from £3 to £13. Queen Street, though full of houses, is nearly a blank as to rating, almost all the residents escaping from local burdens. In regard to this street there is a curious entry—six houses, rated at 4s., having appended to them the note "paid by Mr. Ruston," possibly an early example of the compounding system. In the middle and busiest streets of the town the rates are proportionately as low as in other quarters. In High Street, for example, there are many houses which are not rated at all, and others are plainly rated below their value. Thus William Hutton, the historian, stands at £20, although his business as a stationer was then probably the most important of its kind in the town. The highest ratal in this street is "W. Taylor's house and shopping," £68. Bull Street, another principal thoroughfare, ranges from £10 to £18 in ratal. In Snow Hill the highest amount is £23; Livery Street has few houses rated at more than £2 or £3. In Steelhouse Lane, the highest amount, entered to "Samuel Galton"—the premises used lately as the Children's Hospital—is £50; the rest are rarely higher than £5. In the Square, then a good residential place, Mr. Hector, the surgeon, is rated at £13, "Sampson Lloyd" at £20, and other properties at £8, £10, and £12. These examples are enough to show the comparatively small estimated value of property at that date, and the imperfection of the rating arrangements. To this it should be added that most of the back streets appear to have been entirely left out of assessment, and that in many of the principal streets there are long lists of houses to which no ratals are affixed. It is, however, only an act of justice to the overseers to say that after the publication of the complete list, they vigorously set to work to remedy the omissions disclosed by it. A new assessment was made, and published in sections, as above mentioned; and in this revision many of the assessments were more than doubled, and others were proportionately increased. This proceeding seems to have naturally excited much disapproval on the part of those who had previously escaped, or who now had to make a fair payment. The Overseers consequently prefixed to each section the following explanatory note: "The reason for publishing these Books is, that every House-keeper may have an opportunity of seeing and knowing how they themselves, and their neighbours, are circumstanced by the late assessment; and they are hereby informed that the Churchwardens and Overseers, with the Gentlemen that attended upon the Assessment, and many other respectable Gentlemen of the town, do intend (previous to collecting the new

Rate) to hold a meeting, or meetings, of the times and place of which proper notice will be given in the public papers, for the purpose of hearing the complaints of those persons (if any such there are) who, under an apprehension of being aggrieved, may think proper to appeal." Such a polite and considerate notice ought to have mollified the wrath of the most reluctant ratepayer; but it would seem that the fashion of low rents and low rates continued to prevail in Birmingham, for as late as 1790 Hutton says that he knows of no house in the town that lets at more that £90 a year. Hutton, it may be mentioned, was a strong opponent of the rating of small houses—not on the tenants' account, but because directly or ultimately the landlord would have to pay. In a tract on "The Rating upon Small Houses in Birmingham Considered," issued in 1790, he protests vigorously on the landlords' behalf: "How well (he writes) the landlord's profit will bear the burden has not yet been proved. They can best solve the question who count it. In some instances, I am well informed, it does not exceed 5 per cent., in others the trouble exceeds the profit! As I am possessed of only £14 a year of this moonshine property, mine is upon too small a scale to decide; nor is the whole worth a contention. Perhaps, from the loss of rent, empty houses, and repairs, I lose about half. But whatever be these monstrous profits, which injustice marks out for plunder, they are the proprietor's own, and, as private property, they are sacred. It is a dangerous doctrine, to take a man's money because he is rich." Hutton, however, was not altogether a friend to local governing bodies. He had

F

opposed the nomination of Commissioners of the Street Act, and he now falls foul of the Overseers. "The greatest evil (he says) that ever afflicted Birmingham, was that of constituting twelve Overseers. That enormous number can no more conduct the business than twelve pilots, at twelve helms, can a vessel. Six did mischief, but twelve increases it, like that number multiplied into itself." Possibly religious difficulties had something to do with this feeling. "In conversing with one of the Lichfield Street jury [the workhouse was then in Lichfield Street] half tipsy, he told me 'that no man would be suffered to transact parochial business who did not believe in the Trinity,' and asked *my* opinion of that long-disputed point."

CHAPTER V.

FIRST REGULAR LOCAL GOVERNMENT—THE STREET COMMISSIONERS.

The state of the town being such as we have described, and its extent, population, wealth, and importance generally having out-grown the primitive methods of administration at that time in operation, it was a natural result that the more thoughtful of the inhabitants should endeavour to establish a system of local government of a more regular character, and with powers in some degree proportionate to the necessities of the place. Hutton, as we have seen, states that some idea of the kind had been entertained in the early part of the century, by the application to George the First for a charter of incorporation, in consequence of the failure of which, the historian observes in his own peculiar style, "I am not able to bring upon the stage a mayor and a group of aldermen, dressed in antique scarlet, bordered with fur, drawing a train of attendants, the meanest of which, even the pinder [the pound-keeper] is badged with silver, nor treat my guest with a band of music, in scarlet cloaks with broad laces. I can grace the hand of any Birmingham fidler with only a rusty instrument, and his back with barely a whole coat; neither have I a

Chap. V.
1765.
Street Commissioners proposed.

mace, charged with armorial bearings, for the inauguration of the chief magistrate." If Birmingham had ever desired these adornments of the older Corporations it sought for them no longer, but was content to begin its local government by means of a kind of authorised vestry of the leading inhabitants, and to direct their operations to the humble but useful work of street improvement, the provision of necessary light for the public highways, and the establishment of some kind of force for the maintenance of order and the security of property. The first movement in this direction took place in 1765, when a public meeting was held, on February 7, "at the house of Joseph Cooke, victualler, in the Cherry Orchard" (now Cherry Street), when a resolution was adopted to apply to Parliament for an Act to appoint Trustees, with rating powers not exceeding one shilling in the pound, for the purpose of "repairing, cleansing, and enlightening the streets of the Town," and with power to "purchase lamps, and to appoint scavengers, rakers, lamplighters, and other proper officers," which Act the resolution declares "will be of great use and importance, and tend to the suppression of many disorders, and to the preservation of the persons and properties of the inhabitants." The resolution, however, came to nothing; the standing orders of the House of Commons prevented any private bill from being introduced after the 11th of February, and so the intended application to Parliament was postponed. The projected reform now slumbered until the end of 1768, when another meeting of inhabitants was called, by public notice in the churches, and this meeting was held on the

20th of December, in the chamber over the old Cross, in the Bull Ring, and a Committee was appointed to consider the subject of a bill. Six days later the Committee announced by advertisement, that they had unanimously agreed to petition Parliament for an Act to light and clean the streets of the town, to remove nuisances, to remove the beast market to Dale End, to buy and take down certain houses which blocked up the Bull Ring, and others which actually closed the entrance to New Street—access to which was then afforded only by a gateway; and to levy for these purposes a rate not exceeding eightpence in the pound. This reasonable proposal instantly aroused a violent, though not a very extensive opposition. Hutton's Autobiography discloses, with cynical candour, the origin and the motive of the adverse movement. Under the date of 1768 he writes—"The Lamp Act came upon the carpet. Great opposition arose, and more by my means than any other person's; and that for an obvious reason. I occupied two houses which formed the gateway entering New Street, and they suited me. Both must come down if the Act passed. All the terms the opposition could obtain, and which were all I wanted, after many hundred pounds had been spent, were that the buildings should not come down, nor be included in the Act." The confession is discreditable, considering the lofty professions which the writer made of his desire to promote the public good, and bearing in mind, also, the picture he draws in his History of the state of the town, owing to the absence of the very governing powers which he opposed. At a later period, however—which, to

THE STREET ACT.

Chap. V.
1768.
Hutton's candid Confessions.

complete this reference to him, we may here anticipate— Hutton became a supporter of the Street Act. When an extension of the Act was asked for in 1772, he was an advocate of it—again on selfish grounds, which he states with amusing frankness:—"By an amendment of the Lamp Act, my houses [at the end of New Street] must come down. It happened that the old house where I now reside [in High Street, opposite New Street] was upon sale. I durst not let the opportunity slip, but considered it a tool by which I must carry on trade. I purchased it for eight hundred and thirty-five guineas. It was then under a mortgage for £400. I was obliged to pay the residue; and as the premises would open to New Street were my two houses removed, I now wished them down."

Hutton's Conversion.

In the next year, 1773, Hutton had become so entirely converted to the opposite side that he became a member of the Commissioners' body, though, as will be seen, he soon quarrelled with his colleagues. "My disposition (he wrote in his Autobiography, in 1773) was for active life. Pride and the idea of being useful were the urging motives. I was now chosen a Commissioner of the Lamp Act. This I relished, attended, and considered a large field for reform. The whole inhabitants, I found, had for ages been encroachers on public property. This gave a fine opening to reduce things to order. My plan was to execute the Act with firmness and mildness. I would oblige all to conform. But this plan, I found, could not be adopted. There were clashing interests among the Commissioners. Some would retain their own encroachments, or serve their friends; then how could they vote down others? A rich man met with more favour than a poor one. The blame of some removals fell upon me, being strenuous, a speaker, and not backed by the Board. I lost some friends; as they did not act in a body, nor consistent, I declined attendance."

To return, however, to the opposition raised to the proposed Act. The first note of it came immediately upon the report of the Committee, in the form of a proposal to open a subscription for the removal of nuisances, instead of levying a rate. Then, in January, 1769, appeared in the *Gazette*—through the columns of which both sides made their public appeals—an announcement that a canvass of the inhabitants had been made, and that it showed 237 votes for the proposed Act, and 1,236 against it. Thus, proceeded the advertisement—all the appeals, it should be observed, are anonymous—" it appearing that the general Voice of the People is against the Act" a subscription is opened to resist and " defeat so oppressive and ill-judged a scheme." This provoked a rejoinder from the supporters of the Bill, pointing out its intention and objects, describing the Committee as being composed of " the most respectable persons in the town," alleging that the opposition at the public meeting was confined to " four or five persons," and denouncing the reputed canvass as unfair and misleading, because the persons canvassed were " only asked if they were for a perpetual tax," and " a great many names were put down contrary to the inclinations and express orders of the different persons." Then the advantages of the proposed Act were set out with force and clearness, and the appeal concludes by showing that the rating could not be made oppressive: "No impartial person can imagine that anyone that rents a house of £8 a year can think it a great burden to pay 4s. per annum, if the whole [rate of 6d.] is collected; and if 4d. in the pound will be sufficient, no more than 2s. 8d. per annum will be required, and all other houses in proportion; and the public advantage of having lighted and clean streets will more than compensate for the payment." Some persons, however, objected to clean and lighted streets. One writer, a strong opponent of the Lamp Act, published an indignant appeal in the newspaper of February 13. Birmingham, he says very justly, "is a Place whose very Dependance is on the Sale of its Manufactures, which are vended in all parts of the commercial world, and the cheaper they are carried to market, the greater will be their consumption." Therefore local rating will be hurtful, because it will increase the cost of production; and special circumspection is required, because "the present flourishing state of its Manufactures is looked upon with a jealous eye by many Foreign Nations." Besides, the new taxes—"enslaving themselves and their posterity by a perpetual Act of Parliament"—are wholly needless. They are wanted, it is alleged, to provide lamps. The writer does not see the necessity, and he puts his case in a manner certainly entitled to the credit of ingenuity: "This [the necessity for lamps] does not appear to be the Case, from Experience of the Town having hitherto subsisted without Lamps, and that perhaps fewer Robberies or Accidents have happened to its Inhabitants than any other Town for its Size and Numbers of People, which may perhaps be in Part ascribed to its want of Lamps; for, as according to the Proverb, 'Opportunity makes a Thief,' so Lamps frequently give a Villain an Opportunity of perpetrating Mischief, which is prevented by Darkness, and his fear of being observed prowling about the Streets with a Light; and this seems to be verified by the City of London, which is watched and lighted at a very great expense, yet, nevertheless, Robbery and Mischief is very frequent there, for the Truth of which I appeal to the daily Papers." However, if "the Interested or the Wealthy" desire these "Convenient Improvements" let a voluntary Subscription be opened, and let them "not enforce Money against their Neighbour's Inclination or Abilities, for the Conveniency of lighting the Affluent or Extravagant home from Taverns and Alehouses in dark nights." What is wanted, according to this remarkable writer, is not town improvements, but the promotion of "a true Sense of Religion, Sobriety, Temperance, and other Christian and Moral Virtues among the People," and this is to be effected only by building additional places of worship "for the service of the Great Creator of the Universe, and it is greatly to be lamented that Places for his Divine Worship, according to *his* Established Church, have not adequately increased with the number of houses and inhabitants." Wherefore the writer proposes that instead of a Lamp Act, an Act should be obtained to make two new parishes, and that "a temporary duty of 3d. in the pound" should be levied "to purchase two large Pieces of Ground for burying the Dead,

CHAP. V.
1769.

and erecting two stately Edifices, to the Honor and Glory of God, the Ornament of the Town, and the eternal Felicity of Thousands unborn."

Reasons for the Act.

Despite these proposals of spiritual advantage, the promoters of the Street Act preferred temporal improvements as the duty nearest to them. Consequently they pressed forward with the Bill, and on the 25th of March, 1769, they issued a public statement, the closing sentences of which are worthy of quotation, as indicating the temper of the advocates of improvement:—

"The Petitioners for the Bill totally disavow any arbitrary and oppressive Intentions with regard to their Neighbours. They rest their cause altogether upon its own Equity. If they are so happy as to receive the Countenance of Parliament, they will have a satisfaction from thence, proper timed to the many Benefits which they flatter themselves the Town in general will reap from the Bill: on the contrary, if it should become a Sacrifice to private Interest and groundless Clamours, they will nevertheless have left a Consciousness in the Rectitude of their Views, and their Disappointment will only be an additional Instance to many others, of the best Plans failing of their deserved success."

There was unquestionably much opposition that did not appear upon the surface, and much also, of an open character, of which we have no remaining record. The combined efforts of public and secret opponents, however, proved unsuccessful; the Bill was passed by the House of Commons at the end of April, with only one vote in the negative, was read directly afterwards in the Lords, and at the beginning of May received the Royal Assent; and thus, after a sharp fight, the foundation was laid of regular local government in Birmingham. By successive Acts, passed in 1772, 1784, 1801, 1812, and 1828, the powers of the Commissioners were gradually extended; and special Acts were also obtained for the local government of the hamlets of Deritend and Bordesley, and of Duddeston and Nechells. It will be convenient to present abstracts of these Acts at one view, which is accordingly done as follows:—

CHAP. V.
1869.
The Street Act obtained.

COMMISSIONERS' FIRST ACT, 1769, GEO. III., c. 98.

This was an "Act for laying open and widening certain ways and passages within the Town of Birmingham, and for cleansing and lighting the streets, ways, lanes, and passages there, and for removing and preventing nuisances and obstructions therein."

The First Act.

The preamble of the Act is as follows:—"Whereas the Town of Birmingham, in the County of Warwick is a large, populous, and trading Town. And whereas certain ways and passages within the said Town are too narrow for the commodious issuing and repassing of passengers, waggons, and other carriages, to the great danger and inconvenience of the inhabitants of the said Town, and of persons resorting thereto. And whereas it would greatly tend to the convenience of the said Town if a certain ancient building situate near the Market Place, called the Upper Roundabout House, was taken down, and the ground upon which the same now stands was laid open. And whereas it would add greatly to the safety and advantage of the said Town if the streets, lanes, ways, and passages thereof were kept clean and properly lighted, and kept free from nuisances, obstructions, and annoyances." On this

Preamble.

76 STREET COMMISSIONERS: THEIR POWERS.

CHAP. V.
1769.
Names of the first Commissioners.

preamble, the Act appointed certain Commissioners to execute the powers contained in it. The first Commissioners, named in the Act, were the following:—

John Ash, M.D.
William John Banner.
John Baskerville.
Samuel Bradbourn.
Thomas Bingham.
James Butler.
Samuel Baker.
Henry Carver.
Francis Coales.
Thomas Careless.
John Cope.
Thomas Falconbridge.
John Freer.
Samuel Freeth.
John Ford.
Samuel Garbett, Esq.
Samuel Galton.
Richard Goolden.
John Gold.
Samuel Harvey.
Gregory Hicks.
James Jackson.
John Kettle.
Sampson Lloyd, sen.
Sampson Lloyd, jun.

Michael Lakin.
Thomas Lutwyche.
Thomas Lawrence.
William May.
Benjamin Mansell.
John Moody.
John Oseland.
Thomas Pemberton.
William Russell.
John Ryland.
Thomas Russell.
Richard Rabone.
John Rogers.
William Small, M.D.
Joseph Smith.
John Taylor, Esq.
Joseph Thomas.
John Turner, sen.
John Turner, jun.
Joseph Wilkinson.
William Walsingham.
William Welch.
Elias Wallin.
Joseph Webster.
Thomas Westley.

Qualification of Commissioners.

The Commissioners were to be inhabitants, rated to the poor at not less than £15 a year, or possessed of real or personal estate of the value of £1,000. They were authorised (seven being a quorum) to fill up vacancies in their own body; they were debarred from in any way benefiting personally by holding offices of profit under the Act, and it was provided that "at all their meetings they shall defray their own expenses." The first meeting was appointed in the Act to be held "at the house of John Cambden, known by the sign of the Castle, in Birmingham, on the Tuesday fortnight after the passing of this Act, between the hours of ten of the clock in the forenoon and two in the afternoon, in order to put this Act into execution."

<small>CHAP. V.
1769.</small>

The Act authorised the Commissioners to buy the properties named in the schedule, and in case of disagreement, the Sheriff of the county was to empanel a jury to assess the value. If the value so assessed was greater than the price offered by the Commissioners, they were to pay the costs; if it was no more or if it were less, then the costs were to be borne by the vendors. If the purchase money was not paid within six months from the award, then the bargain was to be "void and of no effect."

<small>Powers to Buy and Sell Properties.</small>

The Commissioners were authorised to sell any surplus land not required for widening the streets; "and also all or any part of the present passage leading out of the Corn Market into Saint Martin's Church-yard:" preference in the sale being given to the former owners.

As to officers, the Commissioners were authorised to appoint and dismiss "such and so many scavengers, rakers, or cleaners of the streets, and lighters of lamps, and so many clerks, treasurers, and other officers as they shall think proper;" they were also to "direct and appoint the number and sort of lamps, how and in what parts of the town they shall be set up, and to what houses, buildings, or other places, they shall be affixed, and for how long time the same shall be and continue lighted." For the convenience of the scavengers the inhabitants were ordered (under penalty of one shilling) "every Friday, between the hours of six in the morning and two in the afternoon," to sweep the streets and ways in front of their premises (excepting dead walls), "and collect and put together the dirt and soil in the said streets, lanes, ways, and passages, with the least obstruction to the way, road, and passage therein respectively that may be, to the end the same may be ready for the scavenger to carry away." This obligation extended to a space of twelve feet from the front of all occupied premises. The space in front of void houses, dead walls, waste land, "churches, church-yards, chapels,

<small>Officers, &c.</small>

<small>Lighting and Cleansing.</small>

CHAP. V.
1769.

meeting-houses, the school called the Free School, and other public buildings," was to be cleansed by the town scavengers; and the scavengers were to give notice by ringing a bell, so that the inhabitants might bring out ashes and other refuse from the houses for removal. By a special provision the Commissioners were authorised to undertake the private sweeping and cleaning above mentioned, on an annual payment by those who chose to make it.

Rain Water.

It appears to have been the custom at that time to discharge rain water directly into the streets, for the Act provides that within nine months "all spouts and gutters which convey water from the tops of the houses, warehouses, shops, and other buildings, directly into the streets, lanes, ways, or public places within the town," shall be removed (on penalty of one shilling per week for each spout) and the water shall be brought down by pipes "into some underground sewer, cistern, or reservoir, or to the ground," at the cost of owners, or in their default by occupiers at the owners' expense, the cost to be deducted from the next rent.

Street Traffic.

Amongst other provisions of the Act there is one prohibiting the carrying through the street of "timber, boards, bricks, tubs, hogsheads, barrels, stalls, benches, crates, pens, waggons, drays carts, or other carriages" larger than is reasonably necessary for unloading or for the purposes of building; or the setting up of "any butcher's gallows, posts, shambles, or block," or the placing of "any steps leading into any cellar or vault," or to do anything otherwise that might cause any obstruction in the streets to the hindrance of passengers; and the Commissioners were authorised to "cause any such obstruction, nuisance, or encroachment to be altered or regulated, removed, taken, carried away, and deposited in such place or places as they may appoint, there to remain until the offender shall have paid the costs of such removal," and a fine of ten shillings for each offence.

Street Obstructions.

Horses and Carriages.

The passage of horses through the town was also regulated by the Act, it being provided that "at all times for the future, when any cart, water cart, sledge, or dray shall be drawn in any street, lane, way, or place," the person driving or conducting such vehicle "shall guide the same by holding in his hand a halter or cord, not less than a yard and a half long, fastened to the head of the shaft horse," under a penalty of 2s. 6d., with power to "any person or persons who shall see the offence committed to seize the offender, and without any other warrant to convey and deliver him into the custody of a peace officer, in order to be secured and conveyed before some Justice of the Peace for the county of Warwick."

Other clauses of the Act regulate the size and thickness of cart wheels; give power to the Commissioners to name the streets and number the houses; authorise them to make contracts for lighting the streets, and for the removal of "dirt, dust, rubbish, ashes, soil, and filth." One clause recites that "the market for the sale of neat cattle within the said town has usually been held in the principal street and greatest thoroughfare, called the High Street, to the great danger and inconvenience of all persons living and resorting there," and it then enacts "that for the future that part of the street called Dale End, which is between the house now in the occupation of Clement Satterthwaite and the end of Chapel Street, and not elsewhere, shall be the place for holding a market for neat cattle."

The rating clauses of the Act provide for the appointment, by the Commissioners, of "six or more inhabitants to be Assessors of the money by this Act directed to be raised." The Commissioners are "once a year, or oftener, as there may be occasion," to issue an order to the Assessors of "how much in the pound shall be raised by taxation," the scale of rating being fixed as follows: All persons renting or occupying "any house, tenement, or building of the yearly rent or value of six pounds and under ten pounds shall be rated and assessed at any sum not exceeding two-pence in the pound in any one year;" occupiers of £10 and under £15, at not more than 3d. in the pound; £15 and under £20, at not more than 4d.; £20 and under £25 and upwards, not more than 8d. in the pound. All occupiers of premises under the annual value of £6 were to be entirely free from rating under the Act. An appeal against assessments was allowed to the Quarter Sessions. Exemptions from rating were conferred upon occupiers of "any gardens, garden grounds, or orchards, during the time they may be occupied for the purpose only of selling the fruit or produce;" and upon occupiers of "any arable, meadow, or pasture ground." It is also provided that "stock in trade, money, or personal estate" shall be exempted from rating. In case of premises void at the time of making any rate, in-coming tenants were to be liable only for a proportion of the rate. Inhabitants were to be liable to serve as rate collectors, but no one person was to be liable "oftener than once in ten years."

The rates were to be applied to the specific purposes mentioned in the Act; it being expressly provided that "no part of the money to be raised by rate shall be applied in laying open or widening any of the said ways, passages, or places, or in purchasing of houses, buildings, grounds, or estates for that purpose or otherwise therein or thereabouts."

Rights of Lord of Manor.

The Act contains a proviso that it shall not in any way "prejudice or affect the Right Hon. Andrew Lord Archer, lord of the manor of Birmingham," or his successors in the lordship "in respect of his rents, stallages, cottage, or any other rights" belonging to him as lord of the manor, "save and except all right as the said lord of the manor has to such fines, amercements, pains, and penalties as may be levied or recovered in pursuance of this Act for or in respect of any nuisances or annoyances whatsoever." There was another proviso, "saving always to the King's Most Excellent Majesty, his heirs and successors, and to all and every other person and persons, bodies politic and corporate, all such estate, use, trust, or interest of, into, or out of the ground whereon the building called the Upper Roundabout House now stands, except any power of building thereon."

Buildings to be Removed.

The schedule to the Act recites the buildings, &c., which the Commissioners are empowered to purchase, and remove, or otherwise deal with—namely, (1) four tenements fronting to High Street, occupied by William Hutton, John Greaves, and Thomas Brueton, with five houses in the rear, or, as the Act says, "backwards." This property had a frontage of sixty-four feet to High Street, and seventy feet to New Street. (2) The Upper Roundabout House, in the occupation of Samuel Willets. This building is described as being about twenty-eight feet by nineteen feet. (3) The house fronting the Corn Market, occupied by Francis Moles—thus described: "The front towards the Corn Market about fifteen feet, on the side towards the passage leading into St. Martin's Church-yard about thirty feet, and the back part thereof towards the said Church-yard about fifteen feet."

<small>Chap. V.
1769.</small>

The second Act obtained by the Commissioners was passed in 1773 (13 George III., c. 36). The preamble cites the former Act of 1769, and recites that "a considerable progress has been made in the execution of the said Act," but the powers thereby given are found insufficient. "From the small number of Commissioners thereby appointed, it is sometimes very difficult to procure a meeting for executing the Act, and whereas by reason a navigation [canal] has lately been made up to the said town of Birmingham, a much greater number of carts and carriages are now used there than formerly, in conveying goods and merchandise, and it is therefore very necessary that some other of the streets, roads, and passages should be widened and made commodious for carrying on the extensive trade and commerce of the said town, without danger and inconvenience to the inhabitants and others resorting thereto; and it is also necessary that the carts and carriages used in the said town, for carrying goods, wares, and merchandise, should be put under proper regulations, the fares for the use thereof to be limited and ascertained, and the behaviour of the owners and drivers thereof restricted; and whereas it would tend very greatly to the safety and convenience of the inhabitants of the said town, if a regular Nightly Watch was established therein." Therefore it was enacted that the following twenty-nine persons should be added to the former Commissioners—namely, and in the order given in the Act:—

<small>1773.
Second Act.
Preamble.</small>

Richard Anderton.	John Francis.
Samuel Aris.	Sampson Freeth.
Matthew Barker.	William Hutton.
William Capper.	William Hodgkins.

<small>Additional Commissioners.</small>

G

STREET COMMISSIONERS: THEIR POWERS.

CHAP. V.
1773.
Additional Commissioners.

Joseph Jukes.
Edmund Wace Patteson.
Edward Palmer.
Samuel Pemberton, jun.
Samuel Ray.
William Ryland.
Josiah Rogers.
Samuel Steward.
Timothy Smith.
John Taylor, jun.
John Ward.
Thomas Wight (grocer).

Daniel Bond.
Thomas Colemore, of Edgbaston Street.
William Dutton.
William Holden, of New Street.
John Harris, of Cannon Street.
Luke Bell.
Walter Oakeley.
Thomas Gisbourne.
Joseph Thomason.

Purchase of Properties.

The Commissioners (fifteen being a quorum) were authorised to buy the properties named in the schedule to the Act, and to lay open the ground so acquired for widening the passages and streets named in the schedule.

The clauses of this Act may be briefly described. They are in substance as follows:—

Commissioners to hire a room for an office and storehouse.

Carmen not to ride on their carts, or on the shafts, but to lead the horse, and not to drive on the footpaths, "other than in case of necessity."

Carts carrying coals or water to have six-inch wheels.

Commissioners to fix rates of cartage, to make rules for carmen, and to mark the distances from the several wharves "near or adjoining to the town."

Night Watch appointed.

Commissioners to appoint "such number of watchmen and night constables as they shall judge proper, and to nominate such able-bodied men to be employed in such services as they shall think best qualified." The night constables appear to have been superior officers, as it is provided that they shall "every night go about the town, and take notice whether all the watchmen perform their duties in their several stations," giving notice to the Commissioners' clerk of any neglect, on which the clerk may suspend the offending watchman until the next Commissioners' meeting, when the offender may be fined five shillings "for every such misbehaviour or neglect," or be discharged, "and be incapable of ever after being employed as a watchman by virtue of this Act." The cost of maintaining the watch was to be paid out of rates sanctioned by the Act.

Street nuisances forbidden. Persons are not to throw into the street or other public place, "any broken glass, earthen-ware, casting pots, brick ends, brick bats, cinders, sleck, casting shop dirt, brass dirt, ashes, or any other rubbish whatsoever," but shall, "at their own expense," cause such matter "to be carried away and laid at some convenient and proper place out of the said town."

Some persons appear to have used the streets as places in which to carry on manufacturing processes. There is a special clause to prevent it: "No person shall at any time wash any brass dirt, or ashes, or any kind of metal" in the streets, or ways, but "all persons having occasion to wash such brass dirt, or ashes, or any kind of metal, shall cause the same to be done in their shops or yards, or else in some convenient place out of the said town, in order to prevent the foul water, dirt, or ashes necessarily arising therefrom intermixing with the dirt or soil" of the streets. Penalty for every offence, ten shillings.

Power was given in the Act to regulate "signs, pent houses, shew boards, &c.," and bulks and bulk sashes, for preventing casks and wheelbarrows being rolled on the foot-pavements, to forbid the erection of stalls in the streets, or in the market place (except those belonging to the Lord of the Manor), and for impounding stray "swine and cattle."

At that period bull-baiting was a popular amusement; so the Commissioners inserted a clause providing that "if any person shall bait, or cause to be baited, any bull, in the manner called bull-baiting, in any part of the said town, such person or persons shall, for every such offence, forfeit and pay the sum of five pounds." Bonfires came in the same category of prohibition,

84 STREET COMMISSIONERS: THEIR POWERS.

CHAP. V.
1773.
Second Act.

but with a tithe of the penalty, a fine of five shillings being imposed upon persons making such fires in the streets, or discharging "any squib, serpent, rocket, or other fireworks whatsoever" in any public place. Breaking or damaging the public lamps was made punishable with a fine of twenty shillings for each offence, to be "paid immediately," on pain of a month's imprisonment for injuring a single lamp, or three months' if more than one.

Rating, Revised Scale of.

The rating authorised by the Act of 1769 was now altered as follows—occupiers of premises of less annual value than one pound, exempt; of the value of £1 and under £10, at a sum not exceeding 3d. in the pound in one year; £10 and under £20, not more than 6d.; £20 and upwards not more than 9d. The rates were to be collected "twice a year, or oftener." Persons who on the ground of poverty were "left out of the rates made for the relief of the poor," were not to be liable to the Commissioners' rate. Provision was made that where occupiers held different properties, "either adjoining together, or situated dispersedly in various parts of the town," the separate rents of which were under £10 or £20 respectively, they should be added together, and the occupier charged upon the higher scale of rating, as if the rentals were derived from single properties. The Commissioners were authorised to spend a tenth part of the rates for the purpose of buying properties for public improvements; and they were further authorised to borrow money "so as the whole money which shall be owing or undischarged in respect thereof, at any one time, do not exceed the sum of £1,000;" and they were also authorised to "assign over or mortgage, for any certain term or number of years, a tenth part or share of the yearly revenue or income to arise from the respective rates or assessments hereby granted," or to sell or grant annuities for lives to the same amount.

Schedule of Improvements

The schedule to this Act specified the properties to be dealt with for public improvements—namely, to widen Moor Street; to widen New Street (by taking in "part of a close belonging to John Meredith," and three perches of land "lying next the road at the end of New Street," to make the street sixty feet wide; to widen Bull Lane, to make "the road by the side of St. Philip's Church-yard

STREET COMMISSIONERS: THEIR POWERS.

thirty feet wide; to widen Smallbrook Street; and to widen "the street or road called Mount Pleasant."

CHAP. V.

1801.

Third Act. New Commissioners.

These Acts of the 9th and 13th of Geo. III. were amended and enlarged by an Act of the 41st Geo. III., 1801, which began by reciting the necessity of further powers for improvement, and for raising additional money. The Act began by adding the following persons to the number of Commissioners:—

Edward Bower.	Thomas Hutton.
Edward Bristowe.	Thomas Keland.
Joseph Blunt.	Matthew Lintwood.
Robert Butcher.	William Lycett.
Thomas Brown.	George Lander.
William Bingley.	William Mewis.
John Clarke, druggist.	Theodore Price.
John Cope, mercer.	Richard Pratchet.
Thomas Clowes.	John Parsons, draper.
John Clarke, Paradise St.	Philemon Price.
Richard Tapper Cadbury.	Thomas Phipson.
William Walter Capper.	Theophilus Richards.
William Chance.	Samuel Rogers.
John Duperoy.	John Ryland.
Vincent Eagle.	George Simcox.
Samuel Galton.	John Startin.
William Gilby, M.D.	Benjamin Stokes.
Thomas Hadley.	John Turner, Snow Hill.
John Heeley.	James Woolley.
Benjamin Hughes.	William Whitmore.
Edward Hughes.	John Webb, draper.

This Act authorised the Commissioners to borrow £5,000 on security of the rates (in addition to the £1,000 authorised by the previous Act). The levying of rates was altered so as to bring all occupiers under £20 under the 6d. rate, thus abolishing the 3d. limit between £1 and £10, and abolishing also the exemptions on the ground of omission from the poor levy, it being now provided that "no person shall be left out of the said rates, or be

Borrowing Powers and Rating.

CHAP. V.
1801.
Third Act.

excused from paying the same, without the consent of the Commissioners."

Other provisions of the Act give power to make bye-laws for regulating "hackney coaches and sedan chairs," which are required for the first time to be numbered. It is provided that owners of "every waggon, cart, sledge, dray, hand cart, and street barrow" shall have his name and residence painted on such carriages "in large white capital letters, on a black ground, two inches high at the least, and of a proportional breadth."

Street Improvements

As to public improvements, the Act authorises the Commissioners to fix the level of new streets, and to regulate the street line, and to cause new buildings to be set back to the line, on compensation by the Commissioners. Owners of property, on laying out new streets, or extending old ones, are required to pave them, according to the provisions in the following clause: "The owners and proprietors of the houses, buildings, and premises adjoining to such street or extension of street, when and so soon as three fourth parts thereof shall be built, shall, and they are hereby required to cause the square of their houses, buildings, or premises in the middle of such new or extended street, both in the carriage and footway, to be paved in such manner as the said Commissioners shall direct; and all such houses, buildings, or premises, and the owners and occupiers thereof respectively, shall, for the space of ten years from the time such pavement shall be completed, be exempted from being charged or assessed to, or paying, any of the rates or assessments commonly called highway levies, within the said town or parish of Birmingham."

Paving.

Boundaries.

It is provided that, "whereas doubts may arise respecting the boundaries or limits" of the town, the Commissioners are "authorised and empowered from time to time, to ascertain and fix the limits and boundaries of the said town of Birmingham, within the parish of Birmingham only," the limits so fixed being directed to be adopted for the purposes of the Commissioners' Acts.

The schedule enumerates the improvements to be made under

the Act, namely—to "widen the lower end of Bull Street" by "taking down the Welch Cross" and four houses; to widen Swan Alley; the lower end of Worcester Street; the lower end of Moor Street (by removing eighteen houses;) to widen the upper end of St. Martin's Lane, by taking down "five messuages or tenements fronting to St. Martin's Lane, and adjoining at the back part to St. Martin's Church-yard," and also a messuage fronting to St. Martin's Lane, and "called the Engine House;" and to widen the Market Place, by removing five houses "adjoining St. Martin's Church-yard," five fronting to Spiceal Street, four fronting to the Corn Market, seven "called the Upper Roundabout Houses," and "the remaining part of the Shambles." CHAP. V.
1801.
Third Act.
Schedule of Properties.

In 1812 the Commissioners obtained another Act of Parliament—52 Geo. III., c. 113—entitled "for better paving, lighting, watching, cleansing, and otherwise improving the Town of Birmingham." By this Act ninety-nine persons named in it were appointed Commissioners, with power to fill up vacancies occurring in their body, it being provided that each Commissioner should be an inhabitant, rated at not less than £15 per annum to the poor rate, and possessed "really and *bonâ fide*" of real or personal estate to the value of £1,000. By this Act the property in all roads, streets, and footways in the town, and in all lamps, &c., is vested in the Commissioners, who are authorised to appoint road-makers, and to contract or to compound with persons who by statute are under obligation to provide haulage and labour in road-making. For the purpose of road repairs the Commissioners are authorised, after notice, and on payment of compensation, to "search for, cut, dig, gather, take, and carry away any stone, gravel, clay, sand, or other materials, out of or from any lands and grounds situate in the parish of Birmingham, with the exception of ground used for yards, orchards, paddocks, or nurseries for trees." 1812.
Fourth Act.
Extended Powers.

Encroachments and projections are forbidden by the Act: the Commissioners may order projecting signs to be fixed upon the fronts of houses, and if this is not done within three months, the Commissioners may "cause such signs, emblems, sign posts, sign irons, pent houses, shew boards, stalls, window shutters and flaps, Encroachments.

porches, sheds, butchers' stalls, bulks, and gallowses, shambles, blocks, or pieces of timber, chopping blocks, watering tubs or troughs, posts, rails, and stumps, and all other encroachments, nuisances, or annoyances whatsoever, to be taken down or removed." Power is also given to regulate window projections, to prevent houses being roofed with thatch or straw, and to make bye-laws for cart and carriage traffic and other purposes. Amongst these provisions is one requiring that " the owners or occupiers of all engines commonly called steam engines," shall " use the mode or method now adopted, or other equally efficacious, to consume and burn the smoke arising therefrom," on penalty of £50 " for every such neglect or default."

By this Act the Commissioners were empowered to treat with the Lord of the Manor for the lease or purchase of his markets, fairs, and other manorial rights; and they were also authorised to establish vegetable markets in the Bull Ring, and to provide a cattle market on the site now known as Smithfield. The clauses relating these powers recite that " whereas the town of Birmingham is become a very large and populous trading town, and the markets there have from time out of memory been held in the streets or places called the Bull Ring, High Street, and Dale End, and whereas the Commissioners have purchased and taken down divers messuages or tenements and buildings situate in the Bull Ring, for the purpose of enlarging and making more commodious the said market place, and it would greatly tend to the convenience of the inhabitants if the markets were in future held there," it is enacted that " the street or place so widened and enlarged, called the Bull Ring, shall be deemed a public highway, and shall be considered and used as the market place for the town of Birmingham " for the sale of " all goods, wares, and merchandises, fruit, vegetables or garden stuff, butchers' meat, or other matter or thing, except neat cattle, horses, sheep, pigs, hay, and straw," and that the lord of the manor may set up stalls for markets and fairs, and collect tolls and rents there. The clause cattle market recites that "

STREET COMMISSIONERS: THEIR POWERS. 89

called Dale End and New Street, to the great danger and inconvenience of all persons living and resorting there," therefore it is enacted that the Commissioners may buy " a piece of land with the buildings thereon, called the Moat and Moat House, belonging to Sir Thomas Gooch, Baronet, and Thomas Francis, Esquire," and may lay open the land " so as the same shall form an area at least one acre and two roods," and " enclose the same for a market place for the sale of neat cattle, horses, sheep, and pigs, hay and straw," and thereupon the use of New Street and Dale End for a cattle market shall cease. There is a proviso that the clause shall "not extend to or interfere with the sale of horses at the two public fairs held in the town, in a certain street there called the Horse Fair," or with the tolls and rents leviable by the lord of the manor at all markets and fairs within the town.

*Chap. V.
1812.
Fourth Act.
Purchase of Smithfield.*

Other provisions of this Act oblige owners to lay out and pave new streets to the satisfaction of the Commissioners; authorise the Commissioners to widen streets; to " ascertain and fix the limits or boundaries of the town "; and to re-sell land not required for the purposes of the Act.

The rating powers are also extended by the Act—properties of less value than £10 yearly are not to pay more than 9d. in the pound; between £10 and £15, not more than 1s. in the pound; and above £15, not more than 1s. 6d. in the pound. Market gardens, and arable, meadow, or pasture lands are wholly exempt from rating; and so also are " the tolls or tonnage of any navigable canal made in the parish." The Commissioners are authorised to borrow the sum of £24,000, on the security of the rates, such money, if they choose, to be raised by annuities.

Rating and Borrowing Powers.

The last Act obtained by the Street Commissioners was passed in 1828, 9 George IV. It repeals the previous Act (52 George III.), and re-enacts all the governing powers contained in that and previous Acts, with additional powers declared to be "necessary for the better governing and improving of the town and parish of

*1828.
Fifth Act.*

CHAP. V.
1828.
Fifth Act.

Peace for the County of Warwick residing within seven miles of the town of Birmingham," and twelve other persons to be elected by the Commissioners; the qualification of the Commissioners being a ratal of £15 a year and the possession of property, real or personal, to the value of £1,000; and it is provided that "the said Commissioners at all their meetings shall defray their own expenses."

Consolidation of Powers.

This Act gives the Commissioners full authority over lighting, watching, paving, cleansing, and draining the town; the regulation of carriage and other traffic in the streets; authorises the making of bye-laws; and generally consolidates and extends the governing powers conferred by previous Acts.

Weighing Machines.

Some of the new and special provisions require to be mentioned. One of the clauses provides that "whereas in one of the principal streets or throughfares leading from Birmingham to Holyhead, called Snow Hill, there is a public weighing machine belonging to the Guardians and Overseers of the parish of Birmingham, which occasions great interruption and danger to the mail and other coaches, and also to persons travelling on the said road, and carts and waggons that continually are standing there and obstructing the free and safe passage along the said road," the Commissioners are authorised to remove the weighing machine, and to construct another in some more convenient place.

Police. Day and Night Watchmen.

As to police, the Commissioners are empowered to "appoint such number of able-bodied watch-house keepers, night constables watchmen, patroles, street keepers and other persons," as they may "think sufficient for the protection of the inhabitants, houses, and property, streets and other places, by day and by night," and may provide them with "such clothing, arms, ammunition, and weapons, as to the said Commissioners shall seem meet." All such watchmen, &c., are to be sworn in as constables before the county justices, and are to have the rights and privileges of constables. Watchmen "disabled or wounded in the execution of their duty" are to be pensioned if the Commissioners please; and all publicans harbouring watchmen while on duty may be fined five pounds.

As to new streets it is provided that the Commissioners shall fix the levels of new streets, or of old ones when altered; that all new streets shall be fourteen yards wide; that gutters shall be made and paved by the Commissioners, the cost being charged to the "ground tenants or owners" of the properties; that owners in new streets "shall be required to cause the square of their houses, buildings, or premises, into the middle of such new street, both in the carriage and footway, to be paved in such manner as the Commissioners shall direct; and all such persons "shall for the space of ten years from the time such pavement is completed, be exempted from paying any of the rates or assessments commonly called the highway levies within the town or parish of Birmingham." It is further provided that in all streets not fully built up, new buildings shall be set back seven yards from the centre of the road; under a penalty of £50 and the demolition of the building. *Chap. V. 1828. Fifth Act. New Streets.*

Power is given to the Commissioners to widen, open, extend, and alter streets, and for this purpose to acquire properties mentioned in the schedule of the Act.

The Commissioners are also authorised to "erect and build one or more market house or houses;" and, when they "see fit," also to build "a corn exchange for the holding therein of the markets for corn and grain." Further powers are given to "enlarge and improve" the Public Office (in Moor Street), which is "now too small and incommodious." *Public Buildings.*

By this Act alterations are made in the rates the Commissioners are empowered to levy. They are now authorised to make one or more rates for the purpose of lighting, cleansing, watching, and otherwise improving the streets, lanes, public passages, and places within the limits of the Act, in the following proportions—houses, &c., under £10 yearly rent and value are not to be charged with more than 9d. in the pound in any one year; above £10 and under £15, not exceeding 1s.; £15 and upwards, not exceeding 1s. 6d. The exemptions from rating are, gardens and orchards, and arable, meadow, and pasture land, "while occupied solely for selling the fruit or produce thereof;" tolls or duties belonging to the lord of *Rating.*

92 STREET COMMISSIONERS: THEIR POWERS.

Chap. V.
1828.
Fifth Act.

the manor; tithes; stock in trade, money, or personal estate; and tolls of any navigable canal in the parish. For the purposes of rating, lodgers occupying apartments are to be deemed occupiers, but may deduct rates paid by them from the rent next falling due.

Town Hall.

The Commissioners are further authorised to build a Town Hall. The clause recites that "by reason of the increase in magnitude of the town, and the number of inhabitants thereof, the public buildings are too small and incommodious for the holding of meetings of the ratepayers and other public meetings." Therefore it is provided that a Town Hall may be built by a special rate levied for that purpose, and that the Hall shall be "capable of containing at least three thousand persons." The Hall, when built, is to be used for all meetings called by the High Bailiff, or two Justices of the Peace for the county, or by ten of the Commissioners. Under the following clause the use of the Hall is reserved at special times for musical festivals:—"The said Town Hall and its appurtenances shall for the space of six weeks before the day appointed for any Musical Festival to be from time to time held in the said town for the benefit of the Birmingham General Hospital, and during the continuance of such Festival, and for seven days afterwards, be under the control and direction of the Committee of Governors of the General Hospital appointed to superintend the arrangement of each Musical Festival. And the said Governors, or such board or committee thereof, shall have power to put up an organ in the said Town Hall, the property of which organ shall be vested solely in them; and they shall have free access thereto at all suitable times for practice and rehearsals, and other necessary purposes connected with or preparatory to the said Musical Festival, and also to erect therein at the period of the said Musical Festival such temporary seats, galleries, scaffolding, and other conveniences as they shall deem requisite, and afterwards to remove the same and deposit the materials in some convenient part of the said Town Hall to be provided for that purpose; they, the said Governors or committee, repairing and reinstating the said Town Hall in such parts thereof as shall be injured in consequence of such use or occupation thereof by them, or any other person under their authority."

Musical Festivals.

Rights of General Hospital.

For the building of the Town Hall the Commissioners are authorised to levy a rate of not more than sixpence in the pound in any one year, under the name of the Town Hall Rate, and from such rate all properties of less yearly value than £15 are to be entirely exempt. On the credit of the Town Hall Rate the Commissioners are authorised to borrow money for the purchase of site and for building, but it is provided that the Town Hall Rate "shall not at any time be charged with a greater sum than £25,000." For general purposes, and on the credit of the general rate, the Commissioners are authorised to borrow the sum of £100,000, including "the monies now due and owing" by virtue of the previous Acts.

CHAP. V.
1828.
Fifth Act.
Town Hall Rate.

There are three schedules appended to this Act—one specifying a large number of properties authorised to be purchased by the Commissioners for improvements in several parts of the town; a second specifying properties to be acquired for the enlargement of the Public Office in Moor Street; and a third showing the tolls, rents, and duties payable in the markets.

An Act for the local government of the hamlets of Deritend and Bordesley was obtained in 1791, 31 George III. The preamble declares that "whereas the streets, lanes, and other public passages and places within the hamlets of Deritend and Bordesley, in the county of Warwick, are not properly cleansed, lighted, or watched, and are subject to various nuisances, annoyances, and encroachments, and are in some places, by reason of the uneven or irregular surfaces thereof, very incommodious and unsafe for passengers and carriages," therefore certain persons named in the Act—sixty in all—are appointed Commissioners for the government of the hamlets, with power to appoint surveyors, scavengers, lamp-lighters, night watchmen, and other officers; and generally to exercise powers similar to those conferred upon the Commissioners for the parish of Birmingham by their local Act. The rating powers were fixed as follows: Properties between £1 and £6 annual value to pay not more than sixpence in the pound in any one year; between £6 and £10, not more than ninepence; between £10 and £15, not more than one shilling; between £15

Deritend and Bordesley.

CHAP. V.
1828.
Fifth Act.

and £20, not more than one shilling and threepence; and £20 and upwards, not more than one shilling and sixpence. On the security of the rates the Commissioners were authorised to borrow £1,000, renewable from time to time by bonds or annuities.

Duddeston and Nechells.

The local government of the hamlets of Duddeston and Nechells was provided for by two Acts, the first passed in 1829 (10 Geo. IV., c. 6) and the second in 1845 (8 and 9 Vict., c. 194). Thirty-three Commissioners were appointed by the first of these Acts, with the addition of "all his Majesty's Justices of the Peace residing within the parish of Aston." The Commissioners were authorised to borrow £3,000 on the security of the rates, and for this and other general purposes, to levy rates in the following proportions—properties under £10, not more than 1s. in the pound yearly; between £10 and £15, not more than 1s. 6d.; £15 or upwards, 2s. The ordinary governing powers of watching, lighting, paving, and general street regulation were given by this Act; and in addition the exceptional power of making and selling gas. Clause 21, confering this authority, ran as follows:—The Commissioners to light the streets with oil or gas, "and it shall be lawful for the said Commissioners to contract with any person or persons for the necessary supply of gas, or to manufacture and sell such gas to any person or persons willing to purchase the same, and for that purpose to establish gasometers, and all apparatus and machinery necessary or convenient thereto, and to purchase any land or ground, not exceeding one statute acre, for the purposes last aforesaid. . . . . Provided that nothing herein contained shall authorise the said Commissioners to lay down any mains or pipes beyond the limits of the said hamlets, or to make, sell, furnish, or supply gas to be used or consumed within the parish of Birmingham." Other provisions required that gas pipes should be laid "at the greatest practicable distance, and, wherever the width of the carriage way will allow thereof, at the distance of four feet at least from the nearest part of any water pipe;" and stringent clauses were inserted

of ascertaining whether such contamination proceed from or be occasioned by the said Commissioners."

This Act, and all the powers conferred by it—the making of gas included—was repealed by the Act of 1845, which greatly enlarged the authority of the Commissioners for the purposes of local government in respect to "lighting, draining, cleansing, and improving" the hamlets. The rating power was also altered, so as to fix on all properties assessed a maximum rate of two shillings in the pound of annual value. The borrowing powers of the Commissioners were increased to £6,000.

CHAPTER VI.

PETITION FOR A CHARTER OF INCORPORATION.

CHAP. VI.
1832.
Influence of Reform Act.

The next movement to promote a reform and extension of local government dates from the period of the Reform Act of 1832, which, as regards the election of representatives in Parliament, recognised the right of many towns previously excluded, and which incidentally dealt a severe and, in effect, a fatal blow at the system of restricted and privileged election, by calling into existence the ten pound franchise in boroughs, and thus creating an extended constituency applicable to all purposes of representative government, national and local. The part which Birmingham took in promoting and carrying the Reform Act is matter of history. The force of the Political Union, and of the principles upon which it was based, and of the desires to which it gave expression, continued to exert itself locally after the immediate purpose of the Union had been accomplished. By the Reform Act, Birmingham was erected into a Parliamentary Borough, and had two representatives in the House of Commons assigned to it.

Anomalies of Local Government.

But while the political rights of the town were thus admitted and established, the local government was left untouched. This remained as it was constituted more than sixty years previously. The powers of the manorial officers were still exercised; justice was administered by county magistrates, holding their petty sessions in the town; the lighting, paving, sewering, and other sanitary work was still vested in the Commissioners of the Street Act, a self-elected body, which was felt to be out of harmony with the new development of the representative principle. The active promoters of Parliamentary reform consequently desired to see reform applied also to local administration, and felt that the time had come to extend the principle of representative government to local affairs. There was, however, no disposition to apply to the Crown for a charter of incorporation, because it was understood that the Ministry intended, as their next great measure, to, undertake the reform of municipal Corporations generally, and to establish throughout the country an uniform system capable of being extended to towns and boroughs which until then had no regular municipal government. With the condition of the then existing Corporations this work has no concern, further than to say that they were mostly self-elected, that their charters—granted at various periods from the Conquest downwards—contained many provisions of a character unsuitable to modern times, and that their funds were very frequently wasted in the grossest extravagance and corruption, and were largely applied to personal uses so flagrantly unjust as to constitute a breach of trust of the worst description. Full evidence on these and other points affecting the older Corporations will be found in the speech of Lord John Russell in introducing the Municipal Corporations Bill on the 5th of June, 1835, and in the

CHAP. VI.
1833.
Local Government in Birmingham.

Character of existing Corporations.

Report of Royal Commissioners.

report of the Commission of Enquiry appointed in 1833, and which presented its first report in 1835. A single extract from the report of this Commission explains generally the causes of dissatisfaction with the older Corporations, and indicates the reason why, until a general measure of reform had been adopted, it was not worth while for the unincorporated towns to apply for charters from the Crown: "There prevails (the Commissioners observe) among the inhabitants of a great majority of the incorporated towns a general, and, in our opinion, a just dissatisfaction with the municipal institutions—a distrust of the self-elected municipal councils, whose powers are subject to no popular control, and whose acts and proceedings, being secret, are not checked by the influence of public opinion—a distrust of the municipal magistracy, tainting with suspicion the local administration of justice —a discontent under the burthen of local taxation, while revenues are diverted from their legitimate use, and are sometimes wastefully bestowed for the benefit of individuals, sometimes squandered for purposes injurious to the character and morals of the people." No indictment could well be more comprehensive; certainly, as the evidence proved, none could be more justly preferred. The Government, however, did not wait for the report of the Commissioners before endeavouring to deal with the subject of Municipal Corporations. Reserving these bodies generally for legislative treatment when the Commissioners' report should have been presented, Lord Brougham (then Lord Chancellor) introduced into the House of Lords, in 1833, a bill to incorporate Birmingham,

Manchester, Sheffield, Wolverhampton, and several other towns which, though returning members to Parliament under the Reform Act, were destitute of representative local government. In connection with this measure Captain Gipps and Mr. Aldridge, two of the Commissioners, visited Birmingham in December, 1833, and made private enquiries as to the most convenient division of the borough into wards, &c., in the expectation that the Chancellor's bill would pass. The measure, however, did not excite special interest in the towns affected by it. In Birmingham, in particular, much objection was expressed to some of its provisions, and especially to the property qualification required for members of Town Councils, and to the nomination of Recorders by the Crown. Ultimately the bill was withdrawn. In the next year the hands of the Government were too full to deal with municipal affairs; but in 1835 their promised efforts at Corporation reform were undertaken in earnest, by the introduction of Lord John Russell's bill, which deserves to be regarded as the Great Charter of the Municipalities of the kingdom. The object of this measure was to abolish special privileges both of election and administration, to reduce all existing Corporations to one model, based upon popular election, to confer upon them extended powers of local government, for sanitary purposes, improvements, the maintenance of order, and the administration of justice. The bill did not directly incorporate any of the large towns; it simply gave power to the Crown to grant charters to them on the petition of the inhabitants. The Government measure provoked a storm of opposition in the House of Commons,

CHAP. VI.
1835.

Resistance to Bill.

Corruption of old Corporations.

Privileges of Freemen.

not, indeed, as regards its principle, for both political parties agreed that reform of the Corporations was necessary, but as to those of its leading provisions which struck directly at class privileges. The chief stand of the Conservative party was made upon the clause of the bill which abolished the freemen in boroughs, excepting those then actually in existence. This clause declared that "no person shall be admitted, or enrolled, a citizen, freeman, liveryman, or burgess of any borough, or by any name member of any body corporate, in respect of any right or title, other than by occupancy and payment of rates within such borough, according to the meaning and provisions of this Act." The object and effect of the clause, and the necessity for it, are clearly exhibited in the following extract from Molesworth's "History of England:" *

"The freedom of a borough, carrying with it the Parliamentary and municipal franchise, might be acquired by birth, apprenticeship, redemption (*i.e.* purchase), marriage, or by the gratuitous gift of the Corporation in each borough. The presentation of the freedom was a compliment often paid to successful military or naval commanders, or other persons of distinction to whom the Corporators of the borough desired to testify their admiration or respect. In some boroughs the freemen enjoyed valuable rights of pasturage, or a share in commons adjacent to the town, and of the proceeds of their sale if they should be sold; in others they possessed the right of selling their wares and merchandise toll-free in any fair or market in the kingdom; in others again, they participated in the monopoly of trading in the town which was possessed by the general body of its freemen. In ancient times, the freemen, as their name sufficiently indicates, constituted a

---

* History of England—1830-1874. By William Nassau Molesworth. Vol. i., p. 369.

sort of privileged caste in each borough; they were the *élite* of its inhabitants, and the fitting electors of the corporate body by which the town was governed. But this had long since ceased to be the case. In almost every borough, the governing class, taking advantage of the power they possessed of admitting whom they chose into the number of the freemen, had selected their own partisans, in order to strengthen and perpetuate their authority; and thus the freemen had gradually come to be, as a class, though no doubt with many honourable exceptions, thoroughly corrupt and degraded, and by long habit had been led to expect a fixed and often very valuable consideration for every exercise of their Parliamentary or municipal franchises. The majority of them were bound to the Tories both by interest and gratitude; for the Tories generally paid them most liberally for their votes, and had preserved to them the Parliamentary franchise when the Whigs had attempted to take it from them."

_{Chap. VI.
1835.
Abuses of old Corporations.
Political bias.}

The endeavour of the Tory party to preserve the power of creating freemen was rejected by the House of Commons; and so also was their attempt to introduce a property qualification for Town Councillors, which was not provided in the Government Bill, a strong opinion, as we have seen, having been expressed against it by the Liberals in Birmingham and elsewhere. The Government likewise maintained another important clause of their measure—one which conferred upon Town Councils the power of granting public-house licenses. As this question has been raised again lately, it may not be out of place to go back for a moment to the speech of Lord John Russell in introducing the Municipal Corporations Bill, and to quote the passage relating to the granting of licenses by Town Councils:—

_{Conservative opposition.
Public-house Licenses.}

CHAP. VI.
1835.
Public-house Licenses.

"With regard to the administration of justice and police within the towns, we propose that the whole work and business of watching the town shall be placed completely under the control of the Council. Then, with respect to another part of this measure, which refers to what I consider a part of the police of the towns, and a part which has often led to very great abuses— I mean the power of granting alehouse licenses—it is proposed that this power shall not be mixed up or confounded with the duty of administering justice, but that it should be left to the Council or a Committee of the Council. I think that the Council elected by the ratepayers, as now proposed, although no doubt many of the members may have a desire to favour their friends or to promote their own private views as a body, will always act under popular control, and be less likely to abuse the power of granting licenses than magistrates, in whose case the robe of justice is sometimes employed to cover a great enormity of abuses."

Hostility of the Peers.

In the House of Lords the bill was rudely dealt with. The Peers were afraid to reject it—public feeling was too strongly pronounced to admit of resistance—but they introduced most of the alterations proposed by the Tory party in the House of Commons, including the property qualification for members of Town Councils. These changes, and the attitude of the Peers generally, excited much indignation in the country. Meetings were held, and memorials presented to the Government, denouncing the conduct of the Peers, and urging Ministers to stand firmly by their measure. Birmingham, as usual, led the van in this agitation. A meeting, called by Mr. Paul Moon James, the High Bailiff, was held on the 24th of August, 1835, and the following resolution was passed on the motion of Mr. Thomas Tyndall, the Low Bailiff, supported by Mr. Thomas Attwood, M.P., and the Rev. T. M. M'Donnell,

Meeting in Birmingham.

a Roman Catholic clergyman who took a prominent share in local political movements on the Liberal side—"That this meeting has witnessed, with grief and indignation, the disappointment of the hopes of the people of England, in the arbitrary interference of a powerful majority in the House of Lords, with the measure of Corporate Reform which especially interests the people, and for the introduction of which we cannot but be grateful to a Liberal and patriotic Minister. That, therefore, we deem it an imperative duty, at this juncture of public affairs, to present to Lord Melbourne [then Prime Minister] an assurance of our confidence and support." This resolution was followed by others, proposed and seconded respectively by Messrs. William Beale, George Edmonds, William Wills, and W. Phipson, thanking the "glorious and patriotic minority in the House of Lords" for their support of the bill, and directing a memorial to be sent to Lord Melbourne. The Ministry, however, were not strong enough to coerce the Peers, and the Peers, on their part, were afraid to resist too vigorously the popular will expressed in such a resolution as that above quoted. Ultimately, therefore, after repeated conferences between the two Houses, a compromise took place. The freemen were limited to those actually in existence, a lower property qualification than that proposed by the Peers was accepted, the duration of office of members of Councils was limited to three years for Councillors and six years for Aldermen, instead of longer periods proposed by the Tories, and the clause conferring licensing powers upon Town Councils was abandoned. The bill received the Royal assent on the 15th of

CHAP. VI.
1837.

Inaction in Birmingham.

Proposed petition for Incorporation.

Appeal to all Classes and Parties.

September, 1835; and thus the Reform Act of 1832 received its necessary and natural complement.

It might have been expected that, immediately on the passing of the Act, measures would have been taken to present a petition for a charter of incorporation for Birmingham. In fact, however, several months were allowed to elapse before any step was taken. The reason for this delay is to be found in the circumstance that the desire for a Corporation existed only amongst the Liberal party, and that the leading Liberals were too busily occupied in general political agitation for the further extension of Parliamentary reform, to give time to purely local affairs. The first movement towards applying for a charter was taken on Wednesday, March 1, 1837—a date which deserves honourable remembrance in the history of Birmingham. On that day a meeting, called by circular, was held at the Public Office, "to make the necessary arrangements for obtaining an incorporation of the borough." The circulars were issued by Mr. Philip Henry Muntz (now one of the Members for Birmingham), and, in explaining what he had done, Mr. Muntz said that he had sent out invitations to "Whig, Tory, and Radical indiscriminately, because he did not consider the question one of party: it was one involving the interests of all classes, and he considered it right and fair that all parties should have a full opportunity of considering the merits of the subject." The action of the Conservatives, however, prevented the movement from being established on this broad and reasonable basis. One Conservative only seems to have attended the meeting—Mr. J. B. Hebbert, secretary of the Loyal and Constitutional Association—but on finding that the circular pledged those in attendance to the principle of a Corporation, he retired; and from that moment the work of incorporation passed exclusively into the hands of the Liberal party, and was vigorously and persistently opposed by the Conservatives. The meeting, which was presided over by Mr. Thomas Bolton, the Low Bailiff, was addressed by Mr. William Wills, Mr. R. K. Douglas (then editor of the *Birmingham Journal*), Mr. William Redfern, Mr. George Edmonds, Mr. P. H. Muntz, and others; and resolutions were unanimously passed approving of the proposal to obtain a charter of incorporation, and appointing a committee to take the necessary steps for that purpose.

Chap. VI.
1837.
Conservatives decline to concur.

The Committee appointed at this meeting put themselves into communication with Lord John Russell, then Home Secretary, with the view of inducing the Government to bring in a general measure to bestow Corporations upon the non-incorporated boroughs, and also with other places in the same position as Birmingham, in the hope of obtaining their co-operation in promoting such a measure. Their efforts proved unsuccessful in both directions. Lord John Russell informed them that the Government had no intention of introducing any such measure, " or for abrogating the various private Acts in force, in order to vest the powers conferred by them on the Councils of boroughs when incorporated; and that in such a borough as Birmingham an application for a

Proposed Government measure.

Government declines to move.

Charter must proceed from all the parishes of the Parliamentary borough; that counsel would probably not be required, even if a portion of the inhabitants were to object to an application for a charter; and that, in consequence, the expense of such an application would not be great."* The returns from the other non-incorporated boroughs are described as "not being of much importance. In some of them, as Devonport, charters have been applied for; in others no such application has been made; in some none has been contemplated. All of them seem rather inclined to wait for an example before they move, than prepared to head the movement in favour of a general Incorporation Act."

Here, so far as action was concerned, the matter rested from June until the end of October; much discussion, however, taking place in the town in the meantime, and the project of incorporation was freely canvassed in the newspapers and otherwise, the grant of a Charter being strongly supported by the Liberals, and as vigorously opposed by the Conservatives, with whom some of the Whig party were passive, if not active, sympathisers. The contention of the opponents of the proposal was that the town was sufficiently well governed by the respective Boards of Commissioners, that needful improvements in the administration of justice could readily be arranged by the County authorities, that the grant of a Charter would

---

* *Birmingham Journal*, June 3, 1837.

entail great expense, and that the Municipal Council would possess powers so restricted as not to be worth exercising. The Liberals denied the alleged probability of greater expense, they contested the assumed good government of the town, they admitted that the Charter would confer very moderate powers, but they insisted that the creation of a Municipal Corporation would inevitably lead to the transfer to it of the powers of all other governing bodies within the borough, and that even if this were not the case, the Corporation would be a good thing in itself, as recognising and establishing the principle of representation in local government. "The local government of Birmingham," wrote one of the strongest advocates of incorporation,[*] "is as close as the closest of Irish municipalities; or as the closest of English municipalities, previous to the Act being passed by which they were thrown open. We have our Court Leet and our Bailiffs, chosen by themselves; our Street Commissioners, chosen by themselves; our Town Hall Commissioners, chosen by themselves; working in the dark, unseen by the public eye, irresponsible to the public voice; appointing their own officers, levying taxes at their pleasure, and distributing them, without check or control, as their inclination shall determine. The only institution in which there is an approach to freedom, is the Corporation of Guardians, which, though its constituents are much too few in number, is—thanks to the operation of the ballot—independently, and to a certain extent popularly chosen. The mere incorporation of the Parliamentary borough will

---

[*] *Birmingham Journal*, October 21, 1837.

CHAP. VI.
1837.
Contemplated union of Local powers in one representative body.

not affect the local Acts by which Birmingham and Aston are governed. It will enable the householders, in the several wards, to elect certain persons to act as a Council of the conjoint borough, and the Council so elected will possess the same powers as the Councils of other Royal boroughs under the Municipal Act, save and except always the restrictions imposed upon their exercise by the local Acts. Such will be the immediate effect of incorporating the borough; and we admit freely that, considered in itself, it is extremely insignificant. It is little else than the scaffolding to a building, the materials of which are yet to seek." But, the writer argues, it is plain that by a general, or by a private Act, "a consolidation of the various local Acts will be effected, and the powers granted by them transferred from the present holders to the Council. In fact, the advocates of an incorporation of the borough must commence by assuming this as true; for otherwise they would be convicted of the most egregious folly that men calling themselves patriots could, under any circumstances, be guilty of. The ultimate effect, then, of the incorporation of the borough would be—the consolidation of the entire of the local Acts, and the concentration of the powers granted by them in one body, and their administration by one set of officers. That body, and those officers, would moreover be the choice of the people; responsible to their voice, removable at their pleasure. They could not abuse their powers at all, unless the people had selected them unwisely; they could not persist in abusing their powers, unless the people weakly permitted them to do so."

Supported by arguments and expectations such as these, active measures were taken to apply for a Charter of Incorporation. A meeting was called by advertisement, to which more than six hundred names were appended. Amongst them may be cited as examples, those of Attwood, Scholefield, Muntz (P. H.), Middlemore, Sturge, Van Wart, Ryland, East (Rev. Timothy), Martineau, Redfern, Barlow, Goddard, Pare, Weston, Hudson, Hutton (Rev. Hugh), Hutton (Samuel), Clark, Bray, Edwards, Messenger, Osler, Buckley, Bache (Rev. S.), Sargant, Peyton, Wills, Hopkins, Room, Deykin, Biggs, Osborne, Hawkes, Beale, Colmore, Baldwin, Brooke Smith, Pountney, Pemberton, Johnstone (Dr. James), Moilliett, Bragg, Phillips, Hadley, R. K. Douglas, &c.

Chap. VI. 1837. Town's Meeting to petition for Charter.

The meeting was held in the Town Hall, on Monday, the 30th of October, under the presidency of Mr. William Scholefield, High Bailiff; and as it is of historic interest so far as Birmingham is concerned, a little space may properly be devoted to some account of it.

Description of Meeting.

"The meeting (says the *Journal* of November 4) was numerous, though not crowded; highly respectable, and unanimous. The movers and seconders [of the resolutions and petition] were composed of the leading men of the Whig and Radical parties. The Tories did not co-operate; but neither did they oppose. The introductory speeches were long; and the business was in consequence protracted until the shades of evening were falling. On the whole, we have no hesitation in pronouncing the meeting to have been a most satisfactory one. There was not that exuberant enthusiasm which more exciting questions have customarily called forth; but there was a peace and order, and calm deliberate attention, which

CHAP. VI.
1837.
Town's Meeting to petition for Charter.

suited well with the occasion. In the absence of anything like argument against the incorporation of the town, it would be a waste of logic to enter on its defence. The organ of the Tories [the *Birmingham Advertiser*] has contented itself, and we presume its readers, with saying that the petition must fail for want of supporters. The alleged thinness of the meeting is the specious ground-work of this notable averment. We took pains to count the meeting, which is not a matter of so much difficulty in a room, however large, as in the open air. The body of the Hall contained about 1,500; the side gallery and the organ gallery about 1,000. This does not indicate, as we have stated, a crowded meeting; but it is absurd to call it a small one. That which was assembled to congratulate the Queen on her last birth-day was scarcely half so numerous; and yet not a few of the Tories assisted at it. The meeting called by the Memorial Committee * was certainly not one third larger; and yet all parties joined in it. But the requisition calling the [Incorporation] meeting offers a much less questionable proof of the interest that the inhabitants take in this question than any assemblage, how crowded soever, could have done. To the requisition were appended more than six hundred names; and of these, three hundred, at least, were the names of known and influential individuals. What requisition that was ever signed in Birmingham can match that? The Committee appointed to carry the resolutions into effect held their first meeting on Wednesday morning. The petition sheets are already being circulated and signed. In a few days it will be seen whether, amongst the people at large, there exists any lukewarmness in this matter. We can state that there will be no lukewarmness on the part of Ministers in giving effect to the wishes of the people. A letter, received yesterday, from Mr. Phillips, Under-Secretary of State, assures the Committee that Lord John Russell will be ready to render any assistance in his power to promote the accomplishment of the wish of the inhabitants of Birmingham for a Charter of Incorporation. So far from

Estimate of numbers present.

---

* A Memorial to Lord Melbourne, the Premier, from a Town's Meeting, October 4, 1837, on the then existing distress, with proposals to remedy it by reforms in the Currency system.

TOWN'S MEETING: PETITION FOR CHARTER.

failing for want of support, we have no more doubt than we have of our own existence, that the Charter will be obtained, and in a shortness of time which the most sanguine of its friends had not ventured to anticipate."

This expectation of a speedy grant of the Charter was a little too sanguine, as will be presently seen, for rather more than twelve months elapsed before the important Charter was received in Birmingham, and publicly read to the burgesses in the Town Hall. At present, however, we have to do only with the meeting at which the petition was agreed to. The report of the speeches, occupying more than two pages of the *Journal*, shows the interest felt in the proceedings. The organ gallery, the report says, "was occupied by a great number of the most respectable and influential persons in the town, all of whom took a deep interest in the proceedings." The names given of those present are "Thomas Attwood, M.P., Joshua Scholefield, M.P., William Scholefield, High Bailiff, Abel Peyton, Low Bailiff, J. Towers Lawrence, James James, Dr. Birt Davies, Messrs. Boultbee, W. Wills, W. Redfern, G. F. Muntz, P. H. Muntz, Thomas Bolton, W. Clowes, S. Hutton, R. H. Taylor, John Betts, Charles Lloyd, Thomas Ryland, J. Clark, F. Room, Henry Knight, Joseph Parkes, Arthur Ryland, T. Clark, George Edmonds, W. Room, J. Drake, B. Hadley, the Rev. T. M. M'Donnell, the Rev. T. East, &c." The resolutions adopted by the meeting, and to which no opposition of any kind was offered, are set forth in the subjoined formal record of the proceedings :—

Marginalia: CHAP. VI. 1837. Town's Meeting. Names of persons present.

CHAP. VI.
1837.
Resolutions of Meeting.

"INCORPORATION OF BIRMINGHAM.

"At a Public Meeting of the Inhabitant Householders, called by advertisement in each of the Birmingham Newspapers, and held in the Town Hall of Birmingham, on Monday, October 30th, 1837, William Scholefield, Esq., High Bailiff of the Town of Birmingham, in the chair, the following Resolutions were unanimously agreed to:—

"Moved by Mr. W. Wills, and seconded by Mr. Thomas Bolton—'That, amongst other important recommendations, a popular system of local government is, in its management, the cheapest, simplest, and most effective; that it harmonises with the spirit of the British Constitution; and is eminently conducive to the formation and maintenance of sound principles, and practical habits of freedom.'

"Moved by Mr. George Frederick Muntz, and seconded by Mr. George Edmonds—'That it is highly expedient that the local government, and the expenditure of the public funds of so large and important a community as that of Birmingham, should be vested in a body popularly chosen, and subject to popular control and responsibility.'

"Moved by Mr. J. T. Lawrence, and seconded by Dr. J. B. Davies—'That as a preliminary essential to the establishment of a responsible local government in Birmingham, a Petition be presented to her Majesty in Council, for a Charter of Incorporation, under the Act 5 and 6 Wm. IV., cap. 76 (the English Municipal Act).'

Petition for Charter.

"Moved by Mr. C. Lloyd, and seconded by Mr. Abel Peyton, Low Bailiff—'That the following be the form of the Petition: "To the Queen's Most Excellent Majesty—The petition of the householders of the Borough of Birmingham, agreed to at a public meeting, called by advertisement in the whole of the Birmingham newspapers, and held in the Town Hall of Birmingham on the 30th day of October, in the year of Our Lord 1837. Humbly Sheweth, That by an Act passed in the 5th and 6th years of his late Majesty King William the Fourth, entitled 'An Act to provide for the Regulation of the Municipal Corporations in England and

Wales,' it is enacted that, in respect of sundry towns in England and Wales, it is expedient that they be incorporated, and that 'if the inhabitant householders of any town or borough in England and Wales shall petition his Majesty to grant to them a charter of incorporation, it shall be lawful for his Majesty, if he shall think fit, by the advice of his Privy Council, to grant the same, to extend to the inhabitants of any such town or borough, within the district to be set forth in such charter, the powers and provisions in this Act contained: provided, nevertheless, that notice of every such petition, and of the time when it shall please his Majesty to order that the same be taken into consideration by his Privy Council, shall be published by Royal proclamation in the *London Gazette* one month, at least, before such petition shall be so considered.' May it therefore please your Majesty, by and with the advice of your Majesty's Privy Council, and with all convenient speed, to grant a Charter of Incorporation to the Borough of Birmingham, pursuant to the provisions of the Act for the regulation of Municipal Corporations aforesaid; and your petitioners, as in duty bound, will ever pray."

"Moved by Mr. Thomas Ryland, and seconded by Mr. Douglas—'That the following gentlemen be a Committee, with full powers to carry these resolutions into effect, and to collect subscriptions for defraying the necessary expenses attendant upon the same: The Members for the Borough, the High and Low Bailiffs, Messrs. Joseph Sturge, Thomas Pemberton, William Wills, J. B. Davies, M.D., James Johnstone, M.D., Samuel Beale, William Gammon, Thomas Ryland, Thomas Bolton, Robert Martineau, Francis Clark, P. H. Muntz, William Barlow, Charles Lloyd, A. Ryland, William Middlemore, Charles Sturge, Samuel Hutton, Solomon Bray, Samuel Buckley, jun., William Boultbee, Isaac Aaron, George Edmonds, G. F. Muntz, Benjamin Hadley, William Redfern, Thomas C. Salt, Samuel Haycock, John Pierce, William Pare, James James, and R. K. Douglas.'

(Signed) "WILLIAM SCHOLEFIELD."

Besides the gentlemen named as movers and seconders of resolutions, the speakers were Mr. William Redfern,

Mr. Russell, Mr. T. Attwood, Mr. Joshua Scholefield, and the Rev. T. M. M'Donnell. The speeches, as a whole, were worthy of the object and of the occasion—dignified, temperate, firm in the assertion of popular right, resolute in determination to obtain representative government, and at the same time fairly marked by courtesy and a conciliatory tone towards the existing local governing bodies, and to those who were opposed to the grant of a charter. Mr. Wills and Mr. Redfern, who were the chief speakers, dwelt exhaustively upon the defects and anomalies of the existing forms of local government, especially in their self-elected character, and upon the advantages, immediate and prospective, which the town would derive from the grant of a charter—the control of the police, the appointment of magistrates, the creation of a Court of Quarter Sessions, and ultimately the absorption by the Corporation of the powers of all the existing bodies. Mr. Redfern likewise combatted with vigour the arguments against the proposed Corporation—that it would be too costly, and that it would be too exclusive, by being composed of one party. On the latter point he said, " He had frequently heard it argued against a charter of incorporation that in all probability the Town Council would be of too exclusive a nature; that it would consist entirely of persons belonging to one particular party—in a word, of Whigs and Radicals. And of whom ought it to consist, but of those in whom the people placed their confidence? He would say that if they were to adopt the uniform practice of the opposite side as their guide, their opponents would have no reason to complain, even though the Town Council were to be as perfectly exclusive as they seemed to anticipate and to fear." Mr. M'Donnell touched upon the same theme: "They were told the Council would consist of Whigs and Radicals. He would not say that such would be the case, or that such ought to be the case, but he would say he sincerely hoped it would fairly represent the people of the town. If the people were Whigs, the Council would be Whigs. If the town were Radical, the Council would be Radical; and if the town happened to be Tory, they would have a Tory Council; and in that case, although he should regret it, yet upon the real principle of liberty, which he wished to see carried out, he should say it was just and equitable that it should be Tory. All they required was that honest men should represent their fellow men, and fairly and impartially administer the laws." Other speakers struck a higher note. "Local institutions," Mr. Douglas said, "alone generated and fostered the conviction amongst the people that government was a matter which every man ought to take an interest in, that it was not a machine which the people at large were to put away from them as not of their concernment, but one to which they must each lend an active and a propelling hand. They were taught by such institutions to work out their freedom and independence at home, or they need never expect to find either abroad. A Corporation was truly a school—a school in which every man, however limited his capacity, might acquire the rudiments of freedom, where by taking part in the election of town councillors, and, if called upon, acting as a councillor, he might prepare himself for the

CHAP. VI.
1837.
Speeches at the Meeting.

Importance of Municipal Government.

higher, but not more important functions of a Parliamentary elector, or, if circumstances called on him, of a Parliamentary representative." Dr. Birt Davies dwelt upon the moral and social benefits of local representative government—"The instruments of the law must be more cheerfully obeyed, the right arm of the law must be greatly strengthened by the fact that its various ministerial organs have been chosen especially for their fitness, by the free act of a majority of the people. And besides advantages in an administrative, in a fiscal, in an economical point of view, the elective system of local policy must operate beneficially upon all around us in its moral consequences. Whenever industry, indigenous here, is found combined with those higher qualities which alone enable a man either greatly to serve or to injure the institutions under which we live, there such a system offers a perpetual premium to good conduct. It presents a man with a constant stimulus to deserve and retain the approval of his neighbours. Upon that foundation is produced a broad road patent to all, and it tends directly to those honours and distinctions which have been hitherto chiefly attained by partisanship, by political servility, by the casual recommendations of those before upon the bench, or by the personal predilections of party lords lieutenant. Under the borough system, the householders who live near, who are the daily witnesses of a man's life, are the sole judges of his fitness for office. And in the newly incorporated towns there will be none of the old leaven. There will be no venal freemen to swamp the more sober and rational. There is none rich enough to bribe a community like this. There is none so high as to prevent or to escape the expression of your disapprobation. In consequence, errors excepted, it will be character and conduct alone that will decide the elections; and as the ultimate result there must be a great improvement in the salubrity of the political atmosphere." Mr. George Edmonds may close these extracts with an observation on the authority of a popularly elected body in directing and representing the town:—"They had heard a great deal from the Tories about the danger to which the peace of the community had been subjected, by exciting and calling out the people. Now the establishment of a body like the Town Council would prevent any of this fancied danger. It would establish a permanent body, with powers to convene the people in a legal manner; with power to give expression to their wants and feelings; and with power to restrain and govern them without danger. The men so elected would have the confidence of their fellow townsmen; and their advice and commands would be cheerfully obeyed. At present the authorities were self-elected, self-delegated, and irresponsible; and hence they had no authority, and commanded no respect, or not such respect as they ought, as rulers of the people, to enjoy."

CHAPTER VII.

OPPOSITION TO GRANT OF CHARTER.

<small>Chap. VII.
1837.
Petition presented.</small>

The petition adopted at the Town's Meeting was immediately presented, and a notice appeared in the *London Gazette* of the 22nd of December, ordering it to be taken into consideration on the 31st of January, 1838. This at once brought the opponents of the Charter into the field, and the contest assumed a distinctly political character; the application for a Charter being supported exclusively by Liberals, mainly of the Radical section, and opposed by Conservatives; the Whigs remaining neutral so far as action was concerned, though their sympathies, in many instances, went in opposition to the Charter. The

<small>First note of opposition.</small>

first note of opposition was sounded—curiously enough, on Christmas Day—by *Aris's Gazette*, in the following paragraph :—

"This is an important crisis in the affairs of Birmingham, and demands the serious consideration of all who are concerned. It is evident that the petition for a Corporation originated with a section only of the inhabitants of the town, politically speaking; and it remains to be proved by how large a proportion of the householders, being rated, the petition has been signed. If it be found that the provisions of the Act have been fulfilled as to the number of inhabitant householders, the Privy Council will in all probability favour the project; but still the fact of a clear month's notice of the hearing being necessary, makes it evident that every proper consideration will be given to such reasons as may be advanced on the part of the other inhabitants, either for the rejection of the measure altogether, or for a modification of it as respects the participation of the several parties in which the town is politically divided, or as to the measure of qualification upon which the franchise shall succeed."

To give effect to these views the opponents of the Charter called a private meeting, Mr. J. F. Ledsam pesiding. A resolution was moved by Mr. James Taylor, then the head of the banking house of Taylor and Lloyds, and seconded by Mr. J. W. Unett, a leading solicitor, both of them Conservatives—" That this meeting are of opinion that a Charter of Incorporation would be highly detrimental to the interests and prosperity of the borough of Birmingham." A report of the meeting explains that "there appeared to be a very prevalent opinion that the trading interests of the town would be most seriously injured by the annual excitement incident to a Corporation; and that the most important objects included in a municipal government would be as effectually and more economically attained, by having one or more stipendiary magistrates appointed for the borough, who should sit every day at the Public Office, and it was suggested that an efficient police should be formed and put under their management, that a House of Correction, of adequate dimensions, should be erected within the borough at the expense of the county, and that sessions for the trial of prisoners should be held in Birmingham every month or six weeks. It was contended that all these ends, if deemed desirable by the inhabitants, could be well attained consistently with the simple municipal regulations under which the town of Birmingham had risen to its present opulence and importance." These propositions bring out with clearness the distinction between the two parties—the advocates of the Charter insisting that, to be just or effectual, local government must be representative, based upon and controlled by the will of the people; and the opponents of the Charter being willing to concede the objects sought to be attained only on condition that the representative principle was excluded. Mainly, therefore, the contest which ensued was a conflict of principle; partly, also, it was a struggle on the part of one side to retain the government of the town in their own hands, by means of self-elected or nominated bodies, and on the part of the other to acquire, by the popular vote, the same control over municipal affairs which had already been established in regard to the Parliamentary representation of the borough. The opposing party followed up their private meeting by holding another meeting in the Town Hall. In the advertisements convening this assembly, it was described as "a meeting of such of the inhabitant householders of the Borough as disapprove of the proposed measure." In the counter petition afterwards presented to the Privy Council, this description was altered in a most material particular, the opposition being described as "a meeting of *the* inhabitant householders of the Borough," a designation which instantly and justly called forth a strong expression of indignation by the advocates of the Charter. It also elicited a further memorial addressed to the Privy

Council by Mr. W. Scholefield, the High Bailiff, who declared in this document that the hostile petition was signed by less than half the number of persons who signed the petition for the Charter; and asked, if it were thought necessary, to be heard by counsel in favour of the latter. The petitioners against the Charter, Mr. Scholefield points out, do not "venture to allege that there will be any interference with the existing municipal administration of the Borough, or any injury to the vested rights of individuals, or that there is anything of a peculiar nature in the circumstances and condition of the Borough of Birmingham to make it an exception to the general rule: all the objections of the said petitioners against the grant of a Charter having reference to the general policy of the new municipal system—a matter which has been already most wisely and constitutionally settled by the passing of the Municipal Corporations Act." Mr. Scholefield's protest was fully justified by the published reports of the opposition meeting. The requisition calling it was signed by 230 persons—all of them of the Conservative party—but the number who took sufficient interest in the matter to give themselves the trouble of attending was very small. "It was expected," says a newspaper of the day,* "that the 230 requisitionists at least, by whom the meeting was called, would have attended to confirm by their presence that which they had set their hands and seals to; but no such thing. The affair was left entirely in the hands of its promoters, some dozen

---

* The *Birmingham Philanthropist*, January 18, 1838.

CHAP. VII.
1838.

Small attendance at Opposition Meeting.

Character of Opposition Meeting.

or two of the Loyal and Conservative [Constitutional] Association, who have taken the Borough under their special protection; and, much to the surprise of all who gave the party credit for industry upon the occasion, when the hour of meeting arrived, the space around the Chairman presented a 'beggarly account of empty benches.' There were about forty or fifty of the requisitionists in the organ gallery, and twenty or thirty more sprinkled over each of the side galleries, with some two or three hundred persons in the body of the hall, who would probably have been set down as 'Conservative operatives,' were it not that a large portion of them kept up a random fire of jokes and raillery during the proceedings. Altogether, the appearance of the meeting, with the exception of the aforesaid Radicals, had a woe-begone air of sober sadness, such as must have excited the commiseration of every one whose feelings were not entirely frozen by the extreme coldness of the day." This, of course, is the sketch of an unsympathising observer, and may be heightened a little in colour; but that it is substantially accurate the report of the meeting affords evidence. The speakers were much interrupted by signs of dissent, by ironical laughter, and by those pertinent interjections which are characteristic of popular meetings in Birmingham, and which often serve very happily to point an allusion; or, as in the instance under notice, to upset an argument. For example, Mr. James Taylor, the banker, was one of the speakers against the Charter. He was a Churchman and Conservative; but his father, a Liberal and a Nonconformist, had been one of the sufferers by the Church and King riots of 1791. To this gentleman

Mr. Taylor made an unlucky reference. He had, he said, looked through his father's papers, and had found one, written forty years previously, arguing that Birmingham had prospered because it had been unshackled by a Corporation—(which was very likely, considering that Corporations were then unreformed)—and "lamenting the spirit of rancour which had prevailed among the people of Birmingham from a difference of opinion upon religion." Here a person in the meeting interrupted the speaker by enquiring "Who burnt his house down?;" and the "great laughter" which followed this pointed question effectually put an end to Mr. Taylor's paternal argument. Other speakers were dealt with in a similar manner; and indeed, their so-called reasons for objecting to a Charter deserved no better treatment. Looking back over the period which has elapsed since this contest, now that all parties are agreed as to the benefit of corporate representative government, it seems wonderful that prejudice and party spirit could have been carried so far, or that such feeble arguments should have been thought sufficient to justify opposition. All the speakers at the meeting, it is needless to say, were Conservatives—the conflict about the Charter having from the outset assumed a distinctly party character. The chief speaker, Mr. J. W. Whateley, grounded his argument against the Charter upon the fact that Birmingham had hitherto prospered not only without a Corporation, but because it had never had one. "In some corporate towns," he said, "heavy restraints had been laid upon trade; and in others persons, unless enjoying certain privileges, were debarred from carrying on trade at all. The men of

Birmingham had enjoyed a free and uncontrolled right to carry on their various businesses. This had been a great boon, and had served to raise the town at large to that important and elevated station which it now occupied in the country." The other principal speaker, Mr. James Taylor, employed the same argument: "His ancestors," he said, "came to that borough when Birmingham was a small country town, and since that period to what pre-eminence had it not arrived? It was now one of the largest towns in the empire; and he would ask why had it increased in this manner? He believed because it had been unshackled by a Corporation." These speakers must have presumed in a remarkable degree upon the ignorance of the audience, for the objections raised by them to a Corporation applied only to those Corporations which had been abolished; and the Municipal Act, under which Birmingham was applying for a Charter, was actually passed to extinguish and prohibit the very restrictions and limitations upon which the opponents of the Charter relied as the chief of their objections to it. Mr. Whateley did, indeed, employ one more argument—or, rather assertion—in support of his opposition—namely, that "from the inspection of the petition which had been presented to Her Majesty, he was justified in saying that it did not represent either the wealth, the intelligence, or the respectability of the borough." In order that the influence of these elements might be maintained, Mr. Whateley proposed an alternative plan of local government—namely, to leave the Commissioners of the Street Act in possession of their powers; to appoint stipendiary magistrates, with the control of a police force in their hands; and to remove the Warwick county sessions, by adjournment, to Birmingham. Upon this, we read, "a person in the body of the hall" put a crucial and most embarrassing question—"He wished to know, merely for the sake of information, what control the town would have over its funds under the mode recommended?" This question, the reporter suggests, "was considered irrelevant," as no reply was given to it. To complete the notice of this meeting, it should be added that the other speakers were Mr. E. Armfield, Mr. Anderton, Mr. David Malins, and Mr. J. M. Knott. Mr. Malins, the only one of the number who now (1877) survives, spoke with emphasis of the desire of himself and his friends to "prevent the introduction into Birmingham of the curse of a municipal Corporation. The people would find (he said) "in the long run that the Tories would turn out their best friends, for they were never more mistaken in their lives than when they supposed that their best friends were those who were seeking for a Corporation." In after years—such is the influence of calmer judgment, based upon experience—Mr. Malins himself became a leading member of the Town Council, and gave several years of useful work in the conduct of its business.

The record of this meeting, and the incidents which preceded and followed it, bring out with clearness the position of the two parties, and the state of feeling in the town. The movement in favour of local representative government was the direct issue of the great series of reforms which had been effected in our own Parliamentary institutions. It was part, indeed, of the steady current of progress which is traceable throughout English history. First, the King is supreme; then the Parliament arises, and gradually limits his power; next the Parliament, become oligarchic by the narrow basis of its elective body, is itself widened in the direction of freedom, antiquated elective privileges are abolished, new classes of voters are created, and new constituencies are called into being. The process thus conducted in the affairs of the nation, is repeated in the municipalities. Ancient restrictions on trade and government are removed; close electing bodies are dissolved; the citizens at large are entrusted with the management of their own affairs; privilege, personal influence, the authority of great landowners, and the abuses incident to these, altogether disappear; and under the Municipal Act, the Great Charter of English municipal freedom—a measure not less important or less beneficial than the Parliamentary Reform Act itself—the boroughs become miniature republics, in which all citizens stand upon a level as regards voting power, and in which a free career is opened to men of capacity, intelligence, and probity. The forces which operated for and against Parliamentary reform, and which had operated throughout history for and against freedom, naturally came into play here also, on the more restricted local stage. Those who were always in favour of limiting the power of the few, and increasing that of the many; those who proclaimed the sound maxim that taxation without representation is tyranny, were in favour of popular government in the local communities as well as in the nation generally. Those who belonged to the privileged class, and who, as members of old corporate or nominated bodies, or as magistrates, had enjoyed the authority of government, had arranged their own methods of procedure, had chosen their own colleagues, and had possessed and exercised the power of excluding one class on the ground of politics, and another on that of religion, were naturally averse to surrendering their position; and honestly believed, no doubt, in many instances, that a change to popular representation would be hurtful to the public interests as well as personally distasteful to themselves. On one side, therefore, we have the advocates of popular right, and on the other the advocates of privilege. In other words, as the contest in Birmingham showed—the Liberal party stood forward as the champions of a representative governing body; while the Conservatives endeavoured to maintain the restrictive means of government then in operation.

CHAP. VII.
1838.
Contending forces: Liberal and Conservative.

In the town itself there was not, and could not be, any question as to which of these parties carried public opinion with it. The spirit which had enabled Birmingham to exercise such a decisive influence upon the passing of the Reform Bill was still vigorous in the town. The very organisation—the Political Union—which guided and animated the country in that crisis, had been revived in order to promote further political reforms. The representation of the Borough was in the hands of the Liberal party. They had brought their force to bear upon the reform of the Corporations as well as the reform of Parliament; and

General feeling of the Town.

CHAP. VII.
1838.

Sectional opposition.

Birmingham and the Government.

they were now endeavouring, with zealous and united efforts, to obtain for their own town those benefits of local self-government which Birmingham had materially assisted to confer upon other places. So far, therefore, as popular feeling was concerned, the Charter was desired and supported by the great majority of the inhabitants, as their meetings and petitions testified, not less than the uniform course of their political movements. But while the town generally was of one mind, the Conservative party, and the small number of Whigs who sympathised with them in this particular object, were by no means to be despised in regard to vigour and influence. If the Charter had depended upon a local and popular vote, it would have been carried by an overwhelming majority. But, by the provisions of the Municipal Act, the power of granting or refusing the incorporation of the borough rested with the Privy Council; and before this body it was possible to maintain a more influential resistance than before a popular assembly. Something, too, was to be hoped for on account of the disposition of the Ministry. True, the Whigs were in office; but the Government was of a distinctly aristocratic cast, and, with the exception of Lord John Russell, the members of it had no sympathy with the Radical section of the Liberal party represented by Birmingham. The reception given to the National Petition presented by Mr. Attwood proved that the Ministers had taken up a hostile attitude towards the Radicals; and private Memoirs published within the last few years indicate that the feeling on their

measures. In the "Greville Memoirs," for example, we find Lord Melbourne described, on his own confession, as being "strongly against any Radical measures or Radical colleagues," and we find him also speaking with contempt of "Attwood and the Birmingham fellows."* Haydon, the painter, also records in his "Journals" indications of the same spirit. He had arranged to paint a great historical picture of one of the Newhall Hill meetings, conducted by the Political Union; and for this work he desired to obtain the patronage of Earl Grey. "I called at Lord Grey's (he writes, June 10, 1832). After waiting some time, in came two Lords, one after the other —one with all the obsequious humbleness of a place-hunter. As I had nothing to do, I sketched the whole scene of the Newhall Hill meeting, changing the position of Hutton [the Rev. Hugh Hutton] to the end, which increased the value and effect wonderfully. One Lord was called out first. Then, after another interval, the other Lord went, and a message followed for me. In I walked. Lord Grey received me in his usual amiable manner. He then said, 'I wish to explain to you that it would not be delicate for me, as a Cabinet Minister, to head any subscription connected with the Unions,' to which I replied, 'Perhaps it was indelicate in me to expect it.' 'But (he said) I should be happy to subscribe to any other subject connected with Reform. Suppose you paint the grand dinner in the

a genuine indication of Whig dislike to really popular agitation. Haydon adds—"Lord Grey did not speak of the Unions as he ought. He seemed to think of them as subjects beneath my pencil; and when I put into his hands the sketch I had made while I waited, he merely replaced it in my own without a word."* The spirit of Lord Grey lingered in the Ministry of 1838. Birmingham Radicalism, heartily directed but a short time previously to the support of a Reforming Government, was now practically in opposition to an Administration which seemed more than inclined to pause in the work of reform. The local Conservatives might therefore not unreasonably conclude that a movement originated by the Radicals, and depending for success entirely upon Ministerial favour, might be opposed with a chance of at least delaying it, if not of defeating it altogether. The disappointments and delays which actually occurred seem to favour this impression, for the progress of the matter showed that Ministers were not inclined to hurry the grant of the Charter for the sake of Birmingham; and it may be not unreasonably inferred that if it could have been refused on any decent pretext, there was at least a section of the Government which would have said "No" to the petition of the Birmingham people.

The opposition party in the town rested their case upon two grounds—first, that a Charter was unnecessary, the requirements of local government being capable of

---

* Life of Benjamin Robert Haydon, vol. ii., p. 344.

fulfilment without it; and on this ground they desired to be heard by counsel against the petition of the promoters. The Privy Council, however, declined to hear counsel: they could scarcely consent to do so after having affirmed in the Municipal Corporations Act the desirability of conferring charters of incorporation upon all the leading towns of the country. The opponents were therefore driven to their second ground—namely, that Birmingham itself did not desire the Charter; and in support of this they took up the position advanced by Mr. Whateley in the speech already quoted—that the petition for the Charter "did not represent either the wealth, the intelligence, or the respectability of the borough."

CHAP. VII.
1838.

The petitions for the Charter having been lodged with the Privy Council, a deputation consisting of Messrs. Attwood, M.P., W. Scholefield, W. Pare, Charles Lloyd, W. Redfern, and R. K. Douglas went to see Lord Lansdowne, then President of the Council, in support of them. These petitions were—one from the town's meeting, agreed to unanimously, one signed by 4,400 inhabitants, one from 68 out of the 108 Guardians of Birmingham parish, and one from 13 out of 18 Guardians of Aston parish. Subsequently another petition was presented, bringing up the signatures in favour of the Charter to a total of 8,700. On the other side a petition was presented against the Charter, signed by 2,700 persons; and this was supported personally by Mr. Barker, a then well-known Conservative solicitor, Mr. Ledsam, Mr. Whateley, and other leading members of the Conservative party. On each side, also,

Movements of the petitioners

Petitions for and against Charter.

CHAP. VII.
1838.

Government delays.

Government Enquiry.

Comparison of petitions.

numerous affidavits were put in, those of the Conservatives alleging that, taking the signatures of ratepayers only, the Liberal petitions fell short, both in number and value of rateable property, of those attached to the opposition petitions; while the Liberal affidavits denied and challenged the accuracy of the Conservative statements. The consequence was that instead of deciding, as was expected, to recommend the Queen to grant the Charter, the Privy Council put off their decision, from the 13th of February until their next meeting on the 5th of March, and directed that in the meantime an enquiry should be made by two Government Commissioners into the numbers of signatures and respective rateable values of the two petitions. The Liberals had previously made an estimate for themselves. It was impossible within any reasonable time to ascertain the rateable value of every petitioner. They proceeded consequently by the method of average, thus explained by the *Journal* of February 17:—"First they instituted a comparison between the first hundred names on the two petitions. It was to be presumed that the majority of these were, in both cases, good names. An accident, in the instance of the petition for the Charter, prevented that petition from exhibiting so strong a muster as it otherwise might have done. Still, in respect of aggregate assessment, it showed a larger sum than the opposing petition did. Second, the Committee took the first five names in each hundred, for the purposes of instituting a more general and accurate comparison between the two petitions. The result of this second method showed, in the petition for a Charter, 47 ratepayers in each 100 signatures with an average assessment of £30 10s.; and in the petition against a Charter, 72 ratepayers in each 100 signatures with an average amount of £34 10s." The general result, applied to all the petitioners, according to the Liberal calculation, was as follows:—

Ratepayers.		Assessments.	
For Charter.	Against.	For.	Against.
3,954.	1,944.	£120,527.	£67,068.

Majority of ratepayers for a Corporation 2,010; of assessment £53,529. At that date the rateable value of the Borough was £446,399; and the number of ratepayers about 18,000. This calculation was put before the Privy Council at its meeting on the 13th of February, when representatives of both parties were in attendance. From an account given a few days later in *Aris's Gazette*, the scene must have been an exciting one for the Birmingham deputations. Each side had put in memorials, and each had interviews both with Lord Lansdowne and with the Council itself. First the promoters of the Charter were called in; then their opponents followed; next came the promoters again; and then, once more the counter-petitioners. Finally, the latter drew up a petition on the spot, asking that "some impartial person might be appointed by the Council to ascertain the truth of the conflicting statements that had been made." To this, adds the report, "the parties in a short time received an answer that two impartial persons should be sent down to Birmingham for that purpose," and the further consideration of the subject was then deferred until the 5th of March.

CHAP. VII.
1838.

Discontent of the Liberals.

A candid opinion of the Whigs.

The Liberals were much dissatisfied with this postponement—"The report (wrote the *Journal* of February 17) on which it is intended that the Privy Council should—we were going to say *proceed*, but their practice hitherto points to a more appropriate term, *sit*—cannot be ready by that day. A further postponement will almost necessarily take place, and a further, until the people are grown sick of pressing the matter. Then perhaps, when they have ceased to take any interest in it, their petition will be granted, and produce, as such protracted concessions always do, as little gratitude in the receiver as it will bestow credit on the giver." On the 24th of February—there having been acrimonious debate in the other newspapers in the meantime—the *Journal* returns to the subject, and ends its criticisms on the opponents of the Charter with another attack upon the Ministry—"The Whigs cannot do a good thing graciously. It was said of the famous John, Duke of Marlborough, that a refusal from him was more pleasing than compliance from others. Of our cold, haughty, aristocratic rulers, it may be as truly said—compliance from them is less grateful than denial from others. We shall get the Charter, of course, after much and long delay—it took two years to settle the Devonport case, and ours cannot be dispatched in less—and when we get it, it will be 'thank ye for nothing,' as O'Connell said of the Emancipation Act."

Visit of Government Commissioners.

At the end of February, Captain Dawson and Mr. Denison, gentlemen deputed by the Privy Council, came down to Birmingham to enquire into the relative value of the two petitions. The enquiry was private, Mr. Scholefield assisting them on the Liberal side, and Mr. Barker on the Conservative side, and the two Committees for and against the Charter also having interviews with them. They were also instructed to ascertain the then actual cost of local management, the limits of the borough, and the best divisions for the several wards, supposing that a Charter should be granted. They did not take long to do the work, their visit lasting only for about a week. It is satisfactory to know that it was not marked by an unpleasant incident—" Of course," says the *Journal*, "there could be but one feeling respecting the Commissioners—to show them every respect that their office, and their message, and the high authority under which they were acting, demanded. Some of the Tory gentlemen were, as usual, a little fidgetty; but, upon the whole, the two deputations seemed each very well satisfied with their opponents' deportment."

The report of the Commissioners was, of course, a confidential document, and was, therefore, neither published nor disclosed to the parties concerned in promoting or opposing the Charter, excepting as regards the numbers of ratepayers who signed the petitions. Mr. Barker, the solicitor to the opponents, applied to Captain Dawson to know the result of the enquiry in this respect, and the request elicited the subjoined letter, addressed to Mr. W. Scholefield, the High Bailiff:—*

---

* *Birmingham Journal*, June 2, 1838.

CHAP. VII.
1838.

"Tithe Commission Office, London,
"June 6, 1838.

"Sir,—Having been applied to by Mr. Barker for information as to the result of the investigation made by Mr. Denison and myself at Birmingham, I beg to apprise you that I have this day sent him the subjoined statement in reply: "The number of names attached to the different petitions praying for a Charter of Incorporation, is 8,707. Of these 1,788 are persons actually paying rates; and the total amount of the sums for which they are assessed is £45,789 11s. 6d. The number of names to the petition against the Charter is 2,841. Of these 1,188 are persons paying rates; and the total amount of the sums for which they are assessed is £47,485 13s. 5d.—I have the honour, &c., ROBERT K. DAWSON, Capt. R.E."

"Although," adds the *Journal*, "this result is not what we certainly expected, yet it is, in all respects, satisfactory; and, had the question not been already settled, would have amply sufficed for that purpose."

Further delays.

The question, however, was not quite settled. The report of the Government Commissioners was obviously conclusive in favour of the Charter, for, at their meeting on the 5th of March, the Ministerial Committee of the Privy Council had informed a deputation of the Charter Committee that "the Lords are disposed to recommend it to the Queen to grant a Charter." The Liberals expected the matter to be decided on that day, and this further delay—for the fuller body had to consider the recommendation of the Committee—was not at all to their taste. "The terms (writes the *Journal*) are peculiar and lordly. It would be too great a mental exertion for such high people to resolve; it is fatigue enough to lean towards a proposition. As it is, we certainly quarrel not with the words provided we have the thing, and that we rather believe we are pretty sure to have before long." The Conservatives, however, held a different opinion. They relied upon their contention that the Charter could not be granted because a majority of the ratepayers had not petitioned for it, and they expected the Privy Council itself to reverse the judgment of its committee. This hope proved fallacious. At their meeting on the 27th of April the Privy Council finally agreed to recommend the Queen to grant a Charter of Incorporation to Birmingham; and the necessary preparations were ordered for the assignment of the wards of the borough, and the completion of the formal business incidental to the grant. The Conservatives still clung to the hope, not of preventing the grant, but of rendering it nugatory, by contesting it in the courts of law. This was the recommendation of the *Advertiser* (May 10, 1838), which used very strong language indeed: "The opposition to the incorporation of Manchester has been conducted with so much activity and zeal as to afford very reasonable grounds to hope that it may be spared the infliction of so bitter a curse on its commercial prosperity and social happiness; while Birmingham, alas! seems doomed to drink the cup of degradation to the very dregs, at the hands of our present Whig governors." Then followed a contention that, as the petition, acording to the Municipal Act, must be that of "the inhabitant householders," it must be necessarily that of a majority of them, and opinions of Sir F. Pollock and Mr. Lawrence Peel were quoted to this effect. The writer

Marginalia: CHAP. VII. 1838. Resolution of Privy Committee in favour of Charter. Legal proceedings threatened. Conservative comments.

proceeded: "The chances are against us, we confess, but drowning men proverbially catch at straws;" and then, speaking for the party, he recommended that when the Charter was granted and the Council elected, the validity of the acts done under it should be tested by appeal to the Court of Queen's Bench.

Influence of Conservative Peers.

There was yet another effort made at opposition before the Charter was finally granted. The Tories presented a petition against it to the House of Lords, and upon this petition a debate occurred on the 1st of June. The Earl of Ripon, who presented the petition, demanded, on behalf of the petitioners, access to the report of the Government Commissioners, and strongly argued against the grant of a Charter on the request of persons who were not actually ratepayers, and "who would not, therefore, be affected by the additional expenses which incorporation would impose." Lord Wharncliffe, another Tory peer, opposed the Charter on political grounds. Mr. Attwood, he said, "had recommended the inhabitants to apply for a Corporation as a great engine for political purposes; and had also told the people of Birmingham that a member of the Government told him in the year 1833, that their object in giving Corporations to the boroughs was to establish real and legal Political Unions in every town." Upon this Lord Wharncliffe insisted that "it was the duty of Government to take care that Corporations were not granted to promote the interests of a political party, else they might become mere schools of factious agitators;" and, as to the particular case of Birmingham,

Debate in the House of Lords.

he alleged that "the anti-corporators were superior to the pro-corporators in number, wealth, and intelligence," and were "entitled to be fairly heard." The Earl of Warwick followed on the same side, alleging that "the cry for a Corporation had been got up for party purposes." Lord Lyndhurst also lent the opponents his powerful support. He insisted that "one of the two parties who had given in contradictory statements having called for enquiry into their respective correctness, was entitled in justice to be furnished with the results of that enquiry," and he urged that "the Privy Council should have proceeded judicially between the opposing parties." In reply Lord Lansdowne, on the part of the Government, explained the rule they had followed, in this as in other cases :—

"The Privy Council had come to the conclusion that applications for Charters ought to be signed by a majority of the ratepayers being inhabitant householders of the town in question. He was not prepared, however, to say that he would always refuse a Charter of incorporation in cases where that majority of ratepayers did not pay the larger amount of assessment. In the case of Birmingham it had been determined to send down persons competently instructed in the nature of their duties, to make examination into the statements of the memorials, and he believed he had succeeded in the object he had proposed to himself of selecting two individuals perfectly free from party bias, and upon the whole well adapted for the office. These gentlemen had prepared a most able report; but with respect to allowing the petitioners to become acquainted with the contents of it, he was not aware that any application but one had been made at the Council Office for that purpose. The question (he continued) had been already fully examined, and he decidedly objected to reopen it, and allow new parties to be heard. It was most important that a limit should be set to the time occupied in discussing these applications, and in this case the same

CHAP. VII.
1838.

facilities for stating their case had been given to the one side as to the other. The Privy Council, he fully admitted, ought not to look to the interests of any political party, but to the general feeling of the inhabitants, whether it were in favour of or against a Charter, and to the predominance of the ratepayers. It was on these grounds alone that their judgment in the present case had been formed."

The Government hesitates

After some further debate, however, Lord Lansdowne so far abandoned his position as to promise that the sealing of the Charter should not proceed until the opponents had had time to make further representations upon the Report of the Government Commissioners. The advocates of the Charter refused to believe in the accuracy of this report;

Renewed delays.

but it seems to have been true, for, during the months of June and July, nothing was done to expedite the grant of the Charter; but, on the contrary, some further enquiries were made locally by the Government. The feeling excited by this delay, and by the obvious hesitation of Ministers, is forcibly expressed in the following paragraph from the *Journal* of August 11 :—

Irritation in Birmingham.

"THE NON-INCORPORATION OF BIRMINGHAM.—We learned yesterday, by accident only, that Captain Dawson, the same person who formerly visited Birmingham, was again here, sent down by the Whig Ministers, to see if he and they could make out a case on behalf of their Tory supporters, for refusing a Charter. We think it necessary to advert to this circumstance, for the purpose merely of stating that the Committee appointed by the inhabitants to conduct the application for a Charter, have not received any communication from Captain Dawson; and that if they had, they would, we feel confident, have treated it with the thorough contempt which the Whig Ministers and their tools, from beginning to end of this business, have so amply and entirely earned."

Another month elapsed—the petition for a Charter had now been nearly nine months before the Privy Council—and Ministers were still indisposed to fulfil the promise they had made so far back as March. On the 15th of September, there is another indignant paragraph in the *Journal*, which shows that the opponents of the Charter had been able to bring powerful influences to bear upon the Government privately, for no public movement of any kind had taken place in the interval on either side :—

Chap. VII. 1838. Another Government Enquiry.

"Some time ago a second investigation of the anti-Corporation petition took place under Government authority. The result, it was reported, added about 500 to the previous number of Tory ratepayers. We have not heard how, in the first calculation, so remarkable an error happened to be committed. Eight or ten days ago the pro-Corporation petition was sent down for re-examination, and on Thursday Captain Dawson and Mr. Denison arrived for the purpose of checking the re-examination; which task, we believe, they finished last night. We know nothing of the result of their labours. The Corporation Committee has had no communication with the Privy Council, nor with its agents, since the first scrutiny (at the end of February); but there is a rumour that the final result is to place the Tories in a worse position than when the re-examination was entered upon. This is their usual destiny here—the further in the deeper."

This opinion seems to have been justified by facts; or at least by the event, for the result of the report of Captain Dawson and his colleague was to confirm the Privy Council in their original decision to recommend the Queen to grant a Charter of Incorporation to the Borough.

Satisfactory Report: the Charter Granted.

CHAPTER VIII.

GRANT OF THE CHARTER.

CHAP. VIII.
1838.
Grant of the Charter.

On the 6th of October, 1838, the following announcement appeared in the *Journal*, printed in the most conspicuous part of the paper, and in the manner given below :—

"INCORPORATION OF BIRMINGHAM.

"THE CHARTER OF INCORPORATION FOR THE BOROUGH OF BIRMINGHAM WAS GRANTED ON THURSDAY. IT IS NOW BEING SEALED. THE COUNCIL WILL BE ELECTED ABOUT THE LATTER END OF DECEMBER; SO THAT THE FIRST MAYOR OF BIRMINGHAM WILL VERY PROBABLY TAKE DINNER IN THE TOWN HALL, WITH HIS FELLOW BURGESSES, ON CHRISTMAS DAY.

"𝕷𝖔𝖓𝖌 𝕷𝖎𝖛𝖊 𝖙𝖍𝖊 𝕼𝖚𝖊𝖊𝖓!"

The Charter of Incorporation was actually received in Birmingham on Thursday, November the First, 1838—it was at once taken to the *Journal* office, and was opened there by Mr. William Scholefield, the High Bailiff, who immediately published it in full in the newspapers, and issued with it the following official notice :—

"CHARTER OF INCORPORATION.

"Whereas her Majesty has been graciously pleased to grant a Charter of Incorporation to the Borough of Birmingham, pursuant to the provisions of the Municipal Corporation Act, and whereas the same has been directed to me, with her Majesty's commands to give effect to it, by making out the first Burgess List, and acting as Returning Officer at the ensuing election of Town Councillors. Now, therefore, I do hereby give Notice that I shall proceed to give publicity to the said Charter at the Town Hall, on Monday next, the 5th of November, at One o'clock p.m.; when and where the inhabitants of the said Borough are hereby invited to attend, for the purpose of hearing the same read.—Dated this 1st day of November, 1838.

"WILLIAM SCHOLEFIELD."

The full text of the Charter will be found in the Appendix. It constituted a Town Council consisting of a Mayor, 48 Councillors, and 16 Aldermen; and divided the Borough into thirteen wards, as follows:—

    1.—Ladywood Ward, returning three Councillors.
    2.—All Saints' .... three ditto.
    3.—Hampton .... three ditto.
    4.—St. George's .... three ditto.
    5.—St. Mary's .... three ditto.
    6.—St. Paul's .... three ditto.
    7.—St. Peter's .... six ditto.
    8.—Market Hall .... three ditto.
    9.—St. Martin's .... three ditto.
  10.—St. Thomas's .... three ditto.
  11.—Edgbaston .... three ditto.
  12.—Deritend and Bordesley ...... six ditto.
  13.—Duddeston and Nechells ...... six ditto.

The preparation of the Burgess List was fixed for the 11th of December, by Mr. Horatio Waddington, the barrister appointed for that purpose; the election of

CHAP. VIII.
1838.

Councillors was fixed for the 26th of December, and their first meeting, to choose a Mayor and Aldermen, for the 27th of December. After giving these particulars the *Journal* adds an exhortation to the inhabitants to attend on the 5th of November to hear the Charter read, " were it for no other reason than that the individuals who assemble may have it to boast, in future years, that they were present on the important day when the emancipation of this great city from the miserable sway of a self-elected Government was first publicly and by authority proclaimed."

Town's Meeting to hear the Charter.

The reading of the Charter took place, as announced, in the Town Hall, on the 5th of November. Mr. Attwood, the senior member for the borough, was unavoidably absent, but his colleague, Mr. Joshua Scholefield, was present, and was elected as chairman. He congratulated the meeting, which was numerous and enthusiastic, on the fact that Birmingham now, for the first time, took its place amongst the self-governed towns of the country, and thus realised "the great difference between slavery and freedom— namely, that the persons in the enjoyment of the latter had power to make the laws by which they were to be governed, and to expend the money which they contributed." On behalf of the town, he thanked the Queen for the grant of the Charter, vindicated the loyalty of Birmingham, spoke with heartiness of its services in the cause of freedom, and declared, amidst cheers, that "there was no town in England in which there invariably existed greater order, in which there was less disposition to tumult or irregularity, or in which less crime was perpetrated." Mr. William Scholefield, the returning officer, then read the Charter of Incorporation; and concluded by holding up the document itself to the view of the meeting—an act which was greeted with great cheering. Several speeches were then delivered. Mr. William Redfern, one of the most active promoters of the Charter, moved a resolution expressive of satisfaction that it had been granted. "They had," he said, "got the Charter at last, and although he sincerely regretted the vacillating policy of the Government in this matter—although he admitted, with pain and sorrow, that it but ill became them, the architects and founders of the new municipal system, to put any difficulties in their way, still, separating the Queen from her Ministers, and believing that whatever was gracious in the proceeding was hers, and whatever was ungracious was theirs, he would say of it that it was a right royal gift—it was a gift which he trusted their children and their children's children would long continue to prize, for the sake of the invaluable rights and privileges it conferred upon them. For the effect of that Charter would be to give them, in place of the close and packed Boards that heretofore had held sway in the town, a popularly elected Town Council—a Town Council consisting of men whom the people delighted to honour, and whom they ought to honour, since through good report and through evil report, some of them in dungeons, like their friend Mr. Edmonds, some of them as the victims to criminal informations, like Mr. Muntz and Mr. Pare, they had held fast by popular principles, and had cloven with constancy to the good old cause."

CHAP. VIII.
1838.
The Charter exhibited.

Speeches at the Town's Meeting: Mr. W. Redfern.

L

CHAP. VIII.
1838.
Validity of Charter.

Referring to a rumour of legal proceedings to test th validity of the Charter, Mr. Redfern said:

Speeches at the Town's Meeting.

"That the opposite parties (the Tories) were aware of the immense advantages we should derive from the new system, of the great power it would put into our hands, was evident from the strenuous efforts they have made to defeat our wishes, from the first moment of their entering the field against us, down to their last intrigue, so slyly carried on by Lord Warwick; and even now there is a strange rumour abroad that they have it in contemplation to call in question our new liberties by means of a *quo warranto*. Be it so. I should like to see these Conservative gentlemen in such a position. I should like to see these Conservative gentlemen—these members of Loyal and Conservative Associations—all of them ready, forsooth, to fight for the Crown, if it be put upon a hedge stake—I should like to see them gainsaying an act of Royal grace and favour; thus disloyally trying to tear the broad seal from the Queen's Charter. At all events, we, the Radicals of Birmingham, who are charged with making the sceptre shake in the Queen's hand, and the crown totter on her brow, we will meet these disloyal men on the floor of the Queen's Bench to vindicate the Royal prerogative; and, God willing, we will beat them again, as we have so often beat them before."

Mr. P. H. Muntz.

Mr. Philip Henry Muntz, who seconded the motion, referred to the petitions against the Charter. They were said to be signed by four thousand persons. "He really did not believe that four hundred of them had ever seriously thought of the matter. He did not believe that forty would have signed if they had not been requested to do so. The truth was there was a little clique who could command a certain number of signatures to any petition, and these gentlemen had by every means in their power obtained a number of signatures. He knew that people had been induced to sign by being told that a Corporation would double the rates. He had not the least doubt in saying that, with the exception of some ten or a dozen of the little clique, the great mass of the inhabitants would be decidedly in favour of a Corporation."

<small>CHAP. VIII.
1838.
Speeches at the Town's Meeting.</small>

Mr. William Wills moved the next resolution: "That this meeting desires to record its gratitude to her Majesty, for having graciously acceded to the prayer of the petition of the inhabitants of Birmingham for a Charter of Incorporation." He dealt chiefly with the character and motives of the opposition to the Charter, all of which had proceeded from one political party. "He felt no small disgust at the allegation that the Charter was likely to engender party strife or ill-will amongst the inhabitants." Those who said so "were themselves of the very extreme of party." The allegation was a pretence. "The real secret of the objection was that the Charter aimed a deadly blow at monopoly—a monopoly which, if it could, would trample its opponents in the dust—a claim urged by a party who claimed for themselves an exclusive infallibility as well in politics as in religion. The cry of party had been loudly raised by a set of wholesale dealers in slander and abuse, towards those who had contributed to the promotion of this measure, and generally to all persons who dared to think for themselves, and act with independence, in a spirit which marked them as the worthy successors of that infamous publication, the *Argus.*"

<small>Mr. W. Wills. Thanks to the Queen.</small>

The Rev. T. M. M'Donnell, who seconded the vote of thanks to the Queen, humorously suggested that as the Conservative party had said and done everything they could against the Charter, they would not take advantage of it. "If they were honest in their profession they would, of course, take care to show their aversion to the Charter by keeping their hands to themselves, and while they would be engaged in taking tea in No. 2 [a well-known room at Dee's Royal Hotel] the people would be proceeding with the election."

Mr. Joseph Sturge, who spoke next, put in a good word for the Commissioners of the Street Act. He had withdrawn from them because they were a self-elected body; but it was only "an act of justice to say that few bodies had, upon the whole, more economically applied the funds at their disposal for the safety and general improvement of the town." Mr. Sturge closed his speech by moving a vote of thanks to the Incorporation Committee, which was seconded by Mr. Boultbee, and acknowledged by Mr. Thomas Bolton, the Chairman of the Committee. Mr. R. K. Douglas, who also replied, gave a strong hint as to the character of the Town Council. "Let it be fairly decided by a majority of the ratepayers. What would the people have said to Mr. Watt if, when he got his steam engine completed, when it was just fit to be set to work, he had committed the trial of its working to men who were strangers to its principles, and who had a direct interest in denying its merits? So would it be if they were to put the machinery of the Corporation into the hands of either Whigs or Tories—men who had always been against the working of it." Mr. Douglas then described the actual reception of the Charter: "He wished the meeting had seen all the members of the Committee on Thursday last, looking out for the arrival of the precious document. They were like children waiting for a fairing, terribly impatient, and almost afraid it would not come after all. Their good friend, Mr. Hutton, went twice to the railway station in search for it; and they told him the second time it had probably gone on to Belfast. At last it arrived, and was uncorded in the *Journal* office, and he (Mr. Douglas) secured the cord, and he meant to keep it with great care. It was a very nice one; precisely of the proper size. If any of the Tories had a desire to try its strength, he had no objection to lend it—(great laughter) —always provided the executors were bound to return it for similar service; for, from their present condition, he thought it very probable it would be wanted more than once."

Mr. George Edmonds moved the last resolution, a vote of thanks to the Chairman. His speech, peculiarly vigorous and eloquent, was devoted to the review of local political affairs for twenty years, with a view of showing the violence and injustice to which he and others had been subjected by the Tory party. From this Mr. Edmonds drew the inference that it would be unwise to allow the Tories to govern the new Corporation. "They were still the same men, actuated by the same spirit; and, if they had the power, would re-enact the worst scenes of Tory physical force." The men who had opposed the Charter "now turned round, and modestly hoped they would be employed to work it." The burgesses should see, as a duty, that "not one of the men whose names were attached to that list had anything to do with the Corporation." The last speaker was Mr. T. Clark, jun.; then Mr. Scholefield returned thanks, and the meeting broke up, amidst loud cheers, after a sitting of over four hours' duration: a memorable day in the annals of Birmingham.

The advice given in these speeches as to the composition of the first Council was emphatically repeated by the newspaper of the Radical party—the *Journal*. On the 10th of November we read:—

"There will be a number of good things going under the Corporation. There will be a most careful economy of the public money, no sinecure will be tolerated, no over-paid office; but there must be offices and officers not a few. The machinery of the Municipal Act renders this essential. These offices will be in the gift of the Council—of the majority of the Council; and the majority of the Council will not give their gifts to neutrals, much less to opponents. . . . The Whigs and the Tories laid on the shelf, there remain only the Radicals to choose from; and from the Radicals the choice will be made. There is a bar in the way of Tory exertion in the present case, which did not exist in the Parliamentary struggle [in which Mr. Stapleton was a Conservative candidate]. Then the borough was all before them. Every vote that they could force or buy, caught up in what corner it might be, told with effect. Now they are cribbed and cabined by ward divisions, which have split up, and mangled, and minced their power without measure or mercy. Bull Street, New Street, High Street, are drawn and quartered. The Tories, in their misery, have got acquainted with strange neighbours. The toe of the huckster galls the kibe of the purse-proud shopocrat. The various degrees, ranks, and offices of electors are mixed and mingled in a confusion out of which, come order or disorder, nothing will emanate which can give satisfaction to the Tories. Every way, then, the respectables, as they are pleased to describe themselves, are sure to have the worst of it."

The first step towards giving effect to the provisions of the Charter was the arrangement and revision of the List of Burgesses. This began on the 11th of December, before Mr. Horatio Waddington, the barrister appointed for the purpose. There was a strong muster of legal gentlemen and others engaged—Messrs. W. Redfern, S. Bray, W. Barlow, Arthur Ryland, and R. K. Douglas for the Liberals; and Messrs. J. B. Hebbert, Smythies, and Cudlipp for the Conservatives. The Conservatives issued 850 objections; the Liberals served only 20. The first case called on raised an interesting point. The voter objected to was a Mr. Nehemiah Buckler, Constitution Hill; and the Liberals insisted upon proof of the service of the objection being given. After some delay this was done by a witness named Gale. Then Mr. Redfern took objection to the insufficiency of the notice, on two grounds—first that the objector was described as "John Palmer, Terrace," which, it was contended, did not allow of his being properly identified—the real description being "Summer Hill Terrace;" and, second, that the name of "Birmingham" was omitted from the notice. On the other side it was contended that Summer Hill Terrace was and always had been known as the "Terrace," and that the objector himself was so described in the Burgess List. A

CHAP. VIII.
1838.
Burgess List:
Conservative
objections.

long debate ensued, and several witnesses were called on both sides. In the course of the discussion Mr. Douglas called upon the Court to reject the objection because the Conservatives had "attempted, by issuing wholesale objections, merely to annoy good voters, for party purposes, and without the slightest knowledge of the parties or examination into their claims." Ultimately, after taking a day to consider the subject, the Barrister decided that the objector's residence was not properly and fully described, and consequently all the objections signed by Palmer fell to the ground. A considerable number of objections, however, were sustained, but a much larger number were rejected or had to be withdrawn.

CHAPTER IX.

ELECTION AND PROCEEDINGS OF THE FIRST COUNCIL.

The election of the first Town Council took place on Wednesday, December 26, 1838. It was preceded by a great deal of commotion in the respective political parties in the borough, and by a division amongst the Liberals. This arose from the formation of a Central Committee to nominate candidates for the respective wards. Some of the Whig party resisted what they termed dictation, and angry meetings and still angrier correspondence occurred in St. Peter's and one or two others of the wards. The Conservatives, too, though they had resisted the Charter, were now desirous of taking part in the new Corporation, and they consequently brought forward a number of candidates. In some instances the Whigs appear to have joined the Conservatives, and in a few cases decided Liberals were included in both the lists put forward. The following return of the election, with the number of votes for each candidate, is extracted from the *Journal* of December 29 :—

"On Wednesday the elections for the various wards of Birmingham, under the Municipal Act, took place, and certainly a more decided expression of popular opinion never was evinced.

FIRST ELECTION OF THE COUNCIL.

Each ward in the borough was contested by Tory candidates, every one of whom were defeated. The election commenced in the different wards precisely at nine o'clock in the morning, under the superintendence of deputy returning officers, and the poll was kept open until four o'clock, when the boxes were conveyed to the Committee Room of the Town Hall, and their contents examined by W. Scholefield, Esq., the returning officer, and the following was declared the result of the elections:—

LADYWOOD.

Radical List.		*Tory List.*	
T. Clark, jun.	66	D. Ledsam	25
J. Betts	65	R. Harris	15
Benjamin Hadley	63	R. W. Winfield	10

ALL SAINTS.

S. Shakespear	221	T. Lane	104
P. H. Muntz	158	— Beynon	66
F. Matchett	135		

Mr. Shakespear was in both lists.

HAMPTON.

G. V. Blunt	159	T. Pemberton	72
J. Meredith	159	W. H. Bates	72
H. Jennings	157	S. Kempson	68

ST. GEORGE'S.

T. C. Salt	128	R. Hollis	109
H. Court	127	J. B. Oram	106
A. Lawden	121	— Waddy	85

ST. PAUL'S.

F. Clark

FIRST ELECTION OF THE COUNCIL.

St. Mary's.

Radical List.		Tory List.	
S. Beale	172	— Phillips	35
R. C. Mason	142	S. Allport	33
J. H. Cutler	140		

Mr. Beale was in both lists.

Market Hall.

T. Aspinall	173	— Warden	87
T. Clowes	163	J. B. Payn	83
T. Bolton	163	T. Perkins	78

St. Peter's.

R. H. Taylor	412	— Butler	218
J. Drake	283	— Osborn	217
W. Scholefield	282	Westley Richards	210
W. Harrold	281	W. Phipson	210
C. Geach	275	S. W. Lucas	202
S. Hutton	266		

Mr. Taylor was in both lists.

St. Martin's.

J. Rodway	110	T. Hill	68
T. Phillips	108	James James	66
T. Weston	105	F. I. Welch	63

St. Thomas's.

W. Middlemore	199	Joseph James	81
Joseph Sturge	144	W. Lucy	71
W. Pare	119		

Mr. Middlemore was in both lists.

Edgbaston.

Charles Sturge	180	R. T. Cadbury	109
		S. Haines	100

DERITEND AND BORDESLEY.

Radical List.			*Tory List.*	
R. Wigley	461		T. Beilby	84
W. Ingall	450		S. Thornton	77
W. Jenkins	446		E. Banks	68
J. Hawkes	397		Isaac Marshall	26
J. Field	387		W. Sumner	24
R. Riley	385		T. N. Fuller	21

DUDDESTON AND NECHELLS.

J. Pierce	520		W. Gammon	452
J. Cornforth	512		J. Haycock	444
T. Hickling	504		Josiah Robins	442
W. Page	492		J. Swingler	441
C. Truman	496		G. J. Green	427
F. Page	489		W. Cracklow	408

It is pleasant to read that "during the day, although the utmost activity and bustle prevailed in the town, not the slightest unpleasantness or interruption took place. The fact was, the whole proceeding was commenced and carried on with a species of religious decorum which reflects the highest credit upon the inhabitants."

The first meeting of the Council was held on the day following the election, in the Committee Room of the Town Hall; Mr. W. Scholefield, as returning officer, presiding. The election returns having been read, a discussion arose as to the principle on which aldermen should be elected, Mr. Weston, Mr. Joseph Sturge, and others contending that they should be chosen only from amongst the members of the Council, in order to maintain the principle of popular election. Mr. P. H. Muntz, while admitting that candidates who had been rejected by the electors ought not to be chosen, urged that it would be unwise to reject good men who had not offered themselves as candidates for the office of Councillor; and this view, as will be seen presently, was, to a limited extent, approved by the Council. Another discussion occurred on the oath which the Municipal Act required to be taken.* There being as yet no Mayor, Mr. Scholefield explained that it was necessary that two justices of the peace should attend to receive the statutory declarations of the members; and that Mr. William Chance and Mr. Francis Lloyd had undertaken this duty. The declaration at that time required Councillors to pledge themselves not to do anything to injure the Church as by law established. Mr. Harrold announced that he could not make that declaration. Mr. Joseph Sturge made the same statement. He should refuse, and should abide by the consequence of doing so. " He had so strong a feeling against Church establishments, he felt so convinced that they were injurious, and that there would be no real peace in this country so long as the present system existed, that he was determined to do all

---

* This oath consisted of the following declarations, which each member was required to make:—

"I, A. B., having been elected [alderman or councillor] for the Borough of Birmingham, do hereby declare that I take the said offices upon myself, and will duly and faithfully fulfil the duties thereof, according to the best of my ability."

"I, A. B., do solemnly and seriously, in the presence of God, profess, testify, and declare, upon the true faith of a Christian, that I will never exercise any power, authority, or influence which I may possess by virtue of the office of [alderman or councillor] to injure or weaken the Protestant Church, as it is by law established, in England; or to disturb the said Church, or the bishops, or the clergy of the said Church, in the possession of any rights or privileges to which such Church, or the said bishops and clergy are, or may be, by law entitled."

CHAP. IX.
1838.
Mr. Joseph Sturge's objection.

he could, in a lawful and constitutional manner, to make a change; and hence he could not conscientiously subscribe to the declaration. He felt he could not be doing right to take that declaration in the morning, and vote against Church rates in the evening. To do one thing as a Councillor, and another as a man, was too nice a distinction for his plain understanding; and rather than run any risk, he would take all the consequences of a prosecution for not taking the declaration." Mr. Pare said he saw no difficulty. "They only declared that they would not injure the Church in their corporate capacity; but they did not surrender their private judgment or individual rights as citizens. He should not hesitate to vote against Church rates, although he should take the declaration." On this Mr. Harrold said that his own scruples had been removed. The two magistrates above mentioned—Mr. W. Chance and Mr. F. Lloyd—here entered the room; and the declaration not to injure the Church, and the oath of office, having been read over, all the Council subscribed them, with the exception of Mr. Joseph Sturge and Mr. Charles Sturge, who declined.

Taking the Oath.

Election of Aldermen.

The election of Aldermen was then proceeded with, the result being as follows:—

Names.	No. of Votes.	Wards.
P. H. Muntz	43	All Saints'.
Thomas Bolton	41	Market Hall.
William Scholefield	40	St. Peter's.
Benjamin Hadley	34	Ladywood.
Joseph Sturge	34	St. Thomas's.

Names.	No. of Votes.	Wards.
Clement C. Scholefield	32	St. George's.
William Jenkins	30	Deritend and Bordesley.
William Ingall	27	Deritend and Bordesley.
John Meredith	26	Hampton.
Samuel Hutton	26	St. Peter's.
* J. Towers Lawrence	25	St. Martin's.
* William Gammon	24	Duddeston and Nechells.
John Betts	24	Duddeston and Nechells.
William Harrold	23	St. Paul's.
Samuel Beale	21	St. Mary's.
H. Van Wart	21	Edgbaston.

The two Aldermen marked with an asterisk were not members of the Council when elected. Votes were also given for the following persons—Mr. Jennings 20, Mr. Wilcox 19, T. Clark, jun, 18, Thomas Phillips 16, Charles Sturge 14, Captain Moorsom 13, J. Pierce 12, W. Phipson 11, T. Weston 10, Abel Peyton 10, Joseph Walker 9, Reuben Wigley 7, William Beale 6, James James 6, Mark Perkins 5, Henry Smith 4.

The Council then adjourned until five o'clock, when a number of burgesses were present, and on the motion of Mr. Hadley special accommodation was provided for the reporters. The first business was the election of Mayor. Mr. Muntz, with a high commendation of his "able, impartial, and excellent conduct," proposed Mr. William Scholefield. The nomination was seconded by Mr. Lawrence, who said "there was only one opinion amongst all classes relative to the competency of Mr. Scholefield. In every sense, and by every one, he was admitted to be entirely

Election of Mayor.

qualified for the office." The motion was then put by Mr. Bolton (who was in the chair) and was "carried with loud and hearty applause, which lasted some time." In order to make the election legally certain, it was put to a show of hands, and was unanimous. The Mayor then took the customary oaths; and thus the Council was duly constituted, and the rule of representative local government in Birmingham was formally established.

Election of Town Clerk, &c.

The Council next proceeded to elect its officers. First came the choice of a Town Clerk. Two candidates were nominated—Mr. William Redfern by Mr. Bolton and Mr. Muntz; and Mr. Solomon Bray by Mr. Hadley and Mr. Salt. In support of Mr. Redfern his proposer and seconder dwelt upon his eminent services in promoting the Charter; and to this the Mayor also bore testimony—Mr. Redfern's exertions "had been incessant: morning, noon, and night he had laboured in the struggle." Mr. Bray's nomination was then put and negatived by a large majority; and Mr. Redfern was elected unanimously. The

Registrar of Mayor's Court

appointment of Registrar of the Mayor's Court followed. This was a court constituted by the Charter for the recovery of small debts, the Recorder being judge, and the Registrar acting as his deputy. Mr. Robert Kellie Douglas was nominated for the office by Mr. Muntz and Mr. Jennings. Some objection was raised on the ground that he was not a lawyer, but it was shown that neither the Municipal Act nor the Charter rendered professional qualifications necessary. Mr. Sturge proposed Mr. William Morgan in opposition to Mr. Douglas; but later, at Mr. Morgan's own request, he withdrew the nomination, and Mr. Douglas was elected, Mr. Muntz testifying "that if it had not been for the labours and the ability of Mr. Douglas they would not then be sitting there as a corporate body." Next came the appointment of Clerk of the Peace, for which Mr. George Edmonds was nominated by Mr. Betts and Mr. Gammon. In supporting the proposal Mr. Harrold bore well-deserved testimony to Mr. Edmonds's merits. "They had before them the oldest man in Birmingham who stood forward upon the platform of religious liberty. He had suffered imprisonment in the cause of liberty; and it was much easier to talk about this, than to endure it with courage." Mr. Hadley added another encomium: "Not only had the people of Birmingham reason to rejoice at the result of the labours of Mr. Edmonds, but the friends of freedom all over England. He had been one of the great pioneers in the battle of freedom; and after all the labours and sufferings he had had to encounter, no man could have come through the fire with cleaner hands." The election, however, it was ascertained, could not then be legally made, as the Town Clerk pointed out that the grant of a Quarter Sessions must be first obtained on petition by fourteen of the Councillors before a clerk of the peace could be appointed. Having arrived at this conclusion, the first meeting of the Council was adjourned.

The election to fill up vacancies caused by the appointment of aldermen took place within a few days after the first meeting of the Council. They resulted in

CHAP. IX.
1839.
The Council completed.

the choice of the under-mentioned burgesses, who, with those previously mentioned, constitute the first Council of the Borough :—

St. Mary's Ward	Mr. W. Stone.
St. Peter's	Mr. E. M. Martin.
	Mr. David Barnett.
	Mr. J. F. Parker.
Ladywood	Mr. W. Jenking.
	Mr. Thomas Hadley.
All Saints'	Mr. T. Lutwyche.
Hampton	Mr. C. Tongue.
Market Hall	Mr. C. Smith.
St. Thomas's	Mr. W. Haslewood Smith.
Edgbaston	Captain Moorsom, R.N.
	Mr. B. Redfern.
Deritend and Bordesley ...	Mr. J. Hardwick.
	Mr. Joseph Rawlins.

1839.
The Oath of Office: New objections.

All the members elected to supply the vacancies were Liberals in politics, like those first elected, and were chiefly Liberals of the Radical section. In regard to religious opinion, the Council was divided; most of its members were Nonconformists, but there were several Churchmen, two Roman Catholics, and one member of the Hebrew community. This gentleman, Mr. David Barnett, attended at the meeting of the Council on the 12th of January, and took the oath of office, but declined to take the second oath, binding him not to use his position as a Councillor to injure the Church of England. His objection, as may be supposed, was to the use of the words "on the true faith of a Christian." He could, he said, take the declaration conscientiously, with the omission of these words, "for his religion strictly commanded Israelites that wherever they might be, they were in duty bound to support the establishment of the country." On this statement the Town Clerk read two letters, one from the Town Clerk of London, and the other from the Town Clerk of Southampton, in both of which places Jews had been elected, had refused to take the declaration "on the true faith of a Christian," and yet had been permitted to act as members of the Councils. These were Alderman Salomons, in London; and Mr. Abraham at Southampton. Ultimately, it was decided by the Mayor that Mr. Barnett must be allowed to take the declaration in his own way, at the risk of incurring any personal penalty to which he might be exposed by so doing. Captain Moorsom then took an objection to the oath. As a Churchman, he demurred to giving any pledge that he would not seek for a reform of the Church, and to test the matter he put this question to the Town Clerk— "Do you consider it the undoubted and inalienable right of the Council to discuss and pronounce an opinion upon all questions of general policy, foreign or domestic, of municipal and fiscal regulations, of religious and civil liberty; on every question, in short, which affects the welfare of society?" To this the Town Clerk replied that, speaking as a lawyer, his opinion was "that the only duties which the Town Council were competent to perform were strictly of a local nature, and that they were not competent to perform duties of any other kind. But when he considered what had been the almost uniform practice of municipal corporations for ages past, and how important a part they had played on some of the most momentous occasions of

Chap. IX.
1839.
Objection to Oath of Office.

Discussion of public subjects by the Council.

CHAP. IX.
1889.
Rule of general debate established.

our history, and when he bore in mind with how universal and prescriptive a consent they had been invested with something of a political character, he felt warranted in saying that they were not bound to confine themselves within the strict limits prescribed by the Municipal Corporations Act, but that it was competent for them to deal with matters of a general and national nature." This, however, did not satisfy the scruple of Captain Moorsom. He still objected to the declaration, on the ground that it hindered his liberty as a reforming Churchman, and also because it maintained the principle of Church establishments, which he believed to be "serious evils and great hindrances to the spread of the Gospel, and a frightful source of discord and contention in society." Accordingly, following the example of Mr. Joseph Sturge and Mr. Charles Sturge, he refused to take the declaration; and consequently, like them, he was admitted without it. Thus, at the outset of its work, the Council raised and decided for itself important questions of principle, on which the judgment of the nation has since been pronounced in the same sense, for the declaration referring to the maintenance of the Church has been repealed by Parliament, and the exclusion of Jews from the Legislature and from municipal bodies has also been repealed, by the withdrawal of the words "on the true faith of a Christian" from the oaths of office. At the same meeting, the Council also decided another point of practice of much importance—namely, whether national as well as local subjects should be open to debate by its members. The occasion was furnished by an application from the

Anti-Corn Law Association for an interview with the Council, with a view of inducing them to "use all the means in their power for the total repeal of the corn and provision laws." Some discussion occurred as to the propriety of dealing with such matters, and of receiving deputations; but, finally, the deputation was received. It consisted of Mr. Joshua Scholefield, M.P., and Messrs. Robert Webb, Thomas Eyre Lee, George Edmonds, William Morgan, and Julius Partrige. At the next meeting of the Council, on the 19th of January, this question again came up, and was thoroughly discussed. Mr. Harrold objected to the municipal representatives travelling out of their proper duties, as laid down in the Municipal Act. Mr. P. H. Muntz proposed to settle the matter by a general resolution, declaring that, "in the opinion of the Council, whenever a respectable number of burgesses request the Mayor to convene a meeting of the inhabitants of the borough, for the purpose of considering any question of importance, either national or municipal, it is expedient that such meeting should be convened." This was objected to, as binding the action of the Council for the future; and Mr. Joseph Sturge moved that the Mayor be requested to convene a town's meeting to consider the propriety of petitioning Parliament for the repeal of the Corn Laws. Alderman Hadley, Mr. Beale, Mr. Weston, Mr. T. Phillips, and others supported this motion, which was carried by a large majority; and thus the discussion of public and political, as well as purely local topics, was decided as the practice of the Council. At a subsequent meeting (January

26, 1839) the Council gave effect to this decision by itself adopting a petition to Parliament for the repeal of the Corn Laws. The debate, and the circumstances attending it, deserve some notice. A strong agitation was then proceeding in the country (with Birmingham as its head quarters, and the revived Political Union as its means) for the promotion of Parliamentary reform, by the extension of the suffrage to all adult males—the ballot, and annual Parliaments: this desire being formally expressed in the National Petition presented to the House of Commons by Mr. Attwood, on the 14th of June, 1839. The advocates of this movement strongly objected to allow any other object to interfere with it, and therefore—although many of them were adverse to the Corn Laws—they considered a motion for the repeal of these laws as inopportune, because it tended to withdraw attention from the purely political designs of the Union and the framers and supporters of the National Petition. Some of them, indeed, went so far in their opposition as to suggest that the discussion of the Corn Laws was merely a Whig device to embarrass the reformers. This opinion was plainly intimated in a series of resolutions adopted by the Radical Reform Society of Duddeston and Nechells, with a direct view to the proposed action in the Town Council. "This meeting (they say) utterly deprecates the attempt now being made by short-sighted men to distract, by the agitation of party and class questions, the attention of the people from the momentous constitutional struggle in which they are engaged. This meeting is of opinion that it would ill become the municipal representatives of this great and enlightened borough to sanction the interested movements of the Whig Corn Law intriguers; and that the high reputation of our important town demands that the first political act of its Corporate body should be in aid of the legal and peaceful movement which is now being made by suffering millions to acquire their indefeasible right of suffrage." These views found supporters in the Town Council. Mr. Weston brought forward the subject by moving that a petition be presented for the repeal of the Corn Laws. This was seconded by Alderman Joseph Sturge; and was resisted by Mr. T. Clutton Salt, who moved the following resolution: "That this court considers it inconsistent with its duty, by petitioning the House of Commons as now constituted, to sanction the belief that any large or liberal measure of justice can possibly emanate from a body so chosen by privileged classes; and that this court deems it accordingly inexpedient to petition a House so constituted." A long and animated debate ensued, much doubt was expressed as to the good effect of a repeal of the Corn Laws, the currency question—then, owing to Mr. Attwood, very popular in Birmingham—was introduced into the discussion, and hard things were said of the House of Commons. Ultimately, however, the amendment of Mr. Salt was rejected by 34 to 12, the motion for a petition for the repeal of the Corn Laws was agreed to, and a petition—a very out-spoken document—was adopted. The resolution of the Council, it is curious to note, was condemned by the newspaper of the party to which all the members of the Corporate body belonged—the *Journal*, which strongly

Chap. IX.
1839.

Disputes in the Council.

CHAP. IX.
1839.

supported the suffrage movement, and looked coldly upon Corn Law repeal, observing that "there seems something like a spirit of domination, which a body elected as the Council is ought of all things to avoid, more especially in the very flush of its recent honours, in authoritatively anticipating the voice of the people."

Dinner to celebrate the Charter.

Before proceeding to describe the business transacted by the Council, and the difficulties which the new Corporation had to overcome, it may be as well to complete the initial stage of municipal history by recording the circumstance that the grant of the Charter was celebrated by a public dinner in the Town Hall, on Thursday, February 21, the Mayor presiding. The Hall was filled by an enthusiastic company, and the scene was one of great interest, as may be inferred from the following desciption of it:—

Description of the Town Hall.

"Immediately above the Mayor's chair there was suspended, in the way of canopy, a large and very handsome Crown, festooned with laurel, and having a union jack waving over it. Over the vice-president's chair there was a splendid silk banner, with the Birmingham arms painted on it, and resting on the rail of the great gallery was placed the well-known symbol, the bundle of sticks, surmounted by a cap of liberty, to indicate that freedom can only be upheld by union, and accompanied by a pair of scales, as emblematic of equal justice to all, the great purpose why liberty ought to be vindicated and maintained. In the organ gallery were two very handsome transparencies, and in the great gallery was a third transparency, of very large dimensions. Banners of blue, purple, and white, were suspended from the candelabra, two from each, and the entire front of the galleries was festooned with laurel branches and artificial flowers and rosettes, the number of the rosettes being not less than fifteen hundred. When to the effect of these very tasteful decorations, we add the attractions of the hall itself, with the blaze of light running along its extensive walls, the cheerful faces of not less than five hundred gentlemen at the tables below, and above all the blooming cheeks and bright eyes of nearly twice that number of elegantly dressed ladies in the galleries, the rich tones of the magnificent organ, and the pealing anthem swelling the note of praise, we shall not be accused of exaggeration when we say that the *coup d'œil* at the moment that 'Non nobis' was being solemnly chanted, was one of very great and rare beauty." *

The chief speakers were the Mayor (Mr. W. Scholefield), Messrs. G. F. Muntz, P. H. Muntz, S. A. Goddard, George Edmonds, R. K. Douglas, the Rev. T. M. M'Donnell, T. Weston, T. C. Salt, and W. Redfern, the Town Clerk. The last-named speaker gave an interesting scrap of information as to the grant of the Charter: "No pains were spared to make the Charter safe. It was prepared by two eminent gentlemen of the bar, under the direction of Mr. Joseph Parkes, as secretary to the Corporation Committee. It was afterwards submitted to the Attorney and Solicitor General, and was approved of by them, and eventually, the Lord Chancellor (Lord Cottenham), than whom a more able lawyer was nowhere to be found, affixed the Great Seal to it, and by so doing, made it law. It had since been entrusted to his (Mr. Redfern's) hands, as Town Clerk, for safe custody. It was a precious deposit: he revered it as the foundation of our local rights and liberties —it was our Magna Charta."

---

* *Birmingham Journal*, February 23, 1839.

CHAP. IX.
1839.
Nomination of Borough Justices.

The appointment of Borough Magistrates engaged the attention of the Council at an early meeting. On the 2nd of January, a resolution was passed appointing a Committee to prepare a list of persons to be recommended for nomination as justices, and reciting by way of preamble "the highly constitutional assurance of the present Home Secretary (Lord John Russell) that in making appointments of Borough Magistrates he should regard the Town Councils as the proper and legitimate organs of their respective constituencies." On the 8th of January the Committee reported a proposed list of justices, which was adopted by the Council, and transmitted to the Home Office, with a petition to the Queen praying for the constitution of a separate Commission of the Peace for the Borough, as "conducive to the prompt administration of justice within the same borough, and otherwise to the good government thereof." The list thus transmitted was composed of the following names:—

Names first proposed.

John Frederick Ledsam, Edgbaston, Esq.
Joseph Webster, Penns, Esq.
Joshua Scholefield, Edgbaston, Esq., M.P.
Thomas Attwood, Harborne, Esq., M.P.
John Towers Lawrence, Balsall Heath, Esq.
William Chance, Birmingham, Esq.

[All these were already in the Commission for Warwickshire.]

Thomas Beilby, Camp Hill, printer.
Philip Henry Muntz, Handsworth, merchant.
Clement Cotterill Scholefield, Birmingham, merchant.

John Birt Davies, Birmingham, doctor of medicine.
Samuel Beale, Edgbaston, lead merchant.
Thomas Bolton, Edgbaston, merchant.
William Scholefield, Edgbaston, merchant, and Mayor.
Robert Webb, Camp Hill, gentleman.
Thomas Clark, sen., Birmingham, gentleman.
Constantine Richard Moorsom, Harborne, captain in the Royal Navy.
Francis Room, Birmingham, manufacturer.
Henry Van Wart, Edgbaston, merchant.

The petition of the Council was granted, a separate Commission of the Peace was established, and early in February a list of twenty-five justices for the Borough was appointed. It was mainly composed of the names recommended by the Council, but with some notable alterations. The Tory party brought considerable influence to bear upon the Government, and presented a memorial setting forth that as the Council was chosen exclusively from one political party, the magistracy ought to be largely composed of the other party. This influence had its effect, for three names were struck out of the Council list—those of Mr. William Scholefield (the Mayor), Mr. Francis Room, and Captain Moorsom—and in place of them those of three members of the Tory party, Mr. Richard Spooner, Mr. W. C. Alston, and Dr. Booth, were inserted. Mr. Charles Shaw, another Tory, was also made a magistrate, and the list was completed by the names of three of the Whig party—Mr. W. Phipson, Mr. Henry Smith, and Mr. James L. Moilliet. On July 17, Lord J. Russell, in a debate on the Birmingham riots,

CHAP. IX.
1839.
Lord J. Russell's explanation.

"From Birmingham a list of twenty-one persons was sent to him by the Town Council, and he received at the same time a representation from the Earl of Warwick, Lord-Lieutenant of the county, who had informed him that he thought it desirable that the county magistrates, and they alone, should be placed in the Commission of the Peace. He (Lord J. Russell) had taken that communication into consideration, and made such enquiries as he could from persons in London, as also from two persons deputed from Birmingham. Some of the parties he consulted agreed with Lord Warwick, and others differed from him. The result was that he (Lord John Russell) did not concur with either party. He put into the Commission for Birmingham eleven county magistrates, some of them Whigs, some Tories, without consideration of their politics. He put in a certain number recommended by the Town Council, and two or three others who were represented to him as persons of great weight and influence in the town." With reference to one magistrate, Lord John went on to explain, he had been troubled with doubts. This was Mr. P. H. Muntz [one of the present (1877) members for the Borough]. "On looking, in the first instance, over the list furnished by the Town Council, he had doubted whether it would be proper to include his name, after the violent part which he had taken in politics; but he had made various enquiries, and was informed that though Mr. Muntz had taken a violent part in politics, he was a man of considerable talent, likely to prove of great use to the town, that his former political violence would not at all prevent him from giving every support to the friends of peace and good order, and that he had totally separated himself from those who wished, by means of force, to bring about a change in the laws. He therefore judged that it would be more likely to produce peace and good order in Birmingham to place Mr. Muntz in the Commission of the Peace than to omit his name."

Corporate Seal: Proposed designs.

It was necessary to devise a Corporate seal for the Borough, and a Committee was appointed to obtain designs for this purpose. At the meeting on the 19th of January the Committee reported. Five designs were laid before the Council. The following description of them, as given in the Committee's report, is worthy of being placed on record:—

"No. 1.—Birmingham Arms. Supporters, on one side a lion passant, denoting courage; on the opposite side a lamb quiescent, denoting peace. Crest, a Locomotive Engine. On a ribbon underneath the arms, the motto 'Unity, Liberty, Prosperity.' The whole surrounded by a Garter, with the inscription 'Common Seal of the Mayor, Aldermen, and Burgesses of the Borough of Birmingham.' In the space underneath the arms, 'Incorporated by Royal Charter, 1838.'

"No. 2.—Birmingham Arms. Supporters, a lion passant, and a muscular figure of a man holding the lictor's axe, signifying justice and strength combined. The Arms surmounted by a helmet. Crest, a Locomotive Engine, and inscription as No. 1. Motto, 'Emporium of the World.'

"No. 3.—Birmingham Arms. Supporters, a lion rampant, and a lamb bearing a banner inscribed 'Peace, Law, and Order,' surmounted by the Cap of Liberty, with helmet, crest, and inscription as No. 1. Motto, 'Fortitudo et Rectum.'

"No. 4.—The Birmingham Arms, encircled with a wreath, under which are the words, 'Incorporated by Royal Charter, 1838.' Around the whole are the words 'Common Seal of the Mayor, Aldermen, and Burgesses of the Borough of Birmingham.'

"No. 5.—A Pillar, around which is entwined a Serpent, assigned to signify prudence joined with constancy. Surmounted with a Lion, for strength and courage. At the base of the column are represented the Birmingham Arms, under which is a scroll for proposed motto, with olive branch, emblematic of peace and concord."

The first three designs were prepared by Mr. E. Lucas, engraver; the fourth by Mr. Halliday; and the fifth by Mr. Harris. The Committee recommended the choice of No. 1; but the Council preferred the design No. 4, and this with the word "Forward," as a motto, was adopted as the Common Seal of the Corporation. The first seal made did not, however, prove successful, and another had to be made in the place of it. The discarded seal was, by an order of the Council, broken into halves; it being directed by resolution that one half should be kept by the Mayor and the other half by the Town Clerk.

A room for the meetings of the Council had also to be provided; and as the Corporation had no property of its own, nor at that time any means of erecting buildings, it was resolved to ask the Commissioners of the Street Act for leave to meet either in their room at the Public Office, or in the Committee Room of the Town Hall, both these places being under the control of the Commissioners. The latter was selected as the place of meeting—the Commissioners, on the 4th of February, 1839, unanimously resolving that they "cheerfully concede the use of the Committee Room at the Town Hall, for the meetings of the Council, *when such room is not otherwise engaged*, and therefore it is necessary that the Council should appoint their ordinary days of meeting, as far as practicable, and that on extraordinary days application should be made to our clerks."

The grant of a Court of Quarter Sessions to the Borough engaged the attention of the Council at a very early period. At a meeting on the 2nd of January, 1839, a Committee was appointed to consider the subject and to report upon it. On the 27th of February the Committee presented its report, an elaborate document, prepared by Mr. Redfern, the Town Clerk, and setting forth, with candour and clearness, the advantages and the cost of the proposed arrangement. From this report it appears that the total expenditure of the county of Warwick, for county purposes, was, on the average of three years, ending Michaelmas, 1838, about £15,835 a year, of which Birmingham contributed £4,073 10s., for the undermentioned purposes:—

Petition for Quarter Sessions.

	£	s.	d.
Prosecutions at Sessions	376	5	0
Prosecutions at Assizes	395	5	0
Conveyance of Prisoners	156	5	0
Expenses of Gaol and Bridewell	1,623	10	0
Clerk of the Peace	153	10	0
High Constables' charges	133	0	0
Coroners' Inquests	191	5	0
Weights and Measures	93	5	0
Bridges	532	10	0
Registration	75	0	0
Treasurer's Salary	37	10	0
Miscellaneous	296	5	0
Total	£4,073	10	0

Birmingham payments to County of Warwick.

CHAP. IX.
1839.
Advantages of Sessions.

All the prisoners committed in Birmingham had then to be sent to Warwick for detention in the County Gaol, and for trial at sessions or assizes. The establishment of a Court of Quarter Sessions for Birmingham would, it was pointed out in the report, relieve the Borough from contributions to the county funds in regard to prosecutions and maintenance of the gaol; but until Birmingham had a gaol of its own an arrangement would have to be made for the use of the County Gaol, and the cost for the conveyance of prisoners to and from Warwick would still continue. The result, it was estimated, would be a total outlay of £8,000 for the Borough, but against this the report set the probable increase of the Birmingham contribution by an increase of the county assessment (no new assessment having been made for twenty-five years), and also the convenience of prosecutors, witnesses, and jurors, and, further, the dignity of the Borough, which, as a community then numbering 200,000 inhabitants, and rapidly growing, required that "even at some small pecuniary sacrifice, it should make all its arrangements, and more especially those which concern the administration of justice, as complete as possible." The report also pointed out that, as compared with the total expenditure of the various governing bodies in the Borough, the proposed outlay would constitute but a very small percentage—not more than 2½ per cent.—of the whole amount.

The following table is given in the report as "a fair

view of the annual expenditure of the Borough, for its various municipal and parochial purposes :—

1. Relief of the poor, Birmingham parish, an average of the last 7 years	£39,832
2. Commissioners of Birmingham Street Act, on an average of 3 years	29,618
3. Commissioners of Deritend and Bordesley, on average of 5 years	674
4. Commissioners of Duddeston and Nechells, on average of 3 years	912
5. Relief of the Poor of Edgbaston, on average of 3 years	1,474
6. Surveyors of the Highways of Edgbaston, during 1838	550
Total	£73,060
To this an estimated sum of	£7,000
Making a General Total of	£80,000

is added for the relief of the poor and the maintenance of highways in those parts of Aston included within the Borough, there being no separate accounts by which this expenditure could be exactly ascertained.

This report was discussed by the Council at some length, on a motion by Mr. P. H. Muntz, seconded by Mr. J. T. Lawrence, "That the Crown be forthwith petitioned for the grant of a separate Court of Quarter Sessions." There was an unanimous opinion in favour of the Sessions; but one or two members thought the subject ought first to be remitted to the burgesses in town's meeting, and Mr. J. H. Cutler moved a resolution to this effect, recalling, in support of it, the fact that when it was

CHAP. IX.
1839.
Petition for Sessions.

proposed to build a Town Hall, the inhabitants were called together at Beardsworth's Repository to give their opinion. To this Mr. Pare replied that "at the time referred to the people had no properly constituted body to decide upon the propriety of any public undertaking. Such was not the case now. The people had elected the Town Council to do what they considered best for the Borough, and it was their business to do so without troubling the inhabitants." This argument prevailed, and the resolution to apply for a grant of Quarter Sessions was agreed to with only two dissentients. The salary which the Council was willing to pay to a Recorder was fixed at £300 a year, and this was duly embodied in the petition presented to the Queen in Council, in conformity with the requirements of the Municipal Corporations Act.

Custody of Prisoners.

Before a grant of Quarter Sessions could be made it was necessary to provide for the safe custody of the Borough prisoners, and for this purpose negotiations were opened with the County Justices to secure the use of the gaol at Warwick. It was finally arranged that, on a Court of Quarter Sessions being assigned to Birmingham, prisoners from the Borough should be received at Warwick, at a charge of 11d. per day for maintenance; and at the Council meeting on the 12th of April the Mayor was desired to inform the Home Secretary of this arrangement, "to the end that there may be no further delay in the granting of a Borough Sessions." This preliminary being settled, the Government did not keep the Council waiting. On the 13th of April Lord John Russell wrote to the Mayor

Grant of Sessions.

to say that he should immediately recommend the grant; and at its meeting on the 7th of May, the Mayor was enabled to lay before the Council the important document which formed the natural complement to the Charter of Incorporation. At the following meeting Mr. Matthew Davenport Hill communicated to the Council his appointment as Recorder of the Borough; and at the same meeting Mr. George Edmonds was appointed Clerk of the Peace. A Coroner was also appointed at this meeting. Before the incorporation of the Borough Mr. J. W. Whateley had been the County Coroner for the division which included Birmingham, and he now offered himself for the Borough Coronership. There were three other candidates—Dr. J. Birt Davies, physician; Mr. Frederick Ryland, surgeon; and Mr. Underhill, solicitor. The last-named gentleman did not go to the poll; and ultimately Dr. Birt Davies was elected by 40 votes; Mr. Ryland receiving 9 votes; and Mr. Whateley 4 votes. At the next meeting, on the 4th of June, the list of Borough officers was completed, by the election of Mr. Henry Knight as Treasurer, by 28 votes, as against 18 given for Mr. Boultbee, who had been actively engaged in the promotion of the Charter. At the same meeting an objection was raised to the legality of the appointment of Mr. R. K. Douglas as Registrar of the Mayor's Court, and the appointment was consequently now confirmed; and at a meeting on June 24, the Mayor's Court, as provided in the Charter, was ordered to be established forthwith. This Court, it may be stated, was for the recovery of small debts. The Recorder was judge; and the Registrar, who

CHAP. IX.
1839.

Appointment of Recorder, Coroner, &c.

Appointment of Treasurer.

CHAP. IX.
1839.
Officers of the Corporation.

practically conducted the business of the Court, was paid by fees. The staff of the new Corporation being thus completed, it may be well to repeat the names of the officers appointed—Mayor, Mr. W. Scholefield; Recorder, Mr. M. D. Hill; Town Clerk, Mr. W. Redfern; Coroner, Dr. J. Birt Davies; Clerk of the Peace, Mr. George Edmonds; Borough Treasurer, Mr. H. Knight; Registrar of Mayor's Court, Mr. R. K. Douglas.

Committee on Rating Powers.

The provision of the money necessary to carry on the government of the Borough naturally engaged the attention of the Council at an early period. A Committee was appointed to consider the rating powers of the Corporation, and this Committee reported on the 12th of April (1839). The proceedings of this meeting were marked by special formality. It was well known that a strong and active party in the town were desirous of embarrassing the Corporation by disputing the validity of its proceedings, and that the levying of a rate might afford the means of beginning a harassing litigation. Consequently the Town Clerk gave formal proof before the Mayor and Council that all the notices summoning the meeting had been duly delivered; and then the Council proceeded to consider the subject of the rate, and to receive the first estimates of the Finance Committee.

Report of the Committee.

The report set out in detail the powers conferred by the Municipal Act, the "plain meaning of which," the Committee added, "is that it shall be lawful for the Town Council, by order made on the Overseers, to levy rates on the several parochial divisions within the Borough, according to the respective amounts of their full and fair rateable value." Two rates, the Committee reported, might be levied—a Municipal Rate for general purposes, and a Watch Rate, for the police; but they recommended that these should be combined in one rate, and the amount of this, on an estimate for six months, they fixed at £12,000, divided as follows:— Police, £5,500; Quarter Sessions, Gaol expenses, Coroner, Recorder, &c., £4,200; "Sundry smaller expenses, which it is impossible at present to estimate, £2,300." The amount of £12,000 represented, the Committee stated, a rate of "about equal to 6d. in the pound; and they recommended that, as a condition precedent to making the rate, the Mayor should issue his precept requiring returns of rateable value to be made by the Overseers of the several parishes. This report was approved, the rate ordered to be levied, and the returns called for. At the next meeting, May 15, the Overseers made their returns of rateable value, as follow:—

	£	s.	d.
Parish of Birmingham	297,383	15	10
Parish of Aston, within Borough	88,502	0	0
Parish of Edgbaston	21,496	13	4
Total rateable value	£407,382	9	2

At the next meeting, on the 4th of June, a Committee was appointed to enquire into the accuracy of the returns made by the Overseers, it being reported that they had not been made on a common and uniform principle, and the Committee were directed "in case they shall find the same, or

CHAP. IX.
1839.
Returns revised and altered by Council.

any of them, to be inaccurate, then to ascertain the annual value of the property "liable to be rated for the purposes of the borough." On the 24th of June the Committee presented a report stating that the return from the Overseers of Aston required no alteration, but that those for the Overseers of Birmingham and Edgbaston fell "considerably short of the full and proper amount, in the former case by £48,658 1s. 2d., and in the latter by £19,347 0s. 2d." On the whole, they added "the full and fair rateable value" ought to be taken to be as follows:—

Revised Assessments.

	£	s.	d.
Parish of Birmingham	346,041	17	0
The Aston Hamlets	88,502	0	0
Parish of Edgbaston	40,843	13	6
	£475,387	10	6

Proportion of Rate to Parishes.

The proportion of rate chargeable upon each of the three parishes was assessed by the Committee as follows:—

	£	s.	d.
Birmingham Parish	8,734	19	8
Aston	2,234	0	4
Edgbaston	1,030	19	11
Total	£12,000	0	0

The report was adopted, and the first Borough Rate was made in accordance with it; special Overseers, as required by law, being appointed to collect the rate in the part of Aston within the Borough.

Although this order was made, it was not acted upon, for difficulties were interposed in the way of obtaining funds by a contest which arose in regard to the validity of the Charter. As the pecuniary troubles of the Council, and the questions referring to the Charter are intimately connected, it will be better to deal with these matters in conjunction; and therefore they may be postponed for a time, in order that another subject of vital importance may be disposed of—namely, the difficulties which occurred in connection with the establishment of a Police Force for the Borough.

CHAP. IX.

1839.

Borough Rate resisted.

CHAPTER X.

THE BIRMINGHAM POLICE ACT.

CHAP. X.
1839.
Police arrangements.

Before the grant of the Charter the police of the town was administered by the Commissioners of the Street Act for Birmingham parish, and by the County Justices for the other parishes afterwards included within the Borough; but there was no regular police force, only a few watchmen being appointed for night duty, and the ordinary arrest of criminals being left to the parish constables. The Municipal Act invested the Town Council with the control of the police, by means of a Watch Committee, by whom the powers of the Act were to be exercised. A sum of money for the establishment of a police force was included in the first estimates laid before the Council on the 12th of April, 1839; but no steps were taken to appoint constables. The threatening state of the town, owing to the political agitation which arose in the early part of 1839—and which culminated in the Chartist meetings in July of that year, and in the Bull Ring riots of the 15th of that month—rendered it necessary that protection should be obtained for life and property; the magistrates consequently applied for the assistance of the London police, and a detachment of the metropolitan force was despatched to Birmingham. In this matter the Town Council, the local and proper authority, was not consulted, and it had no responsibility for the proceeding, or for the lamentable consequences to which it gave rise. The magistrates, however, not only sought the assistance of the London police as a temporary measure, but they pressed upon the Town Council the necessity of constituting a permanent local force. At the Council meeting on the 9th of July, the Mayor (Mr. Scholefield) read to the Council the following memorandum, signed by five of the magistrates, and which, he said, was approved by the whole of them:—

Chap. X.
1839.
The London Police called in.

"The undersigned magistrates of the Borough of Birmingham, being convinced, from recent experience, that the present police force is totally inadequate to preserve the peace and protect the property of the Borough at periods of great excitement, would strongly urge upon the Town Council the immediate necessity of forming a body of police, sufficiently numerous and effective to ensure those most important objects." This was signed by C. Shaw, Joseph Walker, Robert Webb, Thomas Beilby, and J. K. Booth.

Opinion of Justices.

There was a general agreement on the part of the Council as to the necessity of appointing police; but the want of money stood in the way. Alderman Van Wart, indeed, boldly declared that there was no money difficulty, for if "they resolved upon establishing an efficient local police, any of the bankers in the town would advance money for the purpose." Such an advance, however, imposed personal responsibility upon those who obtained it, and the Council generally did not possess the courage of

The Money Difficulty.

Mr. Van Wart. Consequently, on the motion of Alderman Harrold, seconded by Alderman Hutton, the following resolution was passed:—

Resolution of Council.

"That in the opinion of this Council it is highly expedient, with a view to the good order and proper government of the Borough, that an efficient police should be forthwith established. And the Council hereby declares that it will avail itself of the earliest practicable opportunity of carrying this, its opinion, into effect; but that the Council does not deem it prudent to take any further measures in connection with this matter, until it shall be in the actual possession of funds adequate to the accomplishment of so important an object."

Bull Ring Riots.

This, as the event proved, was an unfortunate resolution, for it is probable that had the Council boldly resolved to appoint a police force at once, and to borrow funds for that purpose, the Borough would have been saved from a deep humiliation, and that the principle of responsible local self-government would have escaped a severe blow. On the 15th of July the Bull Ring riots occurred. On the two following days discussions took place in both Houses of Parliament on the conduct of the magistracy, the state of the town, and the inefficiency of the means of protection afforded to the inhabitants. In the Lords the debate was of a peculiarly heated character, the Duke of Wellington repeatedly, and with emphasis, making the monstrous declaration that "he had been in many towns taken by storm, but never had such outrages occurred in them as had been committed in Birmingham;" and this outbreak he connected with the grant of a Charter to Birmingham, and the appointment of

Hostile Debates in House of Lords.

magistrates by the Home Secretary. The influence of this debate in the House of Lords, and of the private movements which it encouraged, were soon apparent in legislation. At first, the Ministry defended the Birmingham magistracy, and endeavoured to assist the Corporation in its difficulties; but, as will be seen, this policy was very soon changed. The Town Council, by the resolution above quoted, had declared that it had no funds for the establishment of a police force, and it was well known throughout the country that the want of funds arose from the disputes as to the validity of the Charter, for this dispute was not confined to Birmingham only, the Conservative party being then engaged also in contesting the legality of the Charters granted at the same time to Manchester and Bolton. On the part of the Government, Lord John Russell (Home Secretary) now proposed to remove the money difficulty, by granting the Corporation of Birmingham a loan of £10,000 to be applied to the provision of a police force. On the 23rd of July he moved that the House of Commons should give the precedence in Committee to a motion authorising the Treasury to make the advance above mentioned. In justifying the plea of urgency, the Home Secretary said that everyone was aware of the recent occurrences at Birmingham. "They had at present there, by means of troops, of the London police, and of the yeomanry, sufficient means for the preservation of the peace of the town, but there were no means of maintaining it, except by means of this extraordinary force, which tended to create disturbance in the minds of the people of Birmingham, and to harass the force employed.

He would, therefore, seeing that some measure for procuring a permanent police for Birmingham was absolutely necessary, ask the House if it would adhere so strictly to the order of proceedings as to risk the continuance of the present state of things in that town? The measure was merely one for enabling the persons in authority there to constitute and organise a police force, and he trusted the House would let the order of the day have precedence of the regular course of proceedings." The proposal to go into Committee was supported by Sir Eardley Wilmot, one of the members for Warwickshire; by Mr. O'Connell, who said "it was no time to stand upon strict forms, when houses were burning, and when they were not able to spare more than 4,000 to 5,000 troops from Ireland"; and by Mr. Scholefield, one of the Members for Birmingham, who said "it was very important that no time should be lost. The people of Birmingham objected strongly to the presence of the London police; and the only way in which they could be got rid of was to enable the magistrates of Birmingham to raise a police force for themselves." It was not only, however, from the Liberal side of the House that the proposal received favour. Sir Robert Peel, as the leader of the Tory party, gave it his support. He said—

"After what had occurred—a great manufacturing town, like Birmingham, in the possession of a mob for two hours and a half—houses set on fire, furniture burned, houses pillaged, and the whole town one scene of anarchy—he thought these facts constituted sufficient reasons to induce the House to accede to the proposition of the noble lord. It was of the greatest importance to provide a civil force in the town of Birmingham, before they removed that which was at present employed there. He could well believe that in the absence of a sufficient civil power, it might be necessary to send down a body of the metropolitan police to prevent great disturbances, but he was also certain that the sooner they could remove that metropolitan force from Birmingham, at the same time replacing it by an effective local police, the better. He regretted the necessity which had existed, because nothing could be more likely to cause irritation. A civil power, acting within its own limits, could act with an extreme rigour which a body of men, strangers to the locality with which they had to deal, could not."

The House then went into Committee, and Lord John Russell moved his resolution. He proposed, " considering the grievous state of the country, as well as the present state of Birmingham, that the State should interpose to advance a sum of money, to be afterwards repaid by the town of Birmingham. He proposed this, not as a vote of supply, but as a vote to form the foundation of a bill to be hereafter introduced; and by that bill he should take means to recover the amount advanced, by a rate to be levied on the borough; that rate to be imposed by an Act of Parliament, totally irrespective of the authority [*i.e.*, the Town Council] which might now impose such rate." He then moved that the sum of £10,000 should be advanced out of the Consolidated Fund, for the establishment of a police force in Birmingham. Mr. Hume supported the motion, " on the ground that the Corporation of Birmingham had not now the power of raising money." Mr. Scholefield explained the inadequacy of the existing force, maintained under the Street Commissioners Act: " Two constables had been appointed, with power to have

The Government Plan.

Proposed Grant of £10,000.

their deputies; there were but twenty men; and the new Corporation had not money at their disposal for the raising of a police force, while the Commissioners alleged that their power no longer existed under the new order of things." Sir Robert Peel asked if this was to be a temporary or a permanent measure; if a stipendiary magistrate was to be appointed, and the police placed under his control; or whether they were to be under the control of the Corporation and the local magistracy? Lord John Russell replied that they were to be under the control of the local magistracy. Sir Robert Peel rejoined that it "would be better to have them under the control of a paid magistrate, like the London police." The resolution was then agreed to, and the House having gone out of Committee, the report was brought up, and Lord John Russell moved for leave to bring in a bill to give effect to the resolution. Leave was granted, Lord John Russell, the Attorney-General, and Mr. Fox Maule were ordered to prepare the bill—which had, of course, been done beforehand; and at the same sitting the bill was brought in, and read a first time.

This bill provided that the Commissioners of the Treasury might

"Advance to the Mayor, Aldermen, and Burgesses of the Borough of Birmingham, out of the Consolidated Fund of the United Kingdom of Great Britain and Ireland, any sum or sums of money, not exceeding in the whole the sum of £10,000, to be employed, under the direction of the Council of the said Borough, for the purposes of the police of the said Borough: provided always, that the said Mayor, Aldermen, and Burgesses, by their Council, shall previously mortgage and charge the police rates to be levied within the said Borough, under the authority of this Act, with the repayment of any sum so advanced, with the interest accruing due thereon, so that the whole sum borrowed, with the interest due thereon, shall be repaid within such time, not being more than ten years at the furthest, as the said Commissioners of the Treasury shall appoint." The repayment of principal and interest, it was further provided, should be made by levying a police rate " by an equal pound rate upon all messuages, lands, tenements, and hereditaments within the borough," and for this purpose the Council were to have all the powers of levying and enforcing rates conferred by the Municipal Act, or any subsequent Act.

<small>Chap. X.
1839.

Rating Powers of Council.</small>

The bill thus introduced was one in every way acceptable. It recognised the authority of the elected representative body—the Town Council; it placed the control of the police of the town in their hands; and by providing funds it relieved the Corporation, in an essential part of its duty, from the pressure and the difficulty imposed by the disputes which had arisen with regard to the validity of the Charter, and which hindered the collection of local rates. Indeed, the action taken by the Government was the direct result of an application made by the Mayor of the Borough to Lord John Russell, as Home Secretary. In consequence of the Chartist riots Mr. Scholefield wrote to the Home Secretary in the following terms:—

<small>Bill approved in Birmingham.</small>

"At every meeting of the magistrates the opinion gains ground among them that there will be no prospect of permanent peace in the town until we are provided with a local police force adequate to the wants of so large a population. So long, however,

<small>Letter from Mr. W. Scholefield.</small>

as a doubt exists as to the validity of our Charter of Incorporation (and your lordship is doubtless aware of the indirect invalidation, or suspicion of its legality, cast upon it by the proceedings commenced in the case of the Manchester Charter), our borough rate, the precepts for which have been already issued, will not, I fear, be paid over to the Council by the Overseers; nor are there any other means by which we can obtain the requisite sums for the purpose in view. Under these circumstances, peculiar at once by reason of the unprotected state of the town, by reason of the recent disturbances, and of the extraordinary character of the obstacles thrown in the way of a Charter bearing about it all the appearances of perfect validity, I venture humbly to represent to your lordship the advisability and urgent importance of a disposition being evinced by the Government to advance, on the security of the Borough Rate, such a sum (say from £5,000 to £10,000) as will enable the Council forthwith to organise an efficient local police, and to keep it in operation until the contested validity of the Charter shall be decided."

Opposition to the Bill. With this request from the town, Lord John Russell, as above stated, complied by the introduction of the Birmingham Police Bill, the provisions of which completely embodied the proposal made by the Mayor. But the bill was not destined to pass in the form in which it was introduced. In the brief discussion upon it Sir Robert Peel had significantly asked if the execution of the measure was to be entrusted to a stipendiary magistrate? The hint thus thrown out was taken up and reduced to practical form by the right hon. baronet and his friends, both in Birmingham and in Parliament. The Conservative party in the town—which, as we have seen, was invariably hostile to the concession of representative government—now saw the chance of striking a double blow against the principle to which they objected, and against the Charter which they had opposed. A petition to the Queen was drawn up, praying her Majesty to annul the grant of the Charter, though the petitioners should have known that no act of the Sovereign—nothing, indeed, short of an Act of Parliament—could revoke the concession which had been made. The petition does not seem to have been proceeded with so far as to bring it before the Privy Council; but its terms are worthy of quotation as showing the height attained by party spirit in the town, and as indicating the feeling not so much of dislike as of hatred with which the new Corporation was regarded by its adversaries. The petition was as follows:— *

"We, the undersigned inhabitants of Birmingham, your Majesty's most dutiful and loyal subjects, humbly pray that the Charter of Incorporation granted to this Borough in October last may be annulled. The incorporation of the town has not promoted the good order or conduced to the prosperity of the inhabitants; but, on the contrary, local agitation has been increased, and local feuds engendered; offices of honour and emolument have been monopolised, general dissatisfaction prevails, and the inhabitants of this populous and important Borough are threatened with heavy rates to support a municipal government which is entirely destitute of their confidence. Under these circumstances we humbly pray that your Majesty will cause the said Charter of Incorporation granted to the Borough of Birmingham to be annulled."

But if this petition was a mere *brutum fulmen*, a more practical step was taken with reference to the Police Bill, and through it against the Charter. If a grant of

---

* *Birmingham Journal*, July 27, 1839.

money were made by the Government to the Corporation, and if the latter were authorised to levy rates to repay the advance, and were formally, by Act of Parliament, entrusted with the administration of the police, it was obvious that no attack upon the validity of the Charter could be successfully conducted. Its opponents, therefore, saw the importance of preventing this recognition of the Corporation, and they communicated with Sir Robert Peel, and through him with the Government, in order to obtain an essential alteration in the Police Bill. The result of this interposition soon became apparent. The Police Bill stood for Committee in the House of Commons on the 29th of August. On the motion for committing the Bill, Sir Robert Peel said he had a proposition to submit to Lord John Russell—namely, that the control of the police for Birmingham should be vested in a Government Commissioner instead of in the Council. He based this proposal upon several grounds—precedent, as in the case of Dublin, and several of the metropolitan boroughs; the doubtful validity of the Birmingham Charter, in reference to which he read an opinion given by Sir William Follett, on a case submitted by the Birmingham Overseers; on the fact that the Birmingham Town Council had been chosen entirely from one political party; and, lastly, that its appointments had been such as to indicate a violent partisan tendency. In support of this declaration Sir Robert Peel cited the case of Mr. Douglas, appointed Registrar of the Mayor's Court, and that of Mr. George Edmonds, appointed Clerk of the Peace. "Could they (he asked), as men of sense, entrust the administration of the police force to men who had appointed to the office of Registrar of the Mayor's Court a delegate to the National Convention," and to the clerkship of the peace a man who had used violent language such as that used by Mr. Edmonds? Here Sir Robert quoted from speeches made by Mr. Edmonds at meetings of the revived Political Union; and he further urged, as a disqualification of Mr. Edmonds, that he had professionally defended Julian Harney, a Chartist prisoner. Then he turned to the Town Council, and insisted that—

> "The country could not see with satisfaction Chartists and Political Unionists in situations where it was their duty to preserve the peace. If the Town Council regarded previous conduct of the kind to which he had alluded as no disqualification for admission to the offices of Clerk of Peace and Registrar of the Mayor's Court, what assurance could he have that the Town Council might not think it their duty to adhere to their partisans, and appoint them to situations high and subordinate in the police force? If they did this, could it be supposed that those who had been kept in a state of constant alarm for the last eight or ten years would with perfect satisfaction and contentment see the powers of municipal authority exercised in this manner? He did not impute to those who, without foreseeing how unable they might be to guide the storm they had raised, had encouraged the Political Union, any participation in the sinister designs of the Chartists. What he said was, that the institution of the Chartists was intimately connected with that of Political Unions, and those who had formed the Political Unions must be content to bear the charge of having encouraged the Chartists."

In conclusion, Sir Robert Peel made quotations from speeches by Mr. Attwood, to show that the Political Unionists, and consequently the dominant party in

Birmingham, sympathised with the Chartists; and he ended with an appeal to the Government to adopt his view. The opposition to the Police Bill, to the Borough Charter, and to the authority of the Corporation was thus distinctly and unreservedly placed upon a political basis. Birmingham had formed the Political Unions; out of the changes promoted by their means had sprung the further demands of the Chartists; the Birmingham Corporation was constituted of Liberals of an advanced type, in harmony with the opinions of the majority of the electors and inhabitants—therefore, let the Corporation of Birmingham be punished for its political opinions, by being declared unfit and unworthy to be entrusted with the control of the police force of the town. This was Sir Robert Peel's argument: the very last, it might have been supposed, likely to influence a Liberal Minister, like Lord John Russell, or to affect and guide the policy of a Liberal Government, like that of Lord Melbourne. Strong protests were instantly made by the Members for Birmingham. Mr. Joshua Scholefield spoke out manfully:

"It was true that the Town Council were opposed to the Tories; they might be called Radicals, perhaps—but they were freely and unanimously chosen, and he did not know that any charge could be brought against the ratepayers for having elected party men. It was a fair fight, and no one could say the Tories did not do all they could to win. All the members of the Town Council whom he knew were as fit to wield the power of the Town Council as anyone then present in that House. As to an exclusive choice of officers, there was nothing unusual in one party excluding another. The principles of the party to which Sir Robert Peel belonged had been exclusion *in toto*. When what was called the high party had power a more determined system of exclusion never existed. They excluded every man who was not a most dogged disciple of their creed. It was said the Charter granted to Birmingham was imperfect, and Sir Robert Peel had expressed surprise at it. It had been a puzzle to the people of Birmingham, for of what use was a Charter unless it gave the Corporation power to levy rates? The moment they proceeded to levy a rate, the Tories said 'No, no; levy a rate as you will, you shall not be paid.' So that they had a Charter, but they had no money. They had not been wise in their generation, nor had the noble lord (Lord John Russell); he had certainly been deficient in the money matter, and Government should back their friends if they wished their friends to back them. As to the proposed alteration of the police, he objected to a system of gendarmerie being established in Birmingham, though he did not object to a constitutional force; and he would sooner pack up his all and leave, than belong to a town that was said not to be fit to take care of its own concerns. Referring again to the Corporation, there was at that moment a striving between Tories and Chartists—a most unnatural one, to be sure—to do away with the new Corporation. Doubtless there was opposition to the Corporation in the town, as Sir Robert Peel had said. It was opposed by persons who had opposed the Reform Bill, and every species of Reform: there was nothing new in that, and they it was who had taken this advantage of the recent disturbances in Birmingham."

Mr. Scholefield also strongly defended Mr. Edmonds, whom Sir Robert Peel had assailed. Mr. Attwood likewise defended Mr. Edmonds and Mr. Douglas, vindicated his own moderation, declared that the police under a commissioner "would be the commencement of a system of gendarmerie, centred in London, and spreading through every parish in England;" and suggested that the recent disturbances in Birmingham, of which Sir Robert Peel and his friends were now taking advantage to injure the town, had actually been instigated by the Tory party: "Some of the retainers of the right hon. baronet had been endeavouring to excite an agitation in the country which might put down the peaceful agitation he (Mr. Attwood) was desirous of encouraging."

The Government gives way.

The protests of the Members for Birmingham proved ineffectual. The probability is that a previous arrangement had been made between Sir Robert Peel and Lord John Russell, for the instant Mr. Attwood had finished speaking, the Home Secretary rose and said that, "taking all the circumstances of the case into consideration, he was inclined to substitute the opinion of the right hon. baronet for his own, as to the appointment of the police. This course was open to many objections—in fact, the whole case was surrounded with difficulties, but he thought, on the whole, the course proposed by Sir Robert Peel was to be preferred. He would propose that some commissioner, some person of discretion and ability in the neighbourhood, should have the whole control and direction of the police for the next two years." Thus, on the suggestion of a political opponent, instigated by local party influences and by general political hostility to Birmingham, the Liberal Minister precipitately reversed the arrangement he had himself devised, in accordance with the wishes of the representative body of the town—a body created by his own act, under a charter granted by the Crown upon his own advice. Thus, also, he threw doubts upon the validity of the Charter, and he discredited the principle of local representative self-government—a cardinal point of his

Sir R. Peel's views adopted.

own political creed. The change of plan elicited an immediate and indignant protest from some of the supporters of the Government. Mr. Joseph Hume "strongly opposed the disgrace which Lord John Russell was about to cast upon the Corporation of the town of Birmingham, and the attack upon local government involved in such an arrangement." Mr. O'Connell defended Mr. George Edmonds, "whom he had long known to be a most honourable man and a thorough Reformer." Mr. Wakley reminded the Home Secretary that he was violating the condition on which the Committee of the House of Commons had agreed to the vote of money—namely, that it should be placed at the disposal of the Town Council. Mr. Hume strongly deprecated the new scheme of the Government, unless the appointment of the Police Commissioner was left to the Town Council. It was all, however, of no avail. The first Bill was withdrawn, in order that another, modelled upon Sir Robert Peel's suggestion, might be introduced.

Chap. X.
1839.
Protests by Liberal Members.

The second Police Bill was immediately brought in— most likely it was prepared even before Lord John Russell announced his intention to comply with the wishes of the Tory party. It was a document which, even after the lapse of nearly forty years, no Birmingham man can look back upon without a feeling of shame and indignation, and an ineradicable sense of wrong. The preamble set out by declaring that "whereas questions are pending as to the powers of the Mayor, Aldermen, and burgesses of the Borough of Birmingham to levy rates by their Council,

A new Police Bill brought in

under the authority of their Charter of Incorporation, and it is expedient to make provision for the police of the said Borough, until such questions shall be determined . . . it shall be lawful for her Majesty to establish a police force in the Borough of Birmingham, and, by warrant under her sign manual, to appoint a fit person to be Chief Commissioner of Police for the said Borough." It then proceeded to enact that the Commissioner so appointed should have a salary of £800 per annum, that he should be authorised to act as a justice of the peace for the county of Warwick [the Borough Commission being thus non-recognised by its exclusion], that he should act under the directions of the Home Secretary, and that he should have sole and full authority over the police force of the Borough. He was authorised, in this capacity, to appoint the constables, all the powers conferred by the Police Acts were entrusted to him, and the whole control of the Borough in reference to police affairs was placed in his hands, to the entire exclusion of the Town Council, and of any local authority whatever. In a word, the Police Commissioner under this measure was declared to be the agent and servant of the Home Office, receiving his appointment from the Government, acting under its instructions, reporting to it, and being responsible only to the Secretary of State. Therefore, the bill proposed to establish, for police purposes, a quasi-military Government, to which the town was to be subjected, without having the power to check or influence it in the slightest degree. But while the Borough was thus placed under centralised administration, the inhabitants were to provide the means of paying an alien governor and a force appointed and controlled by him, as the agent of the Ministry. It was provided that the Treasury might advance to the Police Commissioner (not to the Town Council) the sum of £10,000 for police purposes, at the rate of five per cent. interest; principal and interest to be paid out of a special rate authorised by the Act, to be levied by the Borough Treasurer, and to be paid, together with all other police funds, into a bank to be selected by the Commissioners of the Treasury. The repayment of the loan was extended over a period of "ten years at the furthest;" and it was enacted that the Act "shall continue in force for two years, and from thence until the end of the then next session of Parliament." The Town Council was thus placed in the cruel and humiliating position of being deprived of the control of the police force, secured to it by the Municipal Act, and by the provisions of the Charter, and was consequently—by the act of the Minister who had conferred the right of local representative government upon the great communities of the kingdom—declared to be unworthy of being entrusted with the management of its own affairs; and yet, by a refinement of insult, the Town Council was actually, by the very same Minister, made the unwilling instrument of levying rates upon the population for the purpose of stamping and signalising its own degradation.

It need not be said that this wanton and unlooked-for attack upon the freedom of local government, and upon the honour and reputation of the town, excited the

<small>CHAP. X.
1839.

Special Police Rate.

The Town degraded.

Resentment in Birmingham.</small>

strongest feeling of indignation and resentment in Birmingham, amongst the great bulk of the inhabitants. The Police Bill was read to the Town Council at a meeting on the 6th of August. The reading of it was received with repeated expressions of indignation, which were renewed again and again as the discussion proceeded. The first act of the Council was to petition the House of Commons against the bill. The petition was proposed by Mr. Thomas Weston. It set out the grant of the Charter, the powers given under it to appoint a police force, the resolution of the Council to proceed to such appointment at the earliest possible moment, the difficulties arising as to the levy of rates for this purpose, the promise of the Home Secretary, at the request of the Mayor, to lend the necessary funds from the national Treasury, and the actual embodiment of this pledge in the first bill laid before the House of Commons. The petition then proceeded :—

"Your petitioners have observed, with much pain and surprise, that the original design of the measure in question has been since entirely altered, and that it is now in contemplation to degrade your petitioners, by arbitrarily wresting from them an authority which, as a matter of Royal grace, was granted to them but a few months back by her Majesty's Charter of Incorporation, founded on a solemn act of the Legislature; which is exercised by every other body of a like nature throughout the country; and which, assuredly, has not yet been forfeited by any misconduct or incompetency on the part of your petitioners—whose pride it is to approach your honourable House on this occasion with all the boldness of conscious rectitude—not only unconvicted, but, so far as your petitioners can learn, even unaccused.

"Your petitioners have reason to believe that this measure has been unwarily adopted at the suggestion of a small faction in this town, who have long been distinguished by their violent spirit as members of a political club, styled 'The Loyal and Constitutional Association,' and who, smarting with disappointment at their own exclusion from municipal authority, have never ceased to vilify and to caluminate your petitioners.

"That it is not, however, merely as a local grievance that your petitioners complain of the proposed measure; that, on the contrary, they condemn and denounce it still more strongly as an insidious and alarming step towards that system of centralisation which is so alien from the habits of the people of this country, and from the ancient usages of the Constitution; a system which proceeds upon the false and injurious supposition that the people are incompetent to the management of their own affairs, even in matters of the slightest public interest; which makes the Central Government everything; which begins by treating the people as unfit, and ends by making them really so, to perform the duties of freemen; and which, odious though it be in all its respects, cannot, in the opinion of your petitioners, manifest itself in a shape more offensive, more dangerous, or more unconstitutional, than that of a Government gendarmerie. Your petitioners therefore humbly pray that your honourable House will avert from them the degradation consequent on the passing of the proposed measure; and that it may not be the lot of the large and high-spirited community, on whose behalf they now entreat the just consideration of your honourable House, to be made the subject of experiment which your petitioners hold to be so highly dangerous and unconstitional."

Such was the petition of the Town Council—firm, temperate, dignified, instinct with the true spirit of Constitutional freedom, vindicating the liberty which the Ministers of the Crown proposed that Parliament should violate. The speeches harmonised with the petition. Mr. Weston, in moving the adoption of this protest, spoke of the Police Bill as "a measure opposed to every principle of decency as well as of justice; one which, if carried into operation, would not only be a serious infringement upon their undoubted privileges, but would degrade them in the eyes of the country." He stated and analysed the grounds upon which the proposition was made. Sir Robert Peel, between whom, as leader of the Conservatives, and Lord John Russell, on behalf of the Liberal, or rather of the Whig Ministry, a strange and unnatural alliance had been effected—Sir Robert Peel supported the bill on three grounds: "first, that great opposition had been made to the incorporation of the borough; second, that when the elections took place under the Charter, not a single Conservative was returned; third, that there was a defect in the Charter."

"The first argument," Mr. Weston contended, "was not worth a straw. The Charter was opposed by Sir Robert Peel's political friends, who invariably opposed everything that was for the real good of the people. Everybody knew when the Charter was applied for, that it would be opposed, and they all knew that just in proportion to the extent of that opposition, the inhabitants had a right to appreciate the value of the measure. With respect to the result of the elections, what Sir Robert Peel had stated was quite true. Not a single Tory had been returned. And why? Simply because the people would not elect them. But then the Council did not appoint one Tory to any office in the body. It would, indeed, be very strange if, after Reformers had elected them, they should turn round and tell their constituents there was not in the borough amongst the Liberal body any man capable of filling a public situation, and that they must consequently fill them with Tories—with the very persons who had done everything in their power to oppose the Charter!" After having defended the appointments made by the Council, on the ground of the capacity, character, and fitness of the persons appointed, Mr. Weston proceeded—"What could be the real object of the Government in lending themselves to the Tories he knew not; but one thing was quite clear, that the proposed bill was directly at variance with the principles of the Constitution. If there was one feature stronger than another in the principles of the Constitution, it was the republican principle of self-government. Their ancient institutions were carried on upon the self-governing principle, and now it was proposed to impose upon them an absolute centralised despotism. There could be only one feeling on this subject, and that was of abhorrence and disgust at this attempt to rob the people of their liberties. He should propose that they resist it to the umost legal extremity— that they should represent to the Government in plain terms their abhorrence of the measure—that they should lay before the other Corporations this infamous stab at their rights, and here he would wish it to be borne in mind that the great Corporation of London had already boldly taken up the subject—and if, after having offered every legal resistance, they should fail in averting the evil, he should then say let them, without hesitation, order the Town Clerk to pack up the Charter, and send it back to its givers," a suggestion which was received with loud cheering by the Council. "Was it not a fact (Mr. Weston asked) that Mr. Whateley and Mr. Knott [two leading Conservatives] had been deputed to London in reference to the bill; and was it not equally true that upon their representations, and those of their party, Lord John Russell had shaped his bill? What right had the people of Birmingham to be called upon to submit to a measure emanating from such men?"

CHAP. X.
1839.
The Bill a violation of Self-government.

Source of the Measure.

Alderman Harrold, who seconded the petition, asked "Who could expect that we should have received such treatment from our friends? Who would have thought that our friends in the Government would have so trodden upon our necks, or that they would try to make through us the first experiment upon the liberties of the country?"

Mr. Cutler opposed the bill because it was dictated by the Tory party in Birmingham for political reasons, and because it was a prelude to the general organisation of a Government police for the country. Mr. Blaxland said "he would as soon live under the most absolute despotism as under that bill—a measure which would enable the Commissioner [of police] to arrest any man he might think proper to lay his hands upon." As to the appointments made by the Council, "was it not the height of assurance for the Tories to complain of exclusive appointments? Did they ever appoint a Liberal to any office?" Mr. Mason asked that every member of the Council should enter his protest against the bill. Alderman Sturge "did not wonder at the warmth of expression on the part of the Council. It was difficult for them to restrain their feelings. For some days he could hardly express his own with anything like temper." Alderman Hutton said "he would rather erase his name from the body than remain a member of so degraded a Corporation as that would be if this bill were passed." Mr. Geach said that "from the day of the Bull Ring riots the Tories saw they had a point to work upon, and they lost no time in turning it to their account." The petition was then unanimously approved, and ordered to be sent to the Borough Members for presentation, and a copy to be forwarded to all members of the House of Commons, and to the Corporations of the kingdom. Another resolution, moved by Mr. Weston, was also adopted:—

"That if the bill be persevered in, it will, in the opinion of this meeting, be the duty of our representatives in the House of

Commons to resent so marked an insult to the town with which they are connected, by a total withdrawal of all confidence from the present Government."

A third resolution, moved by Alderman Sturge, was likewise adopted:—

"That the thanks of this Council be presented to those members of the Corporation of London who have so promptly convened that body together to lend their powerful aid in resisting the attempt now making, not only to deprive this Corporation of its constitutional rights, but to establish a precedent which may be fatal to the liberties of the people."

Sympathy from the Corporation of London.

This resolution had reference to a requisition presented to the Lord Mayor by a numerous body of members of the Common Council of London, asking him to call a meeting "to consider the propriety of expressing, in a petition to the House of Commons, the anxiety of this Court that in any provision that may be made by Parliament respecting the police of Birmingham, the House will not sanction any invasion of the ancient and salutary rights of local government which have been inherited by the people of this country from the earliest times as an essential principle of our free Constitution." Such a petition was afterwards agreed to by the Corporation of London, and on the 8th of August was presented to Parliament by the Sheriffs of the city in person; and some opposition was likewise offered from other towns, particularly Manchester and Bolton, which were to be dealt with in the same manner as Birmingham. But the opposition was unavailing. Indeed, there was no time allowed to organise it. In conjunction

Action of the Corporation.

CHAP. X.
1839.
Haste of the Government.

with Sir Robert Peel, the Government had taken their measures in such a manner as to bring forward the Police Bill by way of surprise, and to hurry it through Parliament as rapidly as the technical forms of procedure would permit. This was rendered easier by the fact that Lord John Russell's original bill had not only lulled any suspicion that might have been entertained of Ministerial designs, but had convinced the Corporations affected that Ministers intended to deal fairly with them, and to support with honourable firmness their own work in passing the Municipal Act, and in granting Charters of Incorporation under it. Then, suddenly, at the instigation of their chief political opponent, prompted by a deputation of Birmingham Conservatives, the Government turned round, abandoned their constitutional measure, and brought in their second bill, imposing upon Birmingham a purely Government police, taken out of the control of the local authorities, and responsible only to the Home Secretary—the beginning, obviously, of a force which, under another name, might become practically a second army, and which might be extended to the whole country. If there had been time to make clear the meaning of the Birmingham Bill, and of the corresponding measures proposed for Manchester and Bolton, these bills could never have been passed, for every borough and county in the kingdom was interested, on constitutional grounds, in resisting them. But no time

Opposition in Parliament.

was allowed. The obnoxious bill was brought into the House of Commons at the end of July. The Birmingham Town Council met on the 6th of August, to protest against it, and to organise general measures of resistance. On the

7th of August the Government pushed the bill through the critical stage of the second reading, thus affirming its principle. The second reading, of course, was not carried without a contest. Mr. Attwood moved the rejection of the bill, and explained the dissatisfaction with which it was received in Birmingham, and also insisted upon the unconstitutional character of the measure. Mr. Scholefield seconded the motion. "He was sure the people of Birmingham would not be satisfied with it, for it was meant to keep them down, and all that could be charged against the town was a riot which might have happened anywhere." Sir Eardley Wilmot, one of the members for Warwickshire, supported the bill—"it was well known that difficulties had arisen as to the power of the Corporation to raise rates, and until the question was settled in a court of law, it became necessary to apply to the Government for an advance of money for local purposes; and the Government, in giving the money, annexed its own conditions. There were two parties in Birmingham, strongly opposed to each other, but to neither of these would the Government give the appointment of the police: they said they would retain it in their own hands for two years, until the working of the Corporation should be complete. On this ground he supported the bill. If it were to be a permanent measure, he would oppose it." Mr. Wakley said that the whole transaction was most humiliating to the Liberals in the House of Commons. "By his first bill the Home Secretary proposed to vest the nomination of the police in the local authority, which the Charter had created, and that intention was cheered by the Liberals; but in ten

P

Second Reading carried.

days' time the noble lord came down to the House, and proposed quite a different arrangement, by which the power was vested in the Government, and for that also he was cheered by the Liberals." Sarcasm, argument, and protest were, however, alike thrown away. Secure in the votes of the official Liberals and of the Conservatives, the Ministers did not even trouble to reply. They simply took a division, and the second reading was carried by 74 to 20.

Renewed Protest by the Town Council.

On the next day, Thursday, August 8, the Town Council held another meeting, to consider what could be done in such embarrassing circumstances. Mr. Scholefield, the Mayor, announced that the Police Bill had been read a second time, and was to go into Committee that night. Alderman Muntz proposed a petition praying that the Police Bill should cease to be operative whenever the validity of the Charter might be established. "He did not believe the petition would have any effect, but it was a protest against centralisation. It was incredible that a Ministry laying claim to anything like Liberal sentiments could think of so far deviating from the principles of the Constitution as to propose a measure worse than any that had ever disgraced even the worst Tory reign. The Government had, without waiting for the opinion of the people, hurried the new bill through the House, although they could not but know that ninety-nine out of every hundred in the borough were opposed to its principle. By doing so they had violated the constitutional maxim that taxes raised without the consent of the people were raised contrary to the spirit of the Constitution." Alderman Sturge was for doing nothing more. They should not recognise the bill, or touch it in any way. If they acted coolly, steadily, and firmly, the Police Bill would do more for the cause of general reform than anything that had yet occurred. He moved that they go to the next business; and this motion was carried.

CHAP. X.
1839.
Further opposition in Parliament.

Though the Town Council had thus resolved to do no more in connection with the bill, the opposition to it in Parliament was continued. On Thursday, August 8, on the motion for going into Committee on the clauses, Mr. W. Williams (member for Coventry) moved that the House go into Committee that day three months. The bill, he said, proclaimed that the Town Council and Magistrates of Birmingham were not adequate to self-government. Ministers were "laying the foundation of a system of progressive encroachment, which would eventually spread over the whole country." He called on the people to be on their guard against this attempt. He taunted Lord John Russell with being so ready to follow the lead of Sir Robert Peel, who was known to desire the establishment of a Government police; and he thanked the Corporation of London for the stand they had made in their own case, and against this bill—"As they had preserved their own privileges intact for seven hundred years they had a right to stand forward in defence of others." Mr. Attwood and Mr. Scholefield protested in the name of Birmingham, the former declaring that "many old Whigs of the highest respectability had denounced the bill in

Protest against a Government Police.

Protest of Members for Birmingham.

language so strong that he should have shrunk from using it." The House then went into Committee, Mr. Williams withdrawing his motion, which had no chance of being carried. In Committee an effort was made to divest the bill of its most objectionable feature. Mr. Charles Buller moved that the Commissioner of Police should be appointed by the Town Council, and not by the Home Secretary. Mr. Attwood seconded the motion, but it was rejected by 63 to 20; and then the remaining clauses were agreed to. On the following Monday the report of Committee was received by the House, a motion to reject it, though strongly supported by Mr. Joseph Hume and the Members for Birmingham, being defeated by 38 to 10. In this discussion Lord John Russell made a short speech—the first he had made since the bill was introduced. His object, he said, "was to maintain the peace of the town of Birmingham; but if the people of that town opposed themselves to the means of doing so, on doubt difficulties would be presented. There were three ways by which his object could be attained: one was by a local police under the control of a Commissioner appointed by Government; another was by a portion of the metropolitan police; and the third by the military. He had selected that which seemed to him to be least objectionable, and to that he would adhere, but only as a temporary measure." On the next day the Government proposed the third reading of the bill—their object in thus pressing it forward being evidently to prevent the spread of agitation against such an unconstitutional and dangerous measure. Mr. Scholefield said that "at the wish of the majority of the inhabitants of Birmingham, and the whole of the Town Council," he moved that the bill be read a third time that day three months. Mr. T. Duncombe seconded the motion. True to their policy of speed and silence, the Government made no reply. There was no debate. A division was immediately taken, and the third reading was carried by 38 to 8.

CHAP. X.
1839.
The Bill passed.

The Town Council met on the 13th of August, and resolved to make one more attempt to defeat or to amend the obnoxious measure. Mr. Cutler moved a strong resolution against it :—

Action of the Town Council.

"That this Council having by petition declared its opposition to the bill now before Parliament, entitled 'A Bill for Improving the Police in Birmingham,' hereby offers its firm and unalterable hostility to this measure, both in principle and detail, and further pledges itself to oppose it in practice by all legal means in its power."

This motion was seconded by Mr. Hawkes; but was opposed by Mr. Weston and Mr. Middlemore, who moved, in place of it, a petition to the House of Lords, and a petition was accordingly adopted, and the Mayor, Alderman Sturge, and Mr. Middlemore were appointed a deputation to convey it to London and to see Lord Brougham, who was then in Opposition, and might be induced to give his aid to the Corporation.

The second reading of the bill in the Lords stood for Thursday, August 15, and Lord Brougham, whom the

CHAP. X.
1839.
Proceedings in the House of Lords.

Lord Brougham defends Birmingham.

deputation had seen in the meantime, then presented the petition of the Town Council. He also moved the rejection of the bill, and in doing so made a speech of considerable length and vigour. He said:—

"Government was now proceeding to undo, without any sufficient ground, the very act which they themselves had so lately done. That act [the grant of the Charter] was one of confidence in the town of Birmingham, for it enabled that town to avail itself of the provisions of the Municipal Corporations Act, and to be the first to take advantage of those provisions. He did not know that anything had, as yet, occurred to warrant the Government in altering its course of proceeding, in retracing its steps, and in undoing in August what it had done in October. Why was Birmingham now to be stigmatised, and to be declared unfit to be trusted with the management of its own concerns—one of the most important of which was the preservation of the Queen's peace? There was no use in giving a Charter which did not confer the power of making police regulations. The Government did not propose to take away the Charter; they proposed to continue the Corporation while they set aside all its acts—it was to have the name without the reality; a body was still to be called a Town Council, but functions it was to have none; for it was to be declared unfit to exercise those powers the exercise of which was the only reason for calling the Corporation into existence. He had never heard of suspending the functions of a Corporation without proving an abuse or a non-user of those functions. Now, the Corporation of Birmingham were not only not guilty, but they were not even accused of anything of the kind. No one brought a charge against them. . . . As was truly stated in the petition which he had had the honour to present, the Corporation of Birmingham was unaccused as well as unconvicted, and yet the House was asked to stigmatise not only the Corporation, but the thousands and thousands of inhabitants of that great town, who, by an immense majority, had declared the Town Council fit persons to administer the affairs of the borough, and to be at the head of its police. If any complaint was made against persons who had been appointed justices, that had nothing to do with the conduct of the Corporation. From all he knew of the town of Birmingham, he felt convinced that this bill would aggravate instead of diminishing the bitter party feelings prevailing in that town; that it would keep alive, or rather it would revive, those disturbances which were hardly yet repressed, and that it would lead to a train of disastrous consequences of which the youngest amongst their lordships might not live to see the end."

Lord Brougham, as may well be imagined, had an unsympathetic audience. Lord Melbourne, on behalf of the Ministry, defended the bill on the ground that the Birmingham Charter was disputed, and that the Town Council therefore could not levy a rate for police purposes; and probably he was by no means sorry to have the chance of punishing "those Birmingham fellows," as he had called them a few years before, and who were still as vigorous as ever in their assertion of Radical opinions, and their distrust of the Whigs. Emulating the part played by Sir Robert Peel in the Lower House, the Duke of Wellington came forward in the Lords as the Conservative advocate of the bill. Lord Wilton, another Tory peer, was the only speaker besides those named, and his contribution to the debate was an expression of regret that the bill was not to be made permanent! The second reading then passed without a division. Quick work was made of the successive stages of the measure. On the 16th of August the bill went into Committee. Here Lord Brougham made a suggestion—namely, that the Town Council should appoint the Police Commissioner, subject to the approval of the Home Secretary. This suggestion, he said, "had originated

CHAP. X.
1839.
Lord Brougham's Amendments.

with certain friends of the measure, but who were nevertheless averse to vesting in the Government the appointment of superintendent." The salary proposed for the Commissioner—£800 a year—ought, he also urged, to be reduced. "In other towns the salaries varied from £150 to £400 a year, and he could not see why the superintendent of police at Birmingham should have double the amount of salary of the superintendent of police at Liverpool, which was a larger town." To Lord Brougham's proposal, Lord Duncannon, Under Secretary of State, objected that "as Government had advanced the money, they had a right to the appointment." Lord Brougham replied—"Surely it was not contended that Birmingham was unfit to be entrusted with the management of its own police? His noble friend had very cautiously made use of the ambiguous word 'advance,' but this advance was to be repaid in ten years; and if the people of Birmingham repaid the money, surely they ought to have the appointment of the person spending it?" To this Lord Duncannon replied that "the Town Council had applied for a police." "But," answered Lord Brougham conclusively, "not for *this* police—they applied for a good measure, and you give them a bad one. The application for money was contained in a private letter from the Mayor, without consulting the Town Council; and he (Lord Brougham) was authorised to state that neither the Mayor nor any member of the Town Council would have made any application even for any advance of money, if they had entertained an idea that it would have been made a pretext for saddling them with a foreign police." The Government took time to consider Lord Brougham's proposal, and meanwhile the bill went through Committee. On the following Monday, August 19, it was read a third time and passed, without alteration.

Chap. X.
1839.
The Bill passed without amendment.

The course to be pursued in consequence of the passing of the Police Act was discussed at a Council meeting on the 3rd of September. The strongest indignation was expressed against the measure, and the deepest sense of the insult offered to the town, and of the injury done to the cause of local self-government. Some of the speakers—notably Mr. Clutton Salt—declared that they would not pay the Police Rate, regarding it as unconstitutional; but others, amongst them Mr. Beale and Mr. Lawrence, deprecated the use of violent language, and of threats which could not be carried into effect. The general feeling was that while it was incumbent upon the Council to obey the law, it was also necessary that a solemn protest against the Act should be put on record; and accordingly the following declaration, proposed by Alderman Joseph Sturge, and seconded by Mr. J. H. Cutler, was unanimously adopted, and ordered to be advertised in the Birmingham papers, in the *Times*, the *Morning Chronicle*, and the *Sun*:—

Indignation in Birmingham.

"That the Act, which has just passed through Parliament, entitled 'An Act for Improving the Police of Birmingham,' is, in effect, a measure of confiscation of almost the whole, and certainly of by far the most important, of the municipal rights of this newly-created Corporation.

Formal Protest of the Town Council.

CHAP. X.
1839.
Formal Protest of the Town Council.

"That the measure in question was introduced *unsolicited* and *unsought* by this Council: an assertion, to which it will not be enough to say in answer, that the Mayor had previously addressed a letter to the Secretary of State for the Home Department, suggesting the expediency of assisting the Borough with a loan, for the purpose of establishing a more efficient police; since that letter *was not, nor did it profess to be,* written by the authority or with the privity of the Town Council; but was, on the face of it, merely a private enquiry as to the probable course of the Government in the matter to which it related: whilst the intimation which it contained, that, if the answer were favourable, the Town Council should be convened to consider the subject, told, as plainly as words could speak, that, as yet, the Council had not expressed any opinion with respect to the proceeding. That, moreover, so far was the letter in question from suggesting, or, even in the most distant manner, hinting at the appointment of a Government Commissioner, or the establishment of so odious and unconstitutional a force as a Government police, that it distinctly pointed out the Town Council as the recipients of the loan, and the only proper authority for applying it to its intended purpose.

"That, however the Government may now choose to put a different construction on this communication from the Mayor, it is plain that it was, at first, distinctly understood in this sense, and in this sense alone, by the Home Secretary, who, accordingly, brought a bill into Parliament authorising a loan of ten thousand pounds to the Town Council. Nor was it until Sir Robert Peel, and a deputation from the Birmingham Tories—in perfect consistency with their known hostility to popular institutions and the representative principle—had signified to him *their* wishes on the subject (wishes apparently too much like commands), that he abandoned his original measure, and substituted in its place another, which, if it were not contrived on set purpose, was, at all events, obviously calculated to afford a triumph to the opposite party, by taking away the authority and disparaging the character of the new municipal system.

"That the measure, thus introduced by the Government, on the suggestion of its political opponents, is obviously founded on false pretences. For, though the reason for passing the Act, as alleged in the preamble, is, that 'doubts are entertained as to the authority of the Corporation to levy rates' (doubts, be it observed, which never ought to have existed, and never would have existed, had only proper caution been exercised in framing the Charter), yet, instead of adopting Lord Brougham's suggestion of limiting the duration of the Act to the continuance of those doubts, it fixes, for this purpose, an arbitrary and unnecessarily long period of two years, and 'from thence to the end of the then next session of Parliament'—words of an alarming import, and showing an already half-formed intention to renew the measure on the expiration of the appointed time.

"That, as a further proof of the disingenuousness which has characterised the whole of this proceeding, it is worthy of observation that when Lord Brougham proposed to vest the appointment of the Commissioner in the Town Council rather than in the Government, the suggestion was resisted by Lord Duncannon, on the strange ground, 'that the Town Council had petitioned for a police'—a ground, as has already been shown, false in fact, and even if true, absurdly inconclusive as an argument, since it is surely one thing to have a police, and another to have a Government Commissioner at the head of it.

"That no sooner did the Council become acquainted with the real nature of this measure, than they indignantly repudiated it as a marked insult to the intelligent burgesses of this town, than whom no where can men be found better fitted for the duty of self-government; as an outrage to the representative principle, and as a violation of that system of municipal polity which has ever been deemed, and by none *professedly* more than by the present Ministers, to lie at the foundation of—and to be the best security for—NATIONAL LIBERTY.

"That, unless this usurpation be firmly resisted at the threshold, this Council truly believes, and now warns the people of England to that effect, that the precedent just created will not prove barren, but that, upon one pretence or other, all the municipal

Chap. X.
1839.
Formal Protest of the Town Council.

bodies throughout the country will, before long, be stripped of their rightful privileges and authorities, and reduced to a state of slavish submission to the general Government.

"That, for the above reasons, this Council does now strongly and emphatically PROTEST against the attempt thus made to engraft one of the most pernicious institutions of Continental tyranny on the true English system of popular representation, and hereby declares its conviction that it is in duty bound to avail itself of all just and lawful means to relieve this town, and to guard the country at large from a measure so despotic and unconstitutional.—By order of the Council, W. REDFERN, Town Clerk."

CHAPTER XI.

VALIDITY OF THE CHARTER OF INCORPORATION DISPUTED.

The difficulty which arose with regard to the police force was but one incident—though a most important one —of the general difficulty as to the validity of the Charter; a dispute which lasted for nearly four years, and was finally settled only by an Act of Parliament. When the Municipal Corporations Act was passed, so much opposition was manifested to it in Parliament that Ministers were eager to get it through its various stages, without defining too closely the clauses expressing the conditions on which Charters ought to be granted, and those which related to the divisions of the boroughs created by Charter under the Act. The vagueness of these clauses tempted opposition to the new Charters, or at least indicated too clearly the grounds on which opposition might be founded, wherever there existed a strong and active hostile minority. The result was that several of the Charters granted under the Municipal Corporations Act were challenged by their opponents. The leading case was that of Manchester, in which the Conservatives, intending from the first to resist the Charter, not only petitioned against the grant of it, but abstained from doing, in consequence of it, any public act which might seem to admit its validity. They refrained, for example, from contesting any of the wards in the first election of councillors; and as early as possible afterwards they began the proceedings necessary to test the validity of the Charter in the courts of law. In Birmingham the Conservative opponents of the Charter—for here as well as in Manchester the opposition proceeded on a strictly political ground—did not follow the plan of abstention set in Manchester. They opposed the grant of the Charter, by petition and by private influence, but when it had been granted, they endeavoured to obtain a share in the new government of the town, and for this purpose they appeared in the registration court both as claimants and objectors when the first burgess list was under revision; and in the first elections they boldly and manfully contested every ward in the borough. Not only so, but one of the leaders of the Conservative party, and probably the strongest opponent of the Charter—Mr. Welchman Whateley—offered himself as a candidate for the office of Coroner, which was in the gift of the Town Council. All parties in Birmingham, therefore—Conservatives and Liberals alike—recognised by their acts the validity of the Charter; and it may not unreasonably be presumed that if the Conservative candidates had been moderately successful in the elections (instead of being entirely rejected), and if their candidate for the Coronership had been chosen, there would have been no dispute as to the authority of the document by which the Borough was incorporated. The fact, however, that the burgesses, in the exercise of their discretion and their electoral right, thought fit to confide the administration of the Borough to men of one political party exclusively, stimulated opposition on the part of those of the opposite political opinion; and though the Charter had been practically recognised and accepted on all hands, means were taken to dispute it, and, if possible, to invalidate it. The Police Act encouraged, and in some degree justified these efforts, since its preamble assigned as the reason of passing it that the Town Council could not raise funds in consequence of the validity of the Charter being disputed. The opposition began in a formal way by a movement of the Overseers of the parish of Birmingham. In June, 1839, the Town Council adopted estimates of expenditure, required by precept returns from the Overseers of the rateable value of the parishes in the borough, amended these returns for itself, and upon the basis so amended ordered the levy of a rate. The Overseers of Birmingham demurred to the execution of this order, and after some delay, on being pressed for the rate, they refused to levy it. In arriving at this resolution they acted upon an opinion which they had instructed Mr. Whateley to obtain from Sir Frederick Pollock and Sir William Follett, counsel chosen for their legal eminence and for their political opinions. This opinion was discussed at a meeting of the Town Council held on the 6th of August, 1839, when the Town Clerk (Mr. W. Redfern) made an elaborate report on the subject. The "case" submitted to the counsel above named recited three grounds as affecting the rating authority of the Corporation:—

"1st. That the Borough was divided into wards by the act of the Crown; whereas, it is contended, that according to the

Chap. XI.
1839.

First act of opposition.

Overseers refuse to levy Borough Rate.

Technical grounds of refusal.

Municipal Act (5 and 6 Wm. IV., c. 76) this ought to have been done by a revising barrister, appointed by the senior judge of assize.

"2nd. That the burgess lists, according to the direction of the Charter, were made out by the gentleman who now occupies the Mayoralty (Mr. W. Scholefield), but who was then in no official capacity; whereas it is urged that, according to the Municipal Act, this duty ought to have been assigned to the Overseers of the Poor.

"3rd. That many acts, in connection with the registration of the burgesses, and the election of Councillors and Aldermen, were performed on different days from those specified in the Act of Parliament."

The opinion given by Sir W. Follett (in which Sir F. Pollock concurred) is worthy of quotation, as it states a constitutional question, the settlement of which, as we shall see later, had to be effected by a special Act of Parliament, devised to cure any defect that might exist in the Municipal Act of William IV. :—

"The question now raised on this Charter is one of very great doubt and difficulty. The existing Corporation and Town Council of Birmingham have been formed in a manner altogether different from that provided by the statute 5 and 6 Wm. IV., c. 76, in respect of the ancient corporate towns; and although the Crown, in virtue of its common law prerogative, might grant the Charter in question, and create the mayor, town councillors, &c., who might legally perform all the ordinary functions of a Corporate body, it certainly does not necessarily follow that the Crown could vest in the Corporation, or any portion of it, powers beyond the reach of the prerogative of common law, and which could only be legally conferred by the act of the Legislature. The mode of creating and originally forming the new Corporations contemplated by the 141st section of the statute 5 and 6 Wm. IV., and the 49th section of the statute of 1st Vict., c. 78, and of dividing the towns so to be incorporated into wards, has been altogether unprovided for by these statutes. This omission was, no doubt, an unintentional one on the part of the framers of these Acts, and has left, therefore, in very great doubt the degree of power vested in the new corporate bodies; for it may very fairly be contended, that although the Legislature were willing to give these expanding powers of rating, &c., to councillors elected under the provisions and subject to the guards and restrictions provided by statute, they did not intend to vest such powers in a body constituted under a different authority, and elected in a manner different from that provided by the Act, and that therefore the omission in the statute respecting the original formation of the new Corporations, and more especially that most important, because permanent, provision regarding the division of the borough into wards, could not be sufficient for this purpose by the prerogative of the Crown; and as the Crown could not extend to the inhabitants of this borough all the powers and provisions of the statute, it could not extend them in part only, and give to the new Town Council, elected and formed as this is, the power of taxing the inhabitants of the borough. I think, therefore, in the state of doubt and uncertainty in which the power of the Town Council has been left by the Legislature in this respect, it would not be prudent for the Overseers to obey this precept without the direction and sanction of the Court of Queen's Bench. It is very well known that these doubts do exist, and I should think the better course for both parties would be to arrange to have the point raised and settled, by an application, on the part of the Town Council, for a *mandamus* to the Overseers. Assuming the rate to be valid, and the present Town Council of Birmingham to have the powers granted by the statute 5 and 6 Wm. IV., c. 76, and the statute of 1st Vict., c. 81 [that is, rating powers], the Overseers might be distrained upon, if they refused to obey the order of the Council; but if that course were adopted by the Council, the Overseers might raise the question of the legality of the rate and of the distress, by replevying the distress, or bringing an action of trespass against the magistrates who should sign the warrant."

CHAP. XI.
1839.
Legal opinions on validity of Charter.

CHAP. XI.
1839.
Effect of the opinions.

In other words, the opinion of Sir W. Follett and Sir F. Pollock was that the Charter might be good as a Crown or prerogative Charter, but that this conferred no rating power, until a competent court had declared the Charter to be good according to statute as well as according to common law. Now, a merely Crown Charter was, of course, not worth having, for without the power to rate no power of government practically existed. The Town Clerk's report put the distinction with clearness:—

Difference between a Statutory and a Common Law Charter.

"Here the question naturally presents itself—what is the difference between a statutory and a common law Charter? The difference, it will be found, is all important: under a statutory Charter the Town Council would be at liberty to raise money, and to exercise all the powers granted to Town Councils by the different Municipal Acts; whereas, under a common law or prerogative Charter, though the Town Council might still hold its meetings—though its members might retain the style of Mayor, Aldermen, and Councillors—though it might pass resolutions and express opinions on the passing occurrences of the day—still it would not be competent for it to raise one single farthing of money, or to do any one act, or to make any one arrangement, immediately or remotely accompanied by expense. This, however, is not, I conceive, the kind of Charter for which the people of Birmingham petitioned; it is not the kind of Charter which the Crown intended to grant, nor is it the kind of Charter with which a Town Council, having the least regard to its own character, could rest satisfied."

Modes of raising the question.

His own opinion, the Town Clerk reported, was that the Charter was "good even as a statutory one," but it might possibly be necessary to have a fresh division of the town into wards, and a fresh general election of Councillors. This, however, could be decided only by the judgment of the Court of Queen's Bench, which, he thought, would probably lean to the sufficiency of the Charter. As to the means of obtaining such a decision, it might be done either by a writ of *quo warranto* [a writ requiring some person to show by what warrant he exercised his office] or by a *mandamus* requiring the Overseers to collect the rate. The latter, the report suggested, would be the preferable course, and would not cost more than "from £100 to £200." A distraint on the Overseers he rejected for two reasons—because the case could not be tried until the Lent Assizes, seven or eight months off, and because "the magistrates, under the peculiar circumstances of the case, might feel some hesitation in granting a warrant of distress." Possibly, however, the trial then pending in reference to the Manchester Charter might save cost and trouble by settling the question. Finally, the Town Clerk mentioned a not uninteresting fact—that before the Charter was granted he had, as a member of the Incorporation Committee, pointed out these very difficulties in a letter addressed to Mr. Joseph Parkes, the professional agent of the Committee, urging that particular care should be exercised, as "there was every disposition here to take advantage of any flaw that might be detected in the Charter." In reply, he had been assured that his objection had been submitted to the Attorney and Solicitor General, and to other Crown lawyers, who took a different view of the question:—

The difficulty foreseen.

Carelessness of the Crown Lawyers.

"Against so high an authority (Mr. Redfern proceeded) it would not, of course, have become me to erect my humble opinion still my mind was far from being free from doubt, nor did a closer and more anxious consideration of the matter, after the grant of the Charter, serve to dispel my fears. Anxious to satisfy my mind on a subject of so much importance, I subsequently proceeded to London, in company with Mr. W. Scholefield. We sought and obtained an interview with the Attorney-General [Sir John, afterwards Lord Campbell]. From him, however, we elicited but little information, and experienced still less courtesy; a circumstance by no means unintelligible when it is understood that we went empty-handed. He was evidently not altogether satisfied with the way in which the matter stood, but was not disposed to take any measure for obviating the difficulty. My own opinion then was that the wiser plan would be for us to test the validity of the Charter as soon as possible, by a friendly application for a *mandamus* or *quo warranto*; in which case, had the Charter been decided to be good, no further difficulty would have been experienced, and if it had been adjudged bad, we could, without trouble, have got another. This view I did not fail to urge upon those members of the Council with whom I was then more particularly in habits of communication. I found, however, that my suggestion was not favourably received, and I accordingly dropped it. I now regret that I did not persevere; since, had I done so the question probably before this time would have been set to rest, and both the town and its representatives in this Council would have been rescued from the degradation which it is sought to inflict on them as a cover for the carelessness of the law officers of the Crown."

Hesitation of the Council.

This confession of the Town Clerk's doubts, and of his previous efforts to get the Charter amended, by no means lessened the effect produced by the opinion given by the counsel consulted by the Overseers. The Council certainly was indisposed to resort to legal measures off-hand, and accordingly time for consideration was taken, the following resolution being passed:—

"That the Churchwardens and Overseers of the Poor of the parish of Birmingham having refused to pay their share of the Borough Rate, on the alleged ground of the invalidity of the Charter—resolved, that the Finance Committee be requested to consider what is expedient to be done under these circumstances, and to report thereon to an early meeting of the Council, to be called for that purpose."

A week later, on the 13th of August, the Finance Committee presented their report. It was not a specially comforting document, for the Committee evidently felt that they could make no practical recommendation. There was no disposition to run the risk of heavy expenses, either in legal proceedings by way of *mandamus*, or still less by levying a distraint upon the Overseers. Consequently the Committee recommended an entirely pacific and inexpensive measure, as will be seen from the following report:—

"At a meeting of the Finance Committee, at the office of the Town Clerk, August 12, 1839—present, Mr. Alderman Gammon in the chair, Councillors Wigley, Hardman, Clowes, and Alderman Muntz. The Treasurer stated that the meeting had been convened to afford him an opportunity of appealing to them, as to the course he must adopt, in consequence of his inability, for want of funds, to pay any order that may be made upon him by the Court of Sessions, advertised to be held by the Recorder on the 23rd instant, or any expense attending the same. The Treasurer having reported that a Court of Sessions is advertised to be held by the Recorder on the 23rd instant, resolved—'That the Mayor be requested to communicate to the Home Secretary, that the Town Council has no funds, or means of raising them, to pay the expenses of such sessions, the maintenance of prisoners in gaol, or the holding of inquests, &c.; likewise to call his lordship's attention to the derangement of local government that must ensue therefrom, and

CHAP. XI.
1839.

to request his lordship's advice as to the course proper to be pursued. Resolved, further, that the Town Clerk be requested to attend the Assizes at Liverpool, when the trial of the cause relative to the validity of the Manchester Charter takes place; and that he be authorised to take any opinion there that may appear to him to be desirable.'"

The Council approved of this report without comment, feeling, probably, that as the difficulties of the Corporation had arisen through the neglect of Government officials, it was the business of the Government to devise means of putting an end to the state of embarrassment thus caused. The steps taken in consequence of the resolution above quoted were detailed in a report of the Finance Committee presented to the Council on the 3rd of September. The report stated that, in consequence of the inability of the Town Council to levy a rate, the Mayor was directed to represent the case to Lord John Russell, and "to request his lordship to grant the Corporation pecuniary assistance, in order that they might be relieved from their present difficulties, and be able to proceed with the municipal business." In the first instance, the report stated, "money had been borrowed on the guarantee of certain members of the Town Council,* but the money expended and owing by the Corporation already exceeded the amount guaranteed." To the Mayor's application, Lord John Russell replied that the Government could render no assistance. Then the Mayor and the Borough Treasurer went to London to try what could be done.

Local guarantee for expenses.

---

* The amount was £2,000; the money was obtained from the Midland Bank, and among the guarantors were Messrs. W. Scholefield, P. H. Muntz, Beale, Phillips, &c.

They saw Mr. Joseph Parkes, who went with them to Holland House, to see Lord John Russell. "They informed his lordship that the sessions were at hand—that they were without funds—and added that they should have no difficulty in raising the money themselves, provided the Government would undertake to pay the amount if the Charter of Incorporation should be declared invalid." In reply to this Lord John Russell "expressed a wish to serve the Corporation, if he could," and sent the deputation to the Chancellor of the Exchequer, Mr. Baring, who had just then come into office. He promised to "take the matter into consideration;" but, as the Government was then in a state of change, nothing could be immediately obtained, and the deputation had to come back again empty-handed. The Mayor, however, said that "he indulged hopes that Government would accede to the prayer of the Town Council." This expectation was fulfilled in some degree, for at a Council meeting on the 1st of October the Finance Committee made the following report":— *Chap. XI. 1839. Ministerial promises.*

"That after many interviews with members of her Majesty's Government, and great exertion to obtain the advance of £5,000, towards defraying the expenses of sessions and assizes, and the expenses caused by the late disturbances [the Chartist riots in July], the Mayor has obtained a promise of £3,000, of which sum £1,000 will be paid to the Treasurer of the Borough, to defray the expenses of the Borough Sessions, &c.; and £2,000 will be paid to the Chief Commissioner of Police, to defray expenses arising from the late disturbances, with an understanding that any balance remaining in the Commissioner's hands shall be paid over to the Borough Treasurer, to be applied in like manner as the £1,000." *Funds granted for Sessions.*

It was a most humiliating position for the town and for the Council. But three months earlier an application for a Government loan of £10,000 for the establishment of a police force had been met by the imposition of a special rate upon the town, and by the creation of a police force withdrawn from local control, and placed under the authority of a Government Commissioner. An application for £5,000 to defray the cost of administering justice, under the supplementary Charter by which the Crown had created a Court of Quarter Sessions, was now met, after long-continued pressure and repeated solicitations, with the paltry grant of £1,000 in aid of this department of Corporation expenditure. And all this time the whole difficulty arose from the fault of the Government itself, in omitting or declining to take steps to vindicate the Charter which it had recommended the Crown to grant to the borough. Until the Charter was established as valid, the Council could raise money only by the personal guarantee of its own members, or by begging, under humiliating conditions, from the national Treasury; and yet the Government, who were especially concerned in defending the Charter, left the maintenance of it to the Corporation, which was actually destitute of means to vindicate its position or to validate the Crown commission under which it acted. The Government might have done in 1839, what a Conservative Administration did in 1842—namely, introduce a bill to confirm the Charters granted by the Crown; but, with strange supineness, it neither did anything on its own part, nor advised any course for those whom its own law officers had led into difficulties. The Birmingham

Town Council had, therefore, still to consider for itself the method of settling the question which lay at the root of all its troubles—the legality of the Charter. On this point the advice of Mr. Crompton (afterwards Justice Crompton) was taken. He was of opinion that a *mandamus* to the Overseers could not be obtained, and that the best way of raising the point would be by a nominal distraint, arranged by consent, and stated in a special case for the judgment of the Court of Queen's Bench. The Town Clerk, however, advised that a preferable method would be " by means of an application for a *quo warranto* against some Corporate officer, whom it is not competent for the Town Council to appoint otherwise than under the authority of the Act of Parliament, and with respect to whose appointment the question might be raised whether the Charter were or were not good under the statute." With this view the Town Clerk reported that he had seen Mr. Whateley, who was formerly Coroner for the Birmingham division of the county, and who had been displaced by the election of Dr. Birt Davies as Borough Coroner, and that he had suggested that Mr. Whateley should apply to the Court by way of a writ of *quo warranto,* calling upon Dr. Davies to show by what authority he held and exercised his office. Mr. Whateley, however, replied that in the peculiar circumstances of the case, and considering his personal relations to it, "he should certainly decline taking the initiative in any such measure, but that if the Town Council were to pass a resolution recommendatory of it, it was very probable that his objections on that score might be removed." The Finance Committee consequently

CHAP. XI.
1839.

A Writ of *Quo Warranto* proposed.

234 THE CHARTER DISPUTED.

CHAP. XI.
1839.
Legal proceedings.

recommended that the opinion of counsel should be taken as to whether the question could be raised in the manner proposed, and that in the event of an affirmative reply, an arrangement to that effect should be made with Mr. Whateley. This report and recommendation were approved by the Council; but it does not appear that any such arrangement as that contemplated was entered into.

The Coroner's Right challenged.

Indeed, Mr. Whateley seems at last to have taken the matter into his own hands, in consequence of the proceedings adopted in the case of the Manchester Charter, which also affected Birmingham, as will hereafter be explained. His notice of procedure was contained in the following note addressed to Dr. Birt Davies, the Borough Coroner, and which was read at a Council meeting on the 26th of December, 1839:—

"Waterloo Street, December 12, 1839.

"Dear Sir—In consequence of the opinion recently expressed by the Court of Queen's Bench with reference to the powers conferred upon the newly created Corporations, I think it right to acquaint you that I dispute your title to the office of Coroner for this borough, and that I hold you responsible for interfering with the office, of which I am advised I have never been divested, and for receiving the fees belonging to me as one of the Coroners for the county of Warwick. I have preferred making this communication to you by letter rather than by a formal notice, which I hope, however, you will do me the favour to consider it, and I will thank you to acknowledge the receipt of it.—I am, &c., J. W. WHATELEY."

The validity of the Charter was now questioned in two respects—first, as to the rating powers, by the action of the Birmingham Overseers in refusing to collect a Borough

Rate in obedience to the Mayor's precept; and, second, as to the power of appointment to Corporate office, by Mr. Whateley's challenge of Dr. Davies's right to act as Coroner. A third attack upon the Charter was also imminent on the part of the County Justices of Warwickshire, with regard to the authority of Birmingham Justices to commit prisoners to the county gaol, in accordance with the contract entered into between the borough and the county. These proceedings were taken in consequence of litigation which arose with regard to the Manchester Charter. The first of these, the case of "Rutter v. Chapman," was heard at the Liverpool Assizes on August 26, 1839. It was an action against Mr. Chapman, the Coroner appointed by the Town Council of Manchester, for having held inquests, and the contention was that he had no authority, because the Charter being illegal, his appointment was illegal also. To prove the illegality of the Charter counsel relied upon three points—first, that a majority of resident householders had not petitioned in favour of a Charter; second, that the petitions against the grant of a Charter were more numerously signed than those in favour of it; third, that a majority of those who would become burgesses under a Charter had not petitioned in favour of it. Baron Maule, who tried the case, decided adversely to the plaintiffs on each point, and thus declared the validity of the Charter, on which a bill of exceptions to his ruling was tendered, and the case went to be argued in the Court of Appeal. The appeal in this case was heard in the Court of Exchequer, and the Judges decided (1)— that an adverse petition, though larger in number, did not necessarily deprive the Crown of its right to grant a Charter, but that the determination of the Privy Council to advise the Crown to grant a Charter upon the petition of inhabitant householders was not conclusive as to its validity; (2) that the grant of a Charter is an exercise of the common-law prerogative of the Crown, although it also extends to the new Corporation the powers of the Municipal Act, which the Crown has power to do only by that Act; (3) that a Charter may be granted to a part only of the borough from which the petition emanated [this question arose in the case of Salford being omitted from the Manchester Charter]; (4) that the Crown may, by its common-law prerogative, appoint in the Charter the number and set out the limits of the wards; (5) that the Crown may appoint a person to settle the burgess list; (6) that the Crown may appoint a returning officer for the first election, and may fix days for holding the elections, though not agreeing with those fixed in the Municipal Act. Some of these points, it will be seen, were the same as those on which the validity of the Birmingham Charter was challenged; and therefore the decision was of great importance to Birmingham as well as to Manchester.

The second case arising in connection with Manchester, but also directly affecting Birmingham, was that of "Regina *v.* the Justices of Lancashire," heard in the Court of Queen's Bench on the 23rd November, 1839. The Justices of Lancashire had appointed a committee of their body to treat with the Corporation of Manchester respecting the payments to be made by the borough for the maintenance of borough prisoners in the county gaol, Manchester having no gaol of its own, which was then also the case with Birmingham. A motion was therefore made to have the order of the Justices brought by writ of *certiorari* before the Court of Queen's Bench, the object being to quash the order practically on the ground that, the Charter of Manchester being invalid, no contract could be entered into by the Town Council. The judges, Justice Patteson, Justice Williams, and Lord Denman, were unanimous in their opinion that the order must be brought before them by *certiorari*, because, on their construction of various Acts of Parliament, it was not competent for the Council of a borough which had no gaol of its own to contract for the use of the county gaol.* This decision was reported to the Town Council, at its meeting on December 26, 1839, as one which applied with equal force to the Borough of Birmingham, that borough having no gaol of its own.

In fact, however, the Justices of Warwickshire had made a contract with Birmingham for the maintenance of the borough prisoners, but no money had yet been paid, and at the meeting just referred to (December 26) the bill was presented by the county. The letters then read, and the resolution passed, show the straits to which the Town Council was reduced for want of money, consequent upon its alleged defective rating power. Mr. Beck, Treasurer for the County, writes to Mr. W. O. Hunt, the

---

* Q. B., 11 A. and E., 144.

CHAP. XI.
1839.
Difficulties with the County of Warwick.

County Clerk of the Peace, stating that his own applications for money having met with no reply, the Clerk of the Peace must obtain from the Corporation an order for payment of the amount due—namely, maintenance of 247 borough prisoners in the county gaol up to November 12, at 11d. per head per day, according to agreement, £427 12s. 6d.; ditto, 282 prisoners in House of Correction, £618 10s. 5d.; total £1,046 2s. 11d. Thereupon the Clerk of the Peace writes to the Town Clerk of Birmingham to ask for "a copy of any resolution that may have been entered into by the Council on the subject." The Council considered this letter at its meeting on the 26th of December. Unhappily it had no money, and therefore could give no satisfactory answer; but if a resolution would content the County Justices, they were welcome to it, and accordingly Alderman Scholefield (who had now been succeeded by Alderman Muntz as Mayor) moved the following resolution, which the Council adopted:—

Resolution of the Council.

"That this Council do express its sincere regret that, owing to great difficulties under which the Corporation now labours, and which could not be foreseen when the arrangements for the maintenance of the borough prisoners in the county goal were entered into, the Council is for the present unable to fulfil its part of the contract; that the Council is, however, anxious to discharge to the utmost the obligation which it has incurred with the county justices, and trusts that Parliament, early in the next session, will devise some measure for relieving this borough and the rest of the county from the embarrassed relations in which they stand to one another; and that a copy of this resolution be forwarded by the Mayor to the Chairman of the County Quarter Sessions."

On the same day the Birmingham Quarter Sessions were held, and as the questions which had arisen both in Birmingham and Manchester were then naturally engaging so much attention, Mr. M. D. Hill, the Recorder, discussed them in his charge to the Grand Jury. Were the Birmingham Sessions unlawful; and were the County Justices entitled to refuse to receive prisoners committed by the Borough Justices, or sentenced by the Recorder at the Birmingham Quarter Sessions? These were questions put by the Recorder, and the following is a summary of the statement and argument he addressed to the Grand Jury:—

Chap. XI.
1839.
The Recorder's Opinion.

They were aware that for some time past doubts had been cast upon the validity of the power by which these sessions were held. He was appointed Recorder by command of her Majesty, yet, as the command of the Sovereign in this country could not authorise illegality of any kind, particularly illegality in the frame and construction of a Court of Justice, it became necessary for him to examine the doubts thrown out with respect to the validity of his powers, and to see if they suggested any substantial reasons for his not continuing to hold these sessions. After such consideration, and after obtaining "the opinions of persons in authority," and of "much higher station in the profession than himself," he had come to the conclusion "that these sessions were lawfully held, and that it was his bounden duty to continue to hold them." The doubts thrown upon the validity of the sessions had occurred in the case of "the Queen *v.* the Justices of Lancashire." This case the Recorder stated—"The Justices of Lancashire had received into their custody prisoners who had been committed by the magistrates of the borough of Manchester, and maintained them at the expense of the county. A contract was about to be entered into between the Town Council of Manchester and the Justices of the county, by which the Town Council were to bind themselves to remunerate the County Justices for the maintenance of such prisoners. It

The Recorder on the Validity of the Charter and of the Sessions.

CHAP. XI.
1839.
The Recorder's Opinion: the Right to the County Gaol.

occurred, however, to some ratepayers in Manchester that the Town Council was not bound to enter into such an arrangement, and they argued that, as they could not be compelled to enter into such a contract, they had no authority to make it. A writ of *certiorari* was accordingly applied for to the Court of Queen's Bench, to bring into that Court the order of sessions for making that contract. That step was taken for the purpose of raising the question whether the Town Council and the Justices could enter into a valid contract of remuneration for the maintenance of such prisoners. The case was entered into at length, and from the decision of the Court it appeared that there was no power given by the statutes which were relied upon, by which a valid contract could be made. In the course of the argument doubts were thrown out as to the legality of the grant of the quarter sessions. It was in that view that it became necessary for him to consider the case, and see in what position it placed him and the Birmingham sessions. If it should be found that Birmingham and Manchester were in the same circumstances, and that there ought not to be holden a sessions in either place, then, and not till then, should he refrain from carrying out her Majesty's gracious intentions, and should no longer officiate as Recorder until the instrument conferring the power he had exercised might be differently framed. His decided opinion, however, was that the Birmingham sessions were perfectly legal." The question resolved itself into this—"Suppose Birmingham to be no longer liable to contribute to the county rate, in consequence of the express provisions of the Municipal Act, does this exemption from contribution necessarily infer the absence of the power in the Borough Justices and the Recorder to commit to the county gaol?" The power to commit, he contended, was independent of any contribution towards the cost of maintenance. "What was it that gave the right to commit to a county gaol? At common law the Sheriff of a county had *primâ facie* a right to the custody of prisoners, and such being his right, the correlative duty was cast upon him to receive them into custody, and keep them in the county gaol. No doubt this *primâ facie* duty was restrained in some districts of counties by the existence of franchises which took these districts out of the jurisdiction of the Sheriff, and established that of the lords of such

THE CHARTER DISPUTED.

franchises in its place. In such districts there were common gaols which were not the gaols of the Sheriff. But this borough was no such district; Birmingham was part of the county of Warwick. It had no common gaol, and of necessity, therefore, the gaol of the borough and the gaol of the county were one and the same. It had been said 'What, is the county to maintain the prisoners from Birmingham without any contribution from this borough towards their support?' Now, such was the law. It might be a hardship, but it was the unavoidable result of the slip which had been made in the Act"—which exempted boroughs from contributing to the county rate, and yet, as decided in the Manchester case, failed to give them the power of contracting to pay for the maintenance of prisoners in the county gaol when a borough had no gaol of its own. The Recorder proceeded to illustrate this position by an interesting historico-legal review:—"Going back to the remote period when these rights and duties as to the custody of prisoners grew up, he found this to be the state of the case—county rates did not exist. The Sheriff repaired the county gaol, which he was bound to maintain for the confinement of all prisoners committed thereto, and charge the expense in his account to the Exchequer; and he (the Recorder) also found that when the lord of the franchise held a gaol, he was also bound to repair it. This was the case with the Bishop of Ely and the Earl of Exeter, who were compelled to repair the prisons over which they held jurisdiction, although they could not be reimbursed, and although the inhabitants of the districts where the gaols were situated were not liable, at common law, to contribute to such repair. Then, with respect to the maintenance of prisoners, they were formerly bound to maintain themselves. If the gaoler supplied them with provisions, he had a right of action against the prisoners, to recover the value from them; and if the gaoler refused to supply maintenance, the prisoners had to depend upon the charity of the humane and well-disposed for such a supply. It was not until the time of Queen Elizabeth that legal provision was made for poor prisoners, by a rate on the inhabitants; and then it was only to a limited extent. It seemed quite clear, then, that as there was no burden on the inhabitants for any purpose connected with the detention, prosecu-

Chap. XI.
1839.

The Recorder's Opinion: the right to the County Gaol.

R

CHAP. XI.
1839.

tion, or punishment of prisoners, until centuries after the rights and duties regarding the custody of prisoners had been defined by legal principles, which had no reference to contribution, and settled by long usage, it was impossible to regard contribution as any criterion in law by which to decide upon the right of committal. That the Borough of Birmingham had no other gaol than the county gaol to which to send its prisoners was beyond all doubt. The prison behind that Court was nothing more than a large and convenient lock-up house; and not such a prison as the law contemplated for the committal of prisoners. There were many districts which, until very lately, did not contribute to the county rate, and probably some such still existed where, nevertheless, there was no gaol. But was it ever heard of that any spot could be found in England from which offenders could not be committed to some gaol or other; and if to no other custody, who would say that the Sheriff could refuse to receive them, and hold them, until they were delivered by due course of law? Any other doctrine would hold out an absolute immunity to crime; and if there had been the least pretence for saying the law was so defective they would have had practical proof of its existence long ago."

Proceedings of the County Justices.

This opinion of the Recorder was discussed at the Warwick County Quarter Sessions, which were held on the 31st of December, 1839. Lord Lifford, one of the justices, was for making short work of the matter. He moved that "no more prisoners be received until the legal questions relating to the Borough Quarter Sessions were decided." Mr. Dickins—the present (1878) Chairman of Sessions—moved, as an amendment, that matters should remain as they then were until the next sessions. The Chairman, Sir J. Eardley Wilmot, said he agreed in part of the observations of the Recorder of Birmingham, but thought he had shirked most material points of the case. Mr. Adams asked "if there were not members of the

Corporation of Birmingham who would be willing to give personal security to the county, in the same way in which the Recorder had given personal security to the High Sheriff for the expense of the conveyance of prisoners from Warwick to Birmingham and back?" Finally, the amendment was carried. Another attempt, however, was made to embarrass the Corporation. The Rev. Riland Bedford, Rector of Sutton Coldfield—a leader of the Conservative party in Birmingham, and a strong opponent of the Corporation—moved that the opinion of Sir W. Follett be taken "as to whether the prisoners committed to the county gaol by the borough magistrates ought to be tried at Warwick or Birmingham; and if tried at Birmingham, whether the Recorder had power to send them to the county gaol for punishment." This motion was seconded by Lord Lifford, another Conservative magistrate; but the Bench, feeling that it was a direct attack upon the Birmingham Court of Quarter Sessions, rejected it by a considerable majority—though sixteen justices voted for it.

At the first meeting of the Council in 1840—January 7—the condition in which the Corporation found itself was taken into serious consideration. The money advanced by the Government for the administration of justice at Quarter Sessions had run out, and the Mayor (Mr. Muntz) now announced that on his application the Government had agreed to advance £1,400 in addition. This relief, however—given grudgingly, and after repeated solicitation—was entirely inadequate to its purpose, and was also degrading to the Corporation in the manner in which it was conceded.

CHAP. XI.
1840.

It was plain to everybody that the Corporation could not go on much longer in its then deplorable condition—its authority disputed by an active and resolute political section in the town, its means crippled by inability to levy rates, its capacity to meet the most pressing expenses dependent upon money raised by personal guarantee, or extracted by repeated entreaties from a reluctant Government, legal proceedings being threatened or actually taken against one of its chief officers, and an absolute dead-lock in the administration of justice being prevented only by the temporary forbearance of the County Justices. The Council felt keenly that it was time to bring to a close the discredit and embarrassment caused by this condition of affairs, and Mr. W. Scholefield consequently moved the appointment of a Committee " to consider and adopt such measures as they may deem requisite for effecting an immediate settlement of the difficulties arising out of the contested validity of the Charter." In doing so he spoke out strongly upon the difficulty and degradation of their position :—

Proposals for Action.

Difficulties of the Corporation.

"The situation in which the Council was then placed was humiliating when they reflected what the Town Council was, and what it was intended to be. Within twenty-four hours after the arrival of the Charter, the Town Clerk found it was very defective; and when they appealed to the Government they were smiled at by one high in authority upon such matters. When they attempted to levy a rate they were openly opposed; and when they again appealed to the Government they were told that they must be governed by law. But worse remained behind. In the course of a short time the Government declared the illegality of their own offspring [by the Police Act] and robbed the Corporation of the principal and most important powers with which they had invested it. They must now resolve to be or not to be—to ask her Majesty's Government to remedy the defects in the Charter, or take it back. They ought not to temporise any longer; they had been suing the Government, *in pauperis*, much too long. It was impossible to go on in this manner any longer, for money the Corporation had none, and it could not be expected that the Government, even if they were disposed, could continue to advance large sums for the benefit of the borough."

A Charter Committee was appointed, consisting of the Mayor (Mr. Muntz), Aldermen W. Scholefield, Beale, and James, and Messrs. Pare, Cutler, Jennings, and Palmer. On the 4th of February the Charter Committee reported that they had arranged with Mr. Whateley so to shape his proceedings against the Birmingham Coroner as "to bring the whole question of the validity of the Charter before the Court of Queen's Bench," and that on the 16th of January a rule *nisi* had been obtained by him "on grounds involving most of the principal objections entertained against the legality of the Charter." Since the rule was granted the Manchester Charter case had been set down for hearing, and as this would govern the Birmingham case, the rule applied for by Mr. Whateley had been made absolute, and the writ of *quo warranto* would shortly arrive, but would not be returnable until the following term.

The Borough had now been incorporated for a little more than a year, but it had only the form of representative government, the substance being practically in abeyance. The position of affairs, indeed, was most hurtful to the interests of the burgesses, most humiliating

CHAP. XI.
1840.
Position of the Borough.

to the elected representatives of the several wards, and consequently to their constituents, and, it must be added, with regret, most gratifying to the political opponents of the new Council. These, as we have seen, were to be found in the borough itself; in the county, amongst the Conservative magistrates; in both Houses of Parliament; and even in the ranks of the professedly Liberal Government, for lukewarm friends could scarcely be regarded as other than adversaries. The motives of these various classes of opponents were apparent on the surface. The local opposition was conducted on two grounds. First, there was the political ground, all the opponents of the Charter belonging to the Tory party, and all its advocates to the Whig and Radical parties, chiefly to the latter. The Tories naturally, and no doubt honestly, believed that all measures tending to place the government of the town in the hands of the Radicals were dangerous to the public peace, and they pointed—though most unjustly—to the Chartist agitation and to the riots of 1839, as proofs of the soundness of their contention. This feeling was distinctly shared by the Tories amongst the county magistracy, and by the members of their party in Parliament, whose dislike of Birmingham and its municipal institutions was further intensified by a desire to embarrass the Liberal Government. There was, however, locally, another ground of opposition to the Charter. Previously the government of the town had been conducted wholly on the principle of self-election, and thus the so-called respectable section of the inhabitants had come to regard the choice of rulers as their privilege—as something, in fact, to be arranged in private consultation, and to be managed with reference to the kind of friendly or personal convenience or interest which is inevitably established as the consequence of a close or oligarchical system. It is proverbial that privilege dies hard. What a man has, whether in power, or influence, or money, he desires to keep; and the rule which applies to individuals governs also the proceedings of classes and communities. The representative principle of course prevented the extension of the system of privilege, and threatened to put an end to it altogether; the admission of the ratepayers generally to the right of self-government at once checked the authority and diminished the importance of those who had constituted the restricted and supreme governing class. Here, as in other matters, human nature asserted its characteristics. Those who saw themselves in danger of being ousted from power easily persuaded themselves that they were best fitted to govern, and that they were injured by interference with their prescriptive right. From this conclusion the transition to personal hostility was natural enough, and the privileged class consequently regarded their opponents as personal enemies, inferior in position, lower in capacity, dangerous in purpose, and hostile to established authority. No possible form of words not open to an appearance of gross exaggeration could adequately describe the feeling which these relations engendered. So far was opposition carried that the town was literally split into social as well as political factions. Members of the two parties refused to meet in public or private, to engage in united action of any kind, to join in the

CHAP. XI.

1840.
Motives of Opposition.

Divisions in the Town.

CHAP. XI.
1840.
Divisions in the Town.

same assemblies, or even to speak to each other in the streets. Each side attributed to the other the basest motives and the most dangerous designs; even business relations were not conducted without strain, and indeed, nothing but the strongest considerations of self-interest rendered possible intercourse of any kind. After the lapse of forty years, when the town has grown so largely in education, in wealth, in public spirit, and in the higher forms of tolerance, social, religious, and political,

Contrast with the present time.

it is impossible for us to realise such a condition of affairs as that which has just been sketched. The Charter, then the ostensible bone of contention, has long since been accepted by all parties as essential to the good government of the town. It is now nearly thirty years since the privileged and self-elected governing bodies have disappeared, and since all their powers were merged in the authority of the Corporation; and now, even amongst the strongest political partisans, or the most fervent admirers of ancient methods, it would be impossible to find a single person who would be willing to return to the exploded system which, in 1839, still contested the right of the people to administer their own affairs by means of their own freely elected representatives. At that time, however, the state of things, as we have seen, was very different. It was then possible for a political body, the Loyal and Constitutional Association, representing the Conservatives of the town, to issue a report of which the following is an extract:—

"The evils that had been predicted as likely to result from

the incorporation of the Borough of Birmingham have been too well verified. The precipitation with which the Charter was forced by the Government on the borough during the Parliamentary recess—contrary to the expressed wishes of a large proportion of the ratepayers, and in breach of faith towards the Anti-Corporation Committee—the unfair and illegal manner in which the town was divided into wards, and the burgess roll prepared—could only produce one result. The result was the seating in authority of persons who either had been members or silent abettors of the dangerous practices of the Political Union. The town offices were filled by persons of extreme Radical opinions; and a wide-spread feeling of disgust was speedily produced against the Corporation. This effect was sufficiently manifested by the fact that in a few days after the riots in July, an address, drawn up and published under the direction of your Committee, and forwarded to Lord John Russell for presentation to Her Majesty, praying that the grant of the Charter might be annulled, received upwards of 3,000 signatures. It is worthy of remark, too, that this address contained the signatures of many of those who had formerly prayed for the Charter of Incorporation."*

The menaces expressed in this document were no idle threats. The validity of the Charter was questioned, locally, legally, and in Parliament. The authority of the Town Council to levy rates was denied; consequently, it had no funds. The power of the borough magistrates was disputed, and for a time their jurisdiction ceased to be exercised. For the want of means the borough sessions had to be stopped. The county justices refused to receive Birmingham prisoners. The Corporation was insultingly told by Parliament that it was unfitted to control the police force, and a special authority, with rating powers, was constituted, in contempt of the most

---

* Report of Loyal and Constitutional Association, Dec. 17, 1839.

essential principles of local self-government. All this time, the Government, professedly Liberal, and nominally in harmony with the majority of the Birmingham people—the very Government which had passed the Municipal Corporations Act, and had conferred charters upon Birmingham and other leading towns, stood idle, careless, apathetic, doing nothing to vindicate its own work, or to protect or assist those whom it had invested with a semblance of authority, but to whom, through its own default, the reality of power was denied. It was no wonder that, under such circumstances, the Birmingham Liberals became disaffected towards the Administration, or that, as regarded their local position, they were filled with a sense of shame and indignation at their own humiliating position, enhanced, as this was, by the unconcealed scorn and triumph of their opponents, local and political. Nor could it be a matter of surprise that, stung to resistance, the Town Council at last resolved, without further delay, to exercise such powers as they had, and to levy a rate in order that their authority might be legally tested, or that the Charter itself might be cancelled as the result of defeat.

It was easier, however, to resolve than to act. The Charter Committee appointed in January, 1840, found themselves in March unable to report progress, further than that they had been in communication with the

A resolution of the House of Commons had called for a return of borough rates levied in England, and the Home Office had consequently asked for a return from Birmingham. The reply of the Council was given in the following resolution:—"That a borough rate was made to the amount of £12,000, but that the overseers refused to pay it on the ground of the invalidity of the Charter, and that the question is still in abeyance." At the same meeting another incident of a peculiarly humiliating kind occurred. Addresses were adopted to the Queen and Prince Albert on the occasion of their marriage, and these were described as the addresses of "the Council of the Borough of Birmingham." To this one of the members, Mr. Palmer, demurred on the ground that the proper style was "the mayor, aldermen, and burgesses of the borough of Birmingham," to which the Town Clerk replied that Mr. Palmer was right, but that "it was considered that it might be deemed presumptuous in the Council if they represented the addresses as proceeding from the whole borough, and therefore it was thought best to state it as from the Council of the borough!" At the next meeting of the Council, on the 7th of April, the Mayor was questioned as to whether any progress had been made by the Charter Committee. He replied that the Committee had several times seen Lord Normanby, the Home Secretary, but that nothing had been done. On this, Alderman Hutton, who obviously gave expression to the general feeling, spoke strongly of "the deep humiliation of their position, which was a cause

CHAP. XI.
1840.
Financial and other Difficulties.

much rather see the Corporation put into abeyance altogether, than go on in the state of perplexity in which they were then placed." At the end of this meeting the Council, we read in its minutes, resolved itself into a committee "to consider the present state and prospects of the Corporation;" but no entry of the proceedings is recorded, and the *Journal* of April 11, mentioning the fact, adds that "as the meeting was strictly private, we cannot tell what was done." It is not improbable, however, that the discussion had reference to a project for settling the matter by friendly arrangement, for we find, from newspaper paragraphs, that some persons in London interested themselves in trying to bring about an arrangement. It was, however, rejected by both parties, and came to nothing. The position of the Council financially is illustrated by a report presented at the meeting of the 7th of April. Mr. Knight, the treasurer, on presenting his accounts, showed that the receipts consisted of two drafts on the Treasury—advances made on account of the borough sessions—amounting to £2,148; of which over £2,000 had been spent, leaving a balance of about £145 in hand. The difficulty of the position was now increased by the resignation of Mr. William Redfern, the Town Clerk, on account of business engagements; and at the next meeting, May 5, his place was filled by the election of Mr. Solomon Bray. It is not surprising to find that the difficulties of the Corporation led to some diminution of interest in their work on the part of the members of the Council. At the meeting held on June 2,

Mr. Cutler complained that the Council was kept waiting "on many occasions half an hour, or three quarters of an hour, and sometimes an hour, before they could make a quorum," which showed that little more than one third of the Council attended. It was consequently ordered that a return of attendances for the year should be made out. A long discussion took place at the same meeting as to the appointment of borough magistrates. Those who were in the Commission had, by resignation or other causes, been reduced to nine, and the Mayor (Mr. Muntz) reported that he had received an intimation from the Home Office that "a recommendation from the Council would be acceptable." Opinion was much divided on this question. Some members were in favour of declining to do anything, on account of the difficulties of the Charter, some desired the appointment of a stipendiary magistrate, but ultimately a committee was appointed to draw up a new list; and, at a later period of the year, they presented a report recommending the appointment of several persons, including Mr. Whateley and other Conservatives, but the latter refused to serve.

CHAP. XI.
1840.
Nomination of Borough Justices.

Towards the end of June there was a gleam of hope, arising from a report that the judges had decided to pronounce in favour of the validity of the Manchester Charter, disputed in the case of "Rutter v. Chapman," and that the Government intended to bring in a bill to vest the police of Birmingham, Manchester, and Bolton in the Town Councils of those boroughs. The Birmingham

A Gleam of Hope.

CHAP. XI.
1840.
Another Postponemet.

Conservatives promptly met this intimation by presenting a petition to the House of Lords, praying that the administration of the Birmingham police might be permanently placed in the hands of the Government— a movement which the *Journal* of July 4 bluntly characterises as indicating "an utter and absolute destitution of every honest and neighbour-like feeling." The hope of a settlement, however, proved delusive. The decision in the Manchester case was to have been given at the beginning of July, but when a question was asked about it, the reply of the judges was that it must stand over until next term—that is, until November at the earliest; and consequently, at the Birmingham Council meeting on the 7th of July, the Mayor had the mortification of announcing that the long-pending question of the validity of the Charter was again indefinitely postponed.

The Quarter Sessions suspended.

A more serious blow than mere postponement now fell upon the Corporation. Owing to the delays in settling the validity of the Charter, the course of justice was suspended. The Council, as we have seen, found itself unable to levy rates while the Charter continued in dispute, and the expenses of the quarter sessions were consequently defrayed by advances from the Government. These advances were suddenly stopped, and the result was that the sessions could no longer be held. At the sitting of his Court on the 17th of July (1840) Mr. M. D. Hill, the Recorder, made an announcement to this effect. "Owing," he said, "to a difficulty which had arisen in the construction of the charters given by the Queen to the boroughs of Manchester, Birmingham, and other places, much doubt and difficulty had been thrown upon the validity of these documents; and particular difficulty had arisen in raising funds to defray the expenses of their local government. It was hoped that certain legal points, which were before the Court of Exchequer Chamber for decision, would by the decision of that Court have been put at rest, and so much light thrown upon the subject as would have led to a permanent settlement of the question. But the decision would not be given until the commencement of next term. During the period that this question was being considered, the Lords of the Treasury had made several advances of money to pay the expense of the sessions held in this borough. An advance was made the day before, with an intimation that it was the last money that would be given for that purpose. There would be thus no funds in Birmingham to hold the sessions; and it would be the duty of the magistrates to commit, henceforth, not to Birmingham sessions, but to Warwick [the county sessions]. For this reason he did not anticipate a continuance of the advantage of these sessions. The business which was usually transacted at them would be done at Warwick."

The feeling excited amongst the members of the Corporation, and the burgesses generally, by this announcement may be inferred the following comments in the *Birmingham Journal* of July 18 :—

CHAP. XI.
1840.
The Quarter Sessions suspended.

"The Recorder attributes this most lame and impotent conclusion to the discussions on the validity of the Charter, but this is only the remote and secondary cause. Her Majesty's Ministers have supplied, we believe without exception, the money required for the sessions expenses, from that fund which is ordinarily devoted to the defraying of criminal prosecutions. It would have required a thousand pounds, or thereabouts, to carry on their begun work till the November term arrived, when the judges must have decided one way or the other—and Ministers could not or would not raise it. They could advance ten thousand pounds for the purpose of establishing an odious police force in the borough—as repugnant to the Constitution of England as it was insulting to the men of Birmingham. They could do this at the bidding of Sir Robert Peel and a clique of Tories; but when the question was the maintenance of public justice by a cheap, efficient, and local court—and their own court—they were afraid to go to Parliament for a paltry thousand pounds! We have heard that instructions have been sent to the borough magistrates to examine and remand, but not to commit prisoners, unless their warrant be backed by a county justice! The Queen's warrant, in the making of which Lord John Russell showed so much judgment and liberality, is but a bit of calf's skin after all. We do not know whether the magistrates will be content to perform their prescribed task of journeyman justice, or whether they will leave Lord Normanby to supply their place with another batch. The Tories are 'up' most particularly; and they have a right to be so."

Authority of the Magistrates limited.

With the suspension of the Sessions, the Government also practically suspended the functions of the borough magistrates. But a few weeks earlier the Home Secretary (Lord Normanby) had informed the Mayor that a recommendation from the Town Council as to the appointment of new magistrates would be "acceptable." He now threw most uncalled-for discredit upon the authority of the justices actually appointed, by warning them not to act in the committals of prisoners without at least the concurrence of county justices sitting for the Birmingham division. This warning was conveyed in an intimation, or rather a direction, from the Home Office, as to the committals of prisoners, communicated by Lord Normanby to the Mayor, and also to Mr. Burgess, the Commissioner of Police appointed under the Birmingham Police Act. The letter, dated July 17th, 1840, informed the Police Commissioner that "until the judgment of the Court of Queen's Bench is given as to the validity of the Charter, it will be proper that commitments for offences within the borough should be by county magistrates to the county gaol, for trial at the county sessions or assizes, and that no commitment should be for the borough sessions;" and the Commissioner of Police was directed to confer with the Mayor, and to arrange for the necessary attendance of county justices at the Public Office. Accordingly Mr. Burgess, the Commissioner, summoned a meeting of the Mayor and the county justices acting for the Birmingham division. Twelve of the latter attended. The Mayor (Mr. P. H. Muntz), on being asked what the borough justices intended to do, replied that he had written to remonstrate with Lord Normanby, and should wait for a reply. Then the county justices discussed their course, and resolved that no change need be made until after the assizes, and that they would then comply with the direction of the Home Office. The borough magistrates, acting with a due sense of self-respect, at once ceased their attendance at the

Police Office. The feeling of the town, and especially of the advocates of the Charter, may be inferred from the following comments in the *Journal* of July 25 :—

"The borough sessions are gone. Justice is once more driven from our doors. The act is the act of Ministers; but Ministers in this, as in many other acts, are but the instruments of a Tory faction. The Tory faction it was that withstood the granting of the Charter in the first instance; it was the Tory faction that pronounced the men of Birmingham incapable and unworthy of managing the business of their own town; it was the Tory faction that forced upon them a centralised police, with its irresponsible Commissioner; it was the Tory faction that added thirty per cent. to the rates for upholding that police; it is the Tory faction that, by its hostility to local and responsible government, has deprived the inhabitants of local justice. Every man that is called from his shop or his warehouse to Warwick, as juror, witness, or party, will have to thank the Tory faction for the losses, expenses, and labour to which the journey may subject him."

At the same time the writer upheld the authority of the borough justices—if they chose to exercise it—against the instructions issued by Lord Normanby from the Home Office :—

"The borough magistrates, by the law of the land, are justices of the peace in that district of the county of Warwick which is included within the boundaries of the borough of Birmingham; and in that district their power and authority are as active and ample as are the power and authority of any magistrates in the kingdom. The borough magistrates, in respect to offences charged as committed in Birmingham, can hear and adjudicate in cases of summary jurisdiction, and commit, if not of summary jurisdiction, to the county gaol, which, be it always remembered, is the gaol, not for one part of the county, but for all parts of the county having no gaols of their own. They have done so while the borough sessions were in activity, they may do so while they are in suspension; and let the keeper of the county gaol refuse to receive a prisoner under their commitment, if he dare. Lord Normanby may advise her Majesty to strike any portion of the present magistrates from the borough roll. He may advise her to revoke the borough commission altogether. But while these magistrates remain on the commission, Lord Normanby can neither increase, diminish, nor in any way modify their powers."

This view of the authority of the magistrates was supported by subsequent proceedings in Parliament. Either influenced by the private representations made to them, or ashamed of their own weakness in allowing the administration of justice to be stopped in Birmingham, Ministers brought in a bill "to enable the Treasury to advance money to the Corporation of Birmingham to carry on the administration of justice and the police of that town, until the question now pending as to the validity of the Charter should be decided." On this notice being given by Mr. Fox Maule, secretary to the Treasury, Sir Robert Peel asked on what particular ground the sessions had been suspended in Birmingham, seeing that other sessions had been held since the validity of the Charter had been disputed. To this Mr. Maule (under secretary for the Home Department) replied "that the suspension had not been caused by any doubt as to the power of the magistrates to hold them, but from a want of funds"—thus, on the part of one department of the Government, maintaining the validity of the sessions, and the committing power of the magistrates, which had just previously been contravened by another department, through Lord Normanby's letter from the Home Office! On the following day (July 30) the bill was brought in and read a first time, on the 31st it was read a second time, and on the following Wednesday, August 5, it was read a third time and passed—a clause having been previously inserted in Committee, by Sir John Eardley Wilmot, chairman of the Warwickshire County Sessions, obliging the Borough to pay by a rate, the sums (about £8,000) demanded by the county justices for the maintenance of borough prisoners at Warwick. When the bill reached the House of Lords its fate was very soon decided. On the 7th of August Lord Normanby moved the second reading, and in doing so explained that the bill "left the question of the legality of the Charter wholly untouched." The Earl of Warwick, a consistent and persistent adversary of the Birmingham Charter, moved that the bill be read a second time that day three months. He gave the following reasons for this course:—

"From the length of time the judges had taken for their decision, there must be great doubt as to the legality of the Charter; but his belief was that their decision would be against it. When the Government discovered the doubt, they ought to have stopped their proceedings, and left the administration of justice in the same hands it was in before. The quarter sessions of Birmingham were now held and paid for by funds provided out of the Treasury. The prisoners were sent over first from Birmingham to Warwick goal, then back to Birmingham to be tried, and afterwards were returned to Warwick to be imprisoned. Now, let the Charter turn out how it might, that could not be altered, as there was no goal in Birmingham. That town had hitherto been without a

Corporation, and might it not have gone on in the same way for another year? The Government might now restore matters to the former system, but having got into this danger they called on Parliament to sanction their proceedings. Suppose the Charter was declared illegal? He would ask, in that case, whether the prisoners who had been convicted under the Charter were legally convicted?"

Lord Normanby made a weak reply, which virtually gave up the case. "At first (he said) he thought it would be better if there were no sessions; but the matter had now been going on for nearly two years, and he did not know how they could do without the bill." Lord Wharncliffe doubted if there ever had been any legal quarter sessions in Birmingham. "He believed that every man tried there had been illegally convicted." Lord Calthorpe said it "would be difficult to imagine any circumstances less favourable than those under which it was proposed to admit Birmingham to the functions of a Corporation, especially as regarded the administration of justice. He thought that such an important town ought to have a Corporation, but the present bill would not effect that object; it would give not the reality but the fiction of a Corporation. It was nothing but a bill of indemnity, and he objected to such bills under such circumstances." The bill was then rejected, without a division.

The rejection of the bill afforded much satisfaction to the Conservative party in Birmingham, and to the opponents of the Ministry, who saw in it a defeat for the Government. The *Times*, for example, insisted that the measure was intended as an act of indemnity for Ministers, to protect them from the consequences of having illegally, and without the consent of Parliament, advanced public money for local purposes; and the same journal further alleged that the bill "affords ample illustration of the readiness of the present Government to yield to the dictation of their Radical supporters, however just the course from which those supporters seek to divert them." In fact, however, the Government and the Radicals—so far as Birmingham was concerned—were then, and had for a long time been, in a condition certainly of mutual dislike, and almost of open hostility. The political movements at that period encouraged in Birmingham were of a kind distinctly adverse to the policy of the Government, for, while the latter accepted Lord John Russell's doctrine of "finality" in Parliamentary reform, the Birmingham Radicals were most earnestly pressing for large and immediate advances. As to the object of the particular bill, it was absolutely clear. The Government desired merely that the local administration of justice, once begun under the Quarter Sessions charter, should not cease, and therefore they sought to give the town the means of legally paying the cost of it. There was a second and also important purpose in the bill—namely, to enable Birmingham legally to pay to the county of Warwick the amount expended from the county funds for the maintenance of Birmingham prisoners. By the rejection of the measure this object was defeated:

indeed, Lord Warwick and the Conservatives who supported him inflicted a serious wrong upon the county in their eagerness to discredit and embarrass local government in Birmingham, for they prevented the payment of the money due to the county, by refusing Birmingham the power to levy a rate for the purpose of paying it. The two sides of the question were very clearly put in the following comparison : *

> "The noble head of the county [Lord Warwick was Lord Lieutenant] has, in consenting to officiate as the tool of a few rabid local Tories, while attempting to deal a formidable stroke at the Birmingham Charter, contrived to bestow a hearty thwack on his own head. The results, had the bill been allowed to pass in peace and quietness, would have been—
>
> "1. The continuance to the population (Whig, Tory, and Radical) of the borough of all those seen, felt, and appreciated advantages of cheap and easy justice, that they have enjoyed for the last fifteen months—purchase, say £500.
>
> "2. The payment of the advances made by the Government, by a rate on the borough—say £5,000.
>
> "3. The payment of the expenses of the county for the keeping of the borough prisoners for the last fifteen months, also by a rate on the borough—say £5,000.
>
> "4. The Charter neither shaken, nor corroborated, nor touched.
>
> "The results of the bill being rejected are these—
>
> "1. The discontinuance to the population (Whig, Tory, and Radical) of the advantages of cheap and speedy justice.

Birmingham Journal, August 15, 1840.

The restoration of all the inconveniences of the old system to plaintiffs, defendants, and witnesses—to every one, save jurors.

"2. A receipt in full for the whole of the Government advances.

"3. A receipt in full for the borough share of the county expenses.

"4. The Charter neither shaken, nor corroborated, nor touched."

Discussion at Warwick Quarter Sessions.

The justice of this view was illustrated by a discussion at the Warwick Quarter Sessions (October 20, 1840), when Sir Eardley Wilmot, M.P., the Chairman (himself a Conservative), lamented the failure of the bill. The effect of its rejection, he said, was that it did not in any way affect the case of the Birmingham Charter, but that it prevented the county from recovering any of the money expended on behalf of Birmingham. Some of the county magistrates were for taking strong measures. Mr. Bracebridge had given notice of a motion to include Birmingham in the county rate, and this was moved at the Sessions. It was opposed by Mr. Richard Spooner, who showed the justices that while, by including Birmingham, they would make their own rate illegal, they had no power to raise any rate in the borough of Birmingham. Lord Lifford thereupon proposed that the county justices should refuse to receive Birmingham prisoners at the county gaol. Again Mr. Spooner interfered to set his angry colleagues right, by showing them that the reception of prisoners lay, not with the justices, but with the sheriff. One thing, however, the Quarter Sessions did. They quashed two convictions made

Mr. R. Spooner defends Birmingham.

at the Birmingham Petty Sessions, on the ground that one of the convicting justices, Mr. Muntz, not being a county justice, had no jurisdiction to commit to the "House of Correction" at Warwick. The counsel for the appellants argued that "the conviction was informal, because it was a conviction by one borough and one county justice. He admitted the concurrent jurisdiction of the magistrates, and also that they had power to convict; and had they committed to 'the common gaol of the county,' or had two county justices committed to the House of Correction, the question would not have arisen." The Court allowed this objection, quashed the convictions, and set the prisoners free. On the 23rd of October the Borough Sessions were held—the Recorder explaining that he was compelled to hold four sessions yearly, even though there should be no business to transact. At the present sessions he had no prisoners to try, for they had all been committed to Warwick, there being no funds to pay the costs of trying them in Birmingham, and the borough having no power to raise such funds; but he was able to try appeals, orders, and prosecutions the expenses of which were not defrayed by the public, and the sessions must still be held for these purposes. A libel case was accordingly brought before the Court, and some poor law appeal cases were dealt with.

Another difficulty of a vexatious kind arose in connection with the disputed authority of the borough magistrates—a conflict between the county and borough justices as to the appointment of overseers of the poor. There were two contests of this kind. One of them occurred on the 25th of March, 1840, when the county justices appointed one set of overseers, and the borough justices another set—the former list being exclusively Conservative. The county list was recognised by the Board of Overseers, though, according to the *Journal*, some of the borough list went to the parish offices to qualify, on which they were told by the clerk that "he had his full complement, and would take no more." So, adds the writer, "the Tories have taken possession, and the Radicals, in the humbled spirit that ill luck naturally produces, have sneaked contentedly and quietly out of the way." In parish affairs, indeed, the Liberals do not seem to have had much chance. If they occupied the Town Council exclusively, the Tories had the Street Commissioners' body and the Board of Guardians pretty nearly to themselves. For example, the election of Guardians for the parish of Birmingham, in April, 1840, ended in the return of 99 Conservatives and Churchmen, 6 Whigs, and 3 Radicals. It could scarcely be wondered at, therefore, that an assembly so distinctly of one colour desired to keep the Board of Overseers in its own hands, and this explains why there was a conflict between the two lists, as above described. The contest as to the Overseers was renewed on the 3rd of October, 1840, when the other half of the Board had to be appointed. Two lists were again presented to the magistrates, both county and borough justices being present. Mr. George Whateley, who attended on behalf of the Overseers, candidly explained that they did not recognise the authority of the borough magistrates to appoint, or even to join with the county justices in the appointment. The Rev. Riland Bedford, as a county justice, announced that he would have nothing to do with the borough bench. Mr. J. F. Ledsam and Mr. Charles Shaw, two other county justices, made a similar statement. The borough justices present, Mr. William Scholefield and Dr. Birt Davies, insisted on their right, and an unseemly wrangle occurred. Ultimately, the county justices appointed one set of overseers, and the borough justices another. The former triumphed, however, for Mr. Whateley—pointing to the Borough selection—advised the Clerk to the Guardians "not to touch *that* list;" and accordingly it was left on the table—mere waste paper.

CHAPTER XII.

THE CHARTER ENFORCED AND CONFIRMED.

<small>Chap. XII.
1840.
Resolution to enforce the Charter.</small>

These contests and insults naturally exasperated the Liberal party, and inspired the members of the Town Council with a disposition to do something to vindicate their position and to assert their authority. This feeling received expression at the Council meeting on the 9th of November, 1840, when Mr. P. H. Muntz was unanimously re-elected Mayor. In accepting office, Mr. Muntz announced that he intended to act with vigour in regard to the business of enforcing the Charter. "Feeling convinced," he said, "of the legality of the Charter, and having no doubt as to the powers which the Corporation possessed, he did not intend to allow matters to go on as they had done, even should the judges again defer their decision in the Manchester case. With the sanction of the Council, he proposed to carry out the provisions of the Municipal Act." This declaration was received with loud and long-continued cheers by the Council; and the *Journal*, in explaining the Mayor's proposed course, declared that he meant to levy and enforce a borough rate without delay. "We observe," said the writer, "that the Tories tell the Mayor and Council that they may go on, and burn their fingers. The risk of finger-burning is not a one-handed one. If the Mayor issue his precept, the Overseers may refuse to obey. If the Mayor distrain, the Overseers may replevin. If the Mayor prosecute, the Overseers may defend. Thus far all is equal. But follow out the consequences of the suit. Suppose the Mayor to win? The Overseers must pay the costs of the suit. Is that all? The least part of it. They must pay the levy as well. They can only be saved harmless by a rate imposed during their year of office. If, therefore, they lose, as they certainly will, the loss to them will be some nine thousand pounds, at least. If the Mayor should lose his suit, which he certainly will not, the loss to the Council will not exceed one thousand. The risk of loss to the twelve Overseers will be £750 each; the risk of loss to the sixty-four Councillors will be £15 each."

As was expected, the judges did defer their decision in the Manchester case. They fixed the 14th of December for the re-arguing of the points involved in it, and after argument, they reserved their decision. The Birmingham Council, however, determined to wait no longer. At the meeting of the 1st of December, 1840, the Mayor brought forward the subject of making a borough rate, and stated that he had the advice of eminent counsel in favour of doing so. It would, he said, be "infinitely better for all parties, Whig, Tory, or Radical," to get the question settled on its own merits, his conviction being that the Birmingham Charter was good, whatever that of Manchester might be. There was much discussion as to this proposal, some of the Councillors being timid, others cautious of incurring expense, and one or two hostile to proceeding. One of them, however—Mr. Rodway—spoke out manfully. He said he was "tired of being fooled in that room and out of it. He was tired of coming there and going away without doing anything. He said plainly that at present they met as fools and went away as fools. If they did not, at once and in earnest, commence business, if they did not do that for which they were incorporated, if they did not carry out the Charter, they might as well stay at home." This courageous and common-sense view prevailed, and, with one dissentient (Mr. Hadley), the Council resolved to make a borough rate, and so to bring the validity of the Charter to a practical test. At the Council meeting on January 5, 1841, the Overseers' returns, in obedience to the Mayor's precept, were received, the rateable value of the parishes within the borough being reported as follows:—

Birmingham	£412,922
Edgbaston	31,971
Aston	80,020
Total rateable value	£524,913

On these returns, at the meeting on February 2, 1841, a borough rate of £6,700 was ordered to be "levied, collected, and enforced in due course of law"—the share to be paid by the parish of Birmingham being fixed at £5,161 10s. 6d.; that of Edgbaston at £399 12s. 6d.; and that of Aston at £1,112 15s. The Birmingham Overseers took counsel's opinion as to their power to resist the making of the rate, the counsel selected being Sir Frederick Pollock; and at a meeting of Guardians on the 17th of March, 1841, it was announced that Sir F. Pollock had advised that the Overseers could not legally resist the rate, and that they had consequently decided to pay it; and this resolution was confirmed by a meeting of the Guardians on May 18. As an earnest of this good disposition, it may be noted that on the 25th of March three Liberals were nominated as Overseers—a step (the *Journal* observes) "which has additional value because it has been made by the Conservatives, unprompted and unsolicited, the Reformers having taken no part in it."

Overseers consent to pay it.

The Government now made an effort to settle the difficulties of the new boroughs created under the Municipal Corporations Act. They introduced two bills for this purpose. One of them, called the Criminal Justice Bill, proposed to regulate the administration of justice in Manchester, Bolton, and Birmingham; it legalised the Quarter Sessions, and gave powers for the erection of gaols, and other purposes. The bill did not, however, contain any clause confirming the charters. This measure was approved by the Town Council, so far as the Government

Further Government Measures.

proposals went, but strong opposition was offered to certain clauses introduced by Sir C. Douglas, the member for Warwick, which proposed to give compensation to county coroners and other officers displaced under the new charters. These clauses were rejected in Committee of the House of Commons, and ultimately the bill itself was dropped. The other measure was a Bill "for the Drainage and Improvement of certain Boroughs," and this also affected the boroughs whose charters were disputed. It proposed to authorise the Town Councils to make provision for the drainage and general improvement of their respective towns, and thus it would have conferred upon the Town Council of Birmingham powers equal to those possessed by the Commissioners of the Street Acts, at least in those parts of the borough which were beyond the Commissioners' jurisdiction. As may be supposed, the Town Council heartily supported this bill; but it was very strongly opposed by the Commissioners, who saw their privilege and authority in danger of being transferred from a self-elected to a representative body. They applied to Lord Lyndhurst to take up their case, and Lord Lyndhurst, always ready to do an injury to the Radical Corporation of Birmingham, willingly consented. When the bill reached the House of Lords, and went into Committee, he moved an amendment, "that nothing in the Act should extend to the borough of Birmingham;" though he explained that if the Town Council could be excluded, he should be willing to confer the powers of the measure upon the Street Commissioners. He gave the following reasons for his opposition :—

"The Commissioners," he said, "were men of great respectability, and had exercised the powers with which they were entrusted to the satisfaction of the town. What substitute was to be made for these Commissioners? Why, the Town Council, the most violent and Radical body in the borough, whose conduct had been from the first in strict conformity with its original creation. What was the first act of the Town Council after their election? They had to select a gentleman to fill an office of great trust and responsibility—an office requiring for the performance of its functions a person of considerable legal attainments [the Registrarship of the Mayor's Court]; and whom did the Radical Town Council appoint to that situation? Why a Radical editor of a Radical newspaper of the town. He asked if they would supersede these Commissioners, who had so satisfactorily performed their duties, and substitute in their stead the Town Council of the borough, composed, as it was, of individuals influenced by extreme Radical opinions." The Government made an extremely feeble defence of their measure. They were in a minority in the House of Lords, they did not care much for Birmingham, which distrusted them politically, and so they allowed Lord Lyndhurst to prevail. Nobody thought even of saying that Radical opinions were no hindrance to the management of drainage, or that a popularly elected Liberal might lay out a street or make a sewer quite as well as a self-appointed Conservative. Finally, Lord Lyndhurst's amendment was adopted without a division, Birmingham

CHAP. XII.
1841.

was struck out of the bill, so far as the Town Council was concerned, and on the third reading the powers proposed to be conferred upon the Town Council were conferred upon the Commissioners of the Street Act; and thus the much-needed improvement of the town was delayed for another ten years, for nothing was practically done in this direction until the complete absorption of local governing powers by the Town Council in the Improvement Act of 1851. Well might the Liberals complain of their friends in the Ministry. Well might their newspaper, the *Journal*, exclaim, with reference to the House of Lords—"The Lords do well to talk of political partisanship. If any Radical Council in the kingdom were to exhibit such a specimen of political partisanship as the Lords did on Tuesday, they would deserve to be whipped at the cart's tail from John o' Groat's to Penzance." The further progress of the measures was stopped by the defeat of Ministers on the free trade question, and the dissolution of Parliament.

Financial Movements.

The general election for a time withdrew attention from the affairs of the Corporation; and it was not until September that the Town Council showed any signs of activity. On the 7th of that month a meeting of considerable interest was held. A levy of £5,800 was ordered for the expenses of the half-year ending December 31, 1841, and the Finance Committee recommended the payment of various amounts, including £658 4s. 1d. "the costs of the Charter of Incorporation."

The Mayor reported that since the incorporation of the borough only £3,500 had been spent, and as no county rate had been levied for three years, £19,000 had thus been saved by the incorporation. At the same meeting it was stated that the Government police imposed upon the town had cost £17,000 a year, involving the levying of a shilling police rate.

A curious incident occurred at the meeting of the Council on the 5th of October. It was proposed (in his absence) to make a grant, by way of salary, to Mr. W. Scholefield, for expenses incurred by him on behalf of the Corporation. The motion was opposed, but was ultimately carried, with only two dissentients. At the next meeting, however, on the 20th of October, a letter was read from Mr. Scholefield, declining to receive the allowance; and thus the question of a salary for the Mayor was practically decided in the negative.

The year 1842 opened with new difficulties for the Corporation. The county justices resolved to attempt the levying of a county rate in Birmingham, and served notice to this effect upon the Overseers. The latter body took a legal opinion from Sir F. Pollock and Mr. W. Whateley, and resolved, in consequence of it, to refuse to levy the rate, but to bring the order of the justices before the Court of Queen's Bench to have it quashed, on the ground that, as a borough having a separate Court of Quarter Sessions, Birmingham was not

CHAP. XII.
1842.

liable to the county rate. At the same time the keeper of the county gaol, acting under instructions from the justices, informed the Council that he would not allow the prisoners detained at Warwick to be brought to Birmingham for trial at the Quarter Sessions "until the expenses of their removal had been paid," and the Council was consequently obliged to pay the demand. Application was made to the sheriff for some reduction of the terms, which were thought excessive. Here, again, the Council met with a rebuff, for the under-sheriff replied that "the sheriff cannot part with the custody of the prisoners until they are delivered by due course of law, and therefore they cannot be confided to any other but the county gaoler, and that he cannot take them for less than he does."

State of the Town: Serious Distress.

The state of the town at this time was very serious. Owing to the operation of the Corn Laws trade had fallen off, wages were greatly depressed, and extensive distress prevailed among the artisan and the trading population. Out of 40,000 houses returned in the borough at the census of 1841, not less than 4,000 were void at the beginning of 1842, and these included many in the principal streets as well as in the poorer quarters of the town. The rates were enormously heavy for a period of such distress—the total rating amounting to 8s. 9d. in the pound. So severe were the privations of the working classes that the Rev. Timothy East, speaking at an anti-corn law meeting, said that he had been into all the neighbouring villages, and had entered nearly every cottage; but that in scarcely one of them had he found any person who could tell him the price of meat per pound: this article of food having literally fallen out of the dietary of the poor. While this condition of things existed in regard to the material state of the people, the manifestation of party spirit against the Corporation grew still more intense. Petitions were presented by some of the local bodies, charging the Council with being the cause of the distress, by its alleged increasing rates, and praying for the abolition of the Corporation. "There were," said Mr. P. H. Muntz at a meeting of the Council, "persons infamous enough and disgraceful enough to put forth such statements, and to allege that all the misery and distress of the town was to be attributed to the Corporation. He was perfectly astonished how any person pretending to the name of man, let alone gentleman, could make such misrepresentations; or how it was possible for respectable men, knowing such statements to be utterly false, could sign that petition" —the fact being, as the speaker showed, that from its establishment until 1842 the Corporation had expended only £6,840, and that of this amount only £3,840 had been raised by rates. Such corrections, however, were unavailing to check the opposition raised against municipal institutions. The Conservatives still prosecuted their efforts to get rid of or to embarrass the Corporation; the question of its legality was raised by the challenge of the Coronership, and the county justices insisted on proceeding with their endeavours to levy

CHAP. XII.
1842.
Litigation in the Queen's Bench.

a county rate. It was agreed that this claim should be embodied in a special case to be laid before the Queen's Bench. The Council desired to be heard on the matter, and on their behalf Mr. Hill, the recorder, applied to the Court, but he was refused a hearing, the Court holding that the question was one between the justices and the overseers of the parish of Birmingham alone. The case—that of "The Queen *v.* Boucher and another" [Mr. Boucher being one of the overseers]—was argued in the Court of Queen's Bench on the 23rd of June, before Lord Denman, and Justices Patteson, Williams, and Coleridge: Mr. Mellor (now Justice Mellor) appearing for the county, and Mr. Whateley for the overseers. The contention for the county was that the Charter was invalid, that the grant of Quarter Sessions had not been legally made, because there was no gaol in Birmingham; that the Recorder had therefore no right to try prisoners, or to commit them to the county gaol; and that, consequently, the county was not deprived of its right to levy a rate within the borough. The result of the hearing was that the Court declined to enter into the questions thus raised, and quashed the county rate ordered by the justices. In the course of his judgment Lord Denman said:—

Lord Denman's Judgment: the Rate declared illegal.

"The borough of Birmingham, as duly incorporated, does exist in fact. The same observation applies as to the second Charter of the Queen, and the holding of Courts of Quarter Sessions thereunder. The validity of the first Charter, and of the incorporation by virtue of it, and the legality of the Quarter Sessions under the second Charter is incidentally, and so only, impeached. No person connected with the borough itself complains of that incorporation, or of the holding of the Quarter Sessions as being illegal. The illegality of the Charter is, for the purpose of assessing the borough, assumed—whereas another and more formal method of questioning their legality is open. It is competent by writ of *scire facias* to ascertain whether the grant of a separate Court of Quarter Sessions be invalid or not; and, in the absence of such a proceeding, we think we are not called upon to pronounce any opinion on the effect of this objection, but that the state of things as we find them must be sustained, and that the order of Sessions, for that reason only, cannot be supported."

This difficulty, consequently, was got rid of, and another arrangement was made with the county justices for the reception and maintenance of prisoners; though the justices followed up this arrangement by presenting a memorial to the Treasury, claiming £20,000 as due to them for the maintenance of Birmingham prisoners, and asking that an Act of Parliament might be passed to enable them to get it—an appeal which, as a matter of course, was vigorously and successfully resisted by the Town Council. But though the justices were silenced for a time, the other adversaries of the Corporation continued active efforts at opposition. Mr. Whateley, for example, who claimed the office of Coroner, maintained his application for a writ of *quo warranto*, calling upon Dr. Davies to show by what right he exercised the duties of Coroner in the borough; and in his pleas Mr. Whateley averred that the Charter was illegally granted, and that the letters patent conferring it "were obtained by fraud, covin, and misrepresentation." The character of the Council being thus assailed, that body undertook the

CHAP. XII.
1842.

Negotiations on the Police Act.

defence of its Coroner, and prepared to defend the Charter at all risks and against all comers. Happily, however, it became unnecessary to enter upon this litigation, for the difficulties of the Corporation were now beginning to draw towards their close. The Police Act was to expire at the end of the session of 1842. A private promise had been received from the late Government (Lord Melbourne's) that it should not be renewed. The new Government (Sir Robert Peel's) were of course not in any way bound by this engagement, and they introduced a bill to continue the Act until the end of 1843. The Council instantly protested, and so did the Conservative party: the latter sending a deputation to the Government to allege that if the Corporation were allowed to have the control of the police "there would be no safety for life or fortune in the town." The Council, on their part, sent up a deputation to deny and to disprove this most unfounded and monstrous allegation; the fact being that Birmingham was remarkable for the orderly and peaceful character of its population, and its freedom from serious crime. This deputation saw Sir James Graham, who was then Home Secretary, and their representations prevailed; it was agreed that the Police Act (which affected Birmingham, Manchester, and Bolton) should not be prolonged. The Government kept its promise. A discontinuance bill was introduced; and on the 5th of August, the Parliamentary Committee of the Corporation were enabled to make the following satisfactory report to the Town Council:—

"Your Committee have the highest satisfaction in reporting to the Council that the Police Bill, as altered and amended by Her Majesty's Government, has passed the House of Commons, and is in progress in the House of Lords, under which the Police Acts will expire on the 1st day of October next, when the government of the police of this borough will fall into the hands of this Council. Your Committee remind the Council that a pledge has been given to Government that the Council will take measures for the continuance of an efficient police force, so that, at the expiration of the existing Act, there shall be no interval without an ample and sufficient police, that the public peace and good order of the borough may not be endangered; and suggest that the Council will, at the earliest opportunity, appoint a Watch Committee, and take all necessary steps for managing and providing for the force." The report then proceeded to make another announcement, of the greatest interest and importance to the borough—namely, that the Government had consented to put an end to all difficulties respecting the Charter of Incorporation, by introducing a bill to confirm the Charters granted under the Municipal Corporations Act, and to make compensation to former county officers entitled to such relief—thus disposing of the litigation which had arisen with reference to the office of Coroner. Finally, the report congratulates the Council "on the removal of the difficulties which have hitherto impeded its proceedings, and trusts that by prudence and true economy the

Council will in future be able so to provide for the good order and government of this important borough as to ensure the approval of their constituents and of all classes of the community."

The Charter Confirmation Bill.

These statements were confirmed by Sir James Graham in the House of Commons, on the committal of a bill introduced by Sir C. Douglas, member for Warwick, to give compensation to the county officers displaced in the borough of Birmingham. On the Government engaging to bring in a general bill, Sir C. Douglas withdrew his measure. The officers whom he proposed to compensate were Mr. J. W. Whateley, coroner; Mr. W. O. Hunt, clerk of the peace; and Messrs. W. Spurrier, H. M. Griffiths, and W. H. Gem, magistrates' clerks for the Birmingham division of the Hundred of Hemlingford; all of whom had been displaced by the borough officials, and who, naturally enough, desired to obtain compensation for their loss of emoluments. Mr. Spurrier seems to have been specially energetic in the presentation of petitions and the "lobbying" of Members of Parliament. In one of his petitions he dwells upon his age, his long service (fifty years), and his position as compared with Mr. Gem, who "was more fortunate, since he was appointed a clerk to the borough justices." This petition draws from the *Journal* a sarcastic remark, which probably represented the general feeling: "The argument from the age of the petitioner is a powerful one. It is a serious thing for a gentleman of seventy-three years, and not possessed of more than a couple of hundred thousand pounds, to be deprived of a clerkship of three hundred a year."

The Charters Confirmation Bill (a copy of which is given in the Appendix to this volume) was brought in by Sir James Graham on Thursday, August 4, and was read a first and second time on that day. It was committed on the Saturday following, read a third time on Monday, and, together with the Police Bill, was at once sent up to the House of Lords, where both measures were passed, though not without discussion; the Earl of Wilton, on behalf of the Birmingham Conservatives, having opposed the Police Bill; and Lord Brougham—the former advocate of the Corporation—having, at the same instigation, undertaken to oppose the Charters Confirmation Bill. For this purpose, and to supply him with the materials for his case, Lord Brougham was furnished with a petition from Birmingham; the late Mr. Richard Spooner, and other Conservatives, having gone up to induce him to present and advocate it. Unfortunately for them, Lord Brougham muddled the business. After the Charters Bill had been passed, he appeared in the House of Lords with the petition. The transaction was comical. "He apologised (says a report of the proceedings) to the House and the petitioners for not having presented the petition, in consequence of its having accidentally fallen aside. 'As' (said his lordship—thrusting the petition with some others into the clerk's hands) 'the bill is now passed, it is

CHAP. XII.
1842.
Royal Assent to the Bill.

unnecessary to say anything about the matter.'" On Friday, August 12, the Police Bill and the Charters Confirmation Bill received the Royal assent; and thus the long and bitter contest which had existed in Birmingham to invalidate the Charter came to an end.

Liberal Rejoicings.

The Liberals, as a matter of course, were jubilant at this conclusion of their troubles. Their feeling was promptly and vigorously expressed by their newspaper. In the *Journal* of August 6, we read:—

"The object, the hope, the trust of the more zealous of our local Tories was that the advent of Sir Robert Peel would be the signal for the destruction of the Corporation of Birmingham. We told them that their desires, like their understandings, would prove addle. We entreated them to turn from the error of their ways, with all gentleness and earnestness of entreaty; but they would not listen. They would go on, mud and mire to the contrary notwithstanding; and well muddled and most abundantly mired they are. What is the present position of the institution which these destructive heroes were so fondly bent on levelling?

Summary of Gains.

"1st. The Charter is confirmed by a bill introduced by the Home Secretary of Sir Robert Peel's Administration.

"2nd. The Police Force of the town is committed to the guidance of the Town Council, by a bill introduced by the same right honourable gentleman.

"3rd. The power of building a prison and court is conferred on the same body by a bill introduced by the same high authority.

"Everything we wished from the Whig Ministry, more than we ever looked to get from them, some things which we did not even think of asking from them, have been freely, frankly, in good spirit, and in the best manner, granted by the Tory Ministry. Let us not grudge them one jot of the praise deservedly due to conduct which has been marked by as much liberality as sound judgment."

Again, on the 13th of August, after the bills had passed, and Lord Brougham had made his amusing *fiasco* in opposition, the same paper writes of the local Conservatives and their opposition :—

"Determined to die geese, a last deputation of their number proceeded to London on Tuesday, to make a final effort to move the lords spiritual and temporal. What their expectations were it would be hard to guess, but they carried with them a petition against the two bills. And of all men under the canopy of the sky, to whom did these wise men of Gotham entrust it for delivery—a petition against popular government from half a dozen of Church and King Tories—but to Lord Brougham! And as the *finis* of the farce, Lord Brougham allowed it to fall aside, and only recovered it in time to present it to the House after both the bills against which it had been directed had passed! We have heard of gunners being hoist with their own petards; of men shortening their noses to be revenged of their faces; of pigs, in their striving against the stream, cutting their own throats; but, of all the blind gunners, of all the mad shavers, of all the suicidal pigs, that history and hearing have made us acquainted with, commend us to the veracious, sagacious, and tribulatious gentlemen of the Birmingham Local Rate Committee."

On the 19th of August the passing of the bills affecting Birmingham was announced to the Town Council by Mr. Samuel Beale, the Mayor, who formally presented the Acts, and congratulated his colleagues on the end of their troubles; and at the same meeting

CHAP. XII.
1842.

a Watch Committee was appointed, to arrange for the transfer of the police force, and to take charge of it from the 1st of October, the date at which, according to the provisions of the Police Act, the control of the force was to pass into the hands of the Corporation; and at the next meeting a committee was appointed to consider and report on the erection of a borough gaol.

Review of the Conflict.

Thus, after nearly four years of contention, Birmingham acquired the uncontested right of self-government. The intervening period, as we have seen, was one of extreme difficulty and embarrassment. The grant of the Charter in 1838 aroused both local jealousy and political feeling. Those who had hitherto enjoyed a monopoly of the control of public affairs resisted the establishment of a representative body, because they foresaw that eventually, and at no distant period, the whole of the governing authority of the town must be concentrated in its hands. Those who were adverse to Liberal policy in the national government, naturally strove against the ascendancy of the Liberal party in local administration. Social differences helped to augment the force of opposition, and to intensify its bitterness. How bitter it was the preceding narrative, based entirely upon public proceedings and records, has but feebly borne witness. No words can express the depth of the animosity with which, according to the statements of the survivors of that period, the opposing parties regarded each other. Not only was united public

Estimate of Party Feeling.

action impossible between them, almost for any purpose, however desirable, but private intercourse, and the exchange of the courtesies of social life, were mutually denied. The Tories hated and despised the Liberals and Radicals; the Radicals returned the feeling with interest, for they regarded their opponents as tyrants as well as adversaries: as the embodiment of a system of exclusion and privilege which advancing ideas had rendered intolerable. Under such circumstances, it was no wonder that the Corporation—the realisation of the hopes of one side and the aversion of the other—became the symbol of party and the object of dispute. The form of government which is now happily accepted by all parties as the best, and indeed the only possible method of administration, was then a new and comparatively untried experiment. Even its authors—the Whig Ministry of the day—seemed to distrust it, for they gave its advocates no assistance, and indeed by almost all their proceedings, they seemed disposed to thwart and to discredit their own work. This coldness or insincerity naturally emboldened the hopes of the Conservative party, the opponents of the Charter. By availing themselves of it, they succeeded in offering the Corporation a succession of hindrances and insults. They procured the withdrawal of the police force from the control of the Town Council, and the establishment of a force under Government control. They promoted the resistance of the Overseers to the payment of rates levied by the Corporation, and stimulated the county justices to demands which were disposed of only by harassing

CHAP. XII.
1842.

Contract between Whig and Conservative Ministers.

legal proceedings. They disputed the legality of the appointments made by the Council; they assailed the validity of the Charter; throughout the four years of strife they left unemployed no means, whether of public opposition or of private influence, that might tend to embarrass and to discredit the Corporation, or to conduce to the revocation of the Charter. When a Conservative Administration came into power, the Birmingham Conservatives naturally anticipated the success of their persistent endeavours. But the course of events proved too strong for them. Sir Robert Peel and Sir James Graham were statesmen as well as Conservative politicians. They felt that one of the greatest and most rapidly growing towns of the kingdom could no longer, with justice or with safety, be denied the control of its own affairs. They saw, too, that while the Municipal Act remained in dispute Imperial legislation necessarily failed of its effect, and that serious hindrances were interposed to the development of local government. Acting, therefore, on grounds higher and wiser than those of party, the Conservative Government conferred upon Birmingham the advantages which the Whig Ministry had withheld; and they preferred rather to discourage and to offend their own followers than to continue a system of unjustifiable restriction; or to prolong an arrangement which, however gratifying to political partisans, inflicted serious injury upon public interests. When, therefore, the obligations of Birmingham to Lord John Russell and his colleagues, in the gift of the Charter, are acknowledged, it is no more than an act of justice to acknowledge likewise the patriotic spirit in which Sir Robert Peel and Sir James Graham crowned and completed the work which their predecessors had left imperfect. Record is also due to the Birmingham men who so gallantly and persistently fought out, to a successful issue, the battle of local representative government—those who, in other words, established the freedom of the town, and made it a self-governing community. The names of the workers in this good cause have been mentioned from time to time in this narrative of their labours; but conspicuous amongst them stand out those of William Scholefield, of Philip Henry Muntz, William Redfern, Thomas Weston, William Pare, Robert Kellie Douglas, John Birt Davies, and George Edmonds; and in this honourable list the names of the two first mentioned are entitled to special distinction.

CHAPTER XIII.

UNION OF GOVERNING BODIES IN THE BOROUGH.

Chap. XIII.
1842.
Limited Powers of the Corporation.

The measures incident to the confirmation of the Charter in 1842 established the authority of the Corporation under the Municipal Act, transferred the control of the police to the Town Council, authorised the erection of a Borough Gaol, and put an end to the dispute as to the rating powers of the Corporation. But the authority thus conferred was of a limited character. The actual government of the borough was divided between the Council and the several local bodies created by previous special Acts of Parliament—the Commissioners of the Birmingham Street Act, the Commissioners of Deritend and Bordesley, and of Duddeston and Nechells, and the Surveyors of Deritend and Edgbaston. These bodies had control of the streets, the roads, the drainage, the lighting, and other matters within their respective districts, they levied rates, exercised authority, and absorbed important departments of administration, so that the Corporation was deprived of its natural and necessary powers, and the representative principle was discredited by the rivalry and superiority of the principle of self-election, all the bodies above mentioned being entirely beyond the control of

Conflicting Local Bodies.

the ratepayers, and owing them no account of their proceedings. From 1842, when its right of existence ceased to be questioned, until 1851, when the whole governing authority of the borough passed into its hands, the Corporation was obliged to content itself with a merely fragmentary jurisdiction. Whatever it could do, was done, however, with intelligence and vigour. The police force was reorganised, a gaol was built, a lunatic asylum established, baths and washhouses set up, and some efforts—though they came to nothing—were made to provide public parks and recreation grounds. Such public Acts of Parliament as could be adopted under the powers of the Corporation were put in force, such as the Weights and Measures Act and the Nuisances Act, under the latter of which, however, the Council could appoint only gratuitous medical inspectors. In addition to the matters above referred to, the Council occupied itself with the regulation of the Sessions, the Coroner's Court, and the Mayor's Court for the recovery of small debts, and with the provision, though on an inadequate scale, of buildings for the transaction of corporate business. In the second volume of this work, the steps taken to give effect to the measures here indicated will be recorded under their respective departments of corporate affairs. For the present it is sufficient to deal with them generally, to show the character of the work the Council, with its limited powers, was enabled to take in hand. There were other matters of which mention should be made. The discussion of public questions of political interest,

CHAP. XIII.
1842 to 1851.
Increasing Desire for Union of Powers.

begun in the earliest days of the history of the Corporation, was continued during the period under notice. The management and reform of the Free Grammar School, for example, was repeatedly debated; so also were the wider topics of Parliamentary reform, of cheap postage, the poor law, the window tax, and other subjects of national as well as of local interest—and in all these the Council maintained the breadth and liberality of view and the plainness of expression which characterised its earliest dealings with public questions. No doubt, this interval of limited powers and of restricted interest had its uses, by gradually accustoming the borough to the action of a municipal body, by inspiring the burgesses with greater confidence in the representative principle, and by educating the representatives themselves in the transaction of business under new conditions and with a keener and closer sense of responsibility—thus, in fact, laying the foundation of the broader, stronger, more comprehensive, and more vigorous development of local government now enjoyed by Birmingham in common with the other municipal communities of the country. But, as the process of education went on, and as the ratepayers became more accustomed to representative government, and consequently better qualified to appreciate its value, the system of privilege and restriction which existed side by side with it became increasingly distasteful, and at last intolerable. The advocates of the representative system had from the first foreseen that all other forms of local administration must eventually give way to that now established upon a popular basis, and the confirmation of the Charter, and the subsequent proceedings of the Council, tended to diffuse amongst the community generally the opinion hitherto entertained only by the few. It came to be admitted, as an irresistible conclusion from facts, that the government of the town could not be efficiently conducted by divided authority and under conflicting jurisdiction; that progress was thus rendered impossible; that expense was increased; that necessary reforms were hindered and prevented; and that the health, the prosperity, and the dignity of the community were seriously affected by the absence of a common and indisputable centre of control.

That this would be the case was predicted from the moment when an application was made to the Crown for the grant of a Charter. It was then declared by the advocates of the proposal that the first use to be made of its authority by the Corporation would be to extinguish all other governing bodies within the town, and to transfer their powers to the elected representatives of the ratepayers: the only body which could with right and justice, with economy and efficiency, undertake the government of the community. This inevitable consequence was recognised by the opponents of the Charter as well as by its advocates; and this conviction inspired the former with a determination to resist the grant of a Charter, and, when the grant had been made, to hinder its operation as much as possible. The natural course of events proved, however, too strong for the opposition; and though a long and arduous struggle was maintained—for privilege invariably dies hard—they had finally to succumb. Having regard to the fuller development of public opinion and to the more rapid progress of reform in our own days, it may seem strange that so long a period as ten years was allowed to pass before making a change so obviously necessary, and so manifestly in accordance with the interests of good and efficient local government. There were, however, many causes at work to induce delay. In its earlier years the Council exercised comparatively little influence over the opinion of the town; social prestige and, to a considerable extent, political considerations operated on the side of the self-elected bodies; these, again, had all the stimulus of corporate as well as of personal disposition to maintain their authority, and to this was added the not unnatural desire of their officials to retain their places. Again, the Liberals, by whom the idea of amalgamating the governing powers was mainly advocated, were at variance amongst themselves. The manhood suffrage Radicals, for example, were hostile to the restricted franchise conferred by the Municipal Corporations Act, and were consequently found in opposition to measures which threatened to consolidate local powers without extending the basis of representation. The force of public opinion was necessarily weakened by this opposition, and the resistance of the self-elected governing bodies was proportionately strengthened. Then, it must be confessed, there was great apathy amongst the burgesses

HINDRANCES TO PROGRESS. 295

themselves. Their numbers were few in comparison with the population—for all householders under £10 were excluded—and of the limited number upon the burgess roll, but a very small portion cared to exercise the municipal franchise. No clearer or more startling proof of this apathy could be given than is presented in the following table, extracted from the *Birmingham Journal* (March 5, 1845), showing the population in each ward, the number of burgesses, and the proportion who had taken the trouble to vote at the three previous municipal elections. In some instances, it will be observed, scarcely a man cared to go to the polling place:—

CHAP. XIII.
1842 to 1851.
Apathy of the Burgesses.

WARDS.	Population. 1841.	Burgesses. 1845.	Votes at Elections of Councillors.		
			1844.	1843.	1842.
Ladywood	8,787	226	3	78	6
All Saints'	13,719	397	72	2	2
Hampton	11,037	427	2	2	2
St. George's	19,648	425	203	2	59
St. Mary's	14,685	293	3	106	1
St. Paul's	8,973	358	103	11	2
Market Hall	13,014	388	3	101	124
St. Peter's	16,773	718	404	3	119
St. Martin's	13,325	246	147	3	4
St. Thomas's	18,254	338	143	4	2
Total parish of Birmingham	138,215	3,816	1,083	312	321
Edgbaston	6,609	649	223	9	142
Deritend and Bordesley	18,019	672	234	350	2
Duddeston and					

CHAP. XIII.

1843.
Mr. Beilby's Motion.

Town Council Bill.

1844.
Mr. Jaffray's Appeals.

1845.
The Commissioners' Bill.

Despite apathy and opposition, however, the movement for the amalgamation of the governing bodies of the town was kept steadily before the public mind. As early as 1843, Mr. Thomas Beilby, one of the Commissioners of the Street Act, urged his colleagues to take advantage of the opportunity afforded by the confirmation of the Charter, and to transfer voluntarily to the Town Council the powers which would ultimately have to be transferred by force. His effort, however, was fruitless. In the same year the Town Council itself undertook the preparation of a bill for the purpose of consolidating the governing authority in the hands of the Corporation, and the requisite Parliamentary notices were given, but the intention was finally abandoned. The next year, 1844, lay fallow; but public opinion was being slowly matured by a series of appeals made in the *Journal*, by Mr. Jaffray, who insisted strongly upon the sanitary aspects of the question; and these appeals and efforts were continued, almost without intermission, in the same columns and by the same writer, with most beneficial effect, until the object was finally accomplished. In 1845 the Street Commissioners themselves undesignedly gave a strong impetus to the movement for amalgamation, by preparing a bill for the extension of their own powers, and by thus endeavouring to perpetuate the anomalies of divided government and of self-election. They consequently not only aroused the dormant energies of their opponents, but actually, and with singular indiscretion, challenged the expression of opinion, by formally submitting their proposals to a public meeting of the ratepayers of the parish of Birmingham—the part of the borough over which they exercised jurisdiction. In anticipation of this meeting, the *Journal* vigorously attacked and exposed the existing system, and called upon the ratepayers not only to resist the Commissioners' Bill, but to demand the abolition of the conflicting authorities, and the union of their powers under the authority of a representative government. An extract from this appeal will serve to show the feeling of the town at that time, and to exhibit the condition of practical anarchy into which it had sunk:—*

"The town is sick of a mob of municipal governors. We pay too dear for their amusements. The ratepayers of Birmingham now claim one municipal government for the entire borough. The struggles of the possessors and advocates of self-elect power have naturally begotten a corresponding opposition of extreme opinions. While one party strives to maintain authority for the few, another class would refer all power to the many. The old political aristocracy of the town decry the Town Council as a popularly elected body; an extreme section of the Liberal party will allow no responsibility or independent action to their municipal representatives, and denounce the burgess roll as a limited and incapable elective body. Thus, while our ultra-Conservatives bewail the flood of Democracy let in by our Charter of Incorporation, the ultra-Radicals contend for the submission even of all administrative acts of their Councillors to the veto of public meetings. We are a bye-word in the country for our senseless and self-destructive local factions, and so we shall continue to be till our municipal government is consolidated. Our local taxation is the marvel of our neighbours, as it is the sore burden of the ratepayers. We have no creditable or concentrated governing body to represent

---

* *Birmingham Journal*, May 8, 1845.

us, or secure our interests out of Birmingham. We see the public opinion of every town save Birmingham represented and influenced by a single and active local government. But it is the constant impolicy of Birmingham to present itself before the kingdom as an arena of disgraceful local contentions—as a populous town without self-government; and while other towns are successful applicants to the Legislature for acts of local improvement, we lag behind, and in Parliament we are regarded as a community of rank party spirit and jarring elements of social contention. We do not over-colour the picture. The time was, not many years since, when Birmingham occupied a different political position—when we all acted together. We may yet recover that proud station; but we must begin by better government amongst ourselves."

Defeat of the Commissioners.

The meeting called by the Commissioners was held, but with a result different to that which was intended, for the opposition took the matter into their own hands, and, under the leadership of Mr. George Edmonds, who was the chief speaker, almost unanimously passed a resolution condemning the Commissioners' Bill, and demanding the amalgamation of the governing bodies of the town. This was followed by a town's meeting, (May 28, 1845) called by Mr. Thomas Phillips, then Mayor, on the requisition of more than 2,000 burgesses, to promote the project of amalgamation. Resolutions to this effect were proposed by Mr. Edmonds as a Radical, and by Mr. Robert Allen, a Conservative. They were met by an amendment proposed by Mr. A. Albright and Mr. H. Hawkes, as representing the extreme Radical section, on the ground that it would be unjust and unwise to alter the government of the

Town's Meeting for Union.

borough unless provision was also made to extend the municipal franchise to all householders. The opposition was also fostered by a feeling entertained in some of the local districts—especially in Duddeston and Nechells—that amalgamation would lead to increased rating: a meeting of Duddeston ratepayers having just previously, on the motion of Mr. Hawkes, adopted a resolution that they were "thoroughly convinced that the transfer of the local government of these hamlets to the Birmingham Corporation would generally increase local taxation, and deprive the ratepayers of all effective control over the administration of their public affairs." The opposition, however, failed to convince the town's meeting of the justice of their case; and resolutions in favour of amalgamation were adopted by a very large majority. Upon these resolutions a petition against the Commissioners' Bill was based; and this petition was presented by a deputation to the Town Council, and was adopted by the Council as its own petition. At the same time, in the hope of conciliating its opponents, and of smoothing the way to reform, the Council resolved upon a kind of self-denying ordinance—namely, that the third of its members retiring by rotation at the next election in November should, by voluntary resignation, be increased to one half (including the same proportion of aldermen) in order that the burgesses might have a fair opportunity of altering the composition of the Council, by electing into it members of the other local governing bodies. This offer had no effect upon the opposition, for the Commissioners still pressed forward their bill; but it was ultimately abandoned.

Another phase of the movement now developed itself. The Government introduced the Health of Towns Act, subsequently passed in 1848, under the title of the Public Health Act. This measure created a Central Board, with large powers of interference with local government, particularly in regard to sanitary reforms. It also authorised the Board to prepare and submit to Parliament provisional orders erecting new local governing bodies, consolidating conflicting jurisdictions, and extending the area of united bodies. In principle the bill was regarded as being satisfactory; but strong opposition was aroused in Birmingham by its centralising clauses, and by the extensive right of interference conferred upon the Central Board. The bill was discussed by the Town Council on the 25th of May, 1848, and the view entertained of it was expressed in the following petition to the House of Commons, which was adopted by the Council:—

"That your petitioners are grateful for the proposed salutary measure, inasmuch as the powers of cleansing, lighting, and improving the district comprised in this borough are by local Acts of Parliament now vested in self-elected and other Commissioners, having no uniform action, and who levy and spend in their respective districts, annually, large sums of money without system or coherence, and without reference to the whole extent and area of the borough. That since the incorporation of this borough your petitioners have zealously and promptly carried into effect every Act entrusted to them; that your petitioners object to interference by a Central Board in London with the management of the local affairs of this borough, believing such interference not only unnecessary but in a high degree detrimental to its interests, and in direct contravention to the principle of self-government accorded by the Municipal Reform Act. That your petitioners consider that in this borough, where no district is necessary to be added, the Council appointed under the provisions of the Municipal Corporations Act should be entrusted with and have the control of carrying out the provisions contained in this bill, in the same manner as the Council transacts its general business. Your petitioners therefore pray that such alterations may be made in the bill as will preserve the functions of the Corporation of this borough independent of any interference or control by a Central Board in London."

Chap. XIII.
1848.
Centralisation objected to.

This petition, and others to the same effect from other towns, produced the desired result. At a subsequent meeting (July 11th) the committee appointed to oppose the bill were able to report that an amended bill had been passed by the Commons, "in which the clauses objected to by the Council have been expunged or satisfactorily altered, and that in the event of the bill being passed into law, and being brought into operation in this borough, the Council will constitute the Local Board of Health, and be empowered to carry out its provisions." The bill was passed in the same session (1848), and steps were immediately taken to give effect to it, as under its provisions it was now rendered possible to amalgamate all the conflicting local governing bodies, and to establish one government for the town. The method prescribed by the Public Health Act had this great advantage — it would save the expense of a private bill, and would avoid the long

The Bill amended.

Chap. XIII.
1848.
Petition for Adoption of the Act in Birmingham.

and wearisome conflict necessarily incident to the preparation and promotion of such a measure. Consequently the Council resolved to proceed under the Public Health Act; and it really seemed as if, at last, the government of the borough was about to be placed upon an uniform and a satisfactory footing. The steps necessary to this purpose were the presentation of a memorial to the Board of Health; asking for an enquiry into the sanitary condition of the borough; then, upon the report of the enquiring inspector, the Board was empowered to introduce into Parliament a provisional order applying the Public Health Act to the town; and by Act of Parliament this provisional order would become law—its terms being specially adapted to local requirements. The Act directed that the memorial for an enquiry should be signed by at least one-tenth of the ratepayers. This number was easily obtained, the memorial was presented, and Mr. Robert Rawlinson, C.E., was appointed to hold the enquiry. For this purpose Mr. Rawlinson visited Birmingham on the 12th of February, 1849, when the enquiry occupied four days, and again on the 1st of May, 1849, when he again sat for several days, besides making a thorough personal examination of the town. All the local governing bodies were represented at the enquiry, and witnesses on their behalf, as well as independent witnesses, were examined. Indeed, there was a general willingness to offer evidence, so that the inspector had abundant materials for his report to the Central Board.

Government Enquiry by Mr. Rawlinson

Mr. Rawlinson's Report, dated May, 1849, constitutes a volume of one hundred pages. It deals fully with the history, government, population, and sanitary arrangements of the borough, and contains much information which is of value to the local historian. The number of houses is given as 43,000, the population as 220,000, of whom "50,000 are congregated in 2,000 courts." The situation of the town is favourable to health and to efficient sanitary measures: it "stands upon the new red sandstone, the outcrop of the same formation passing in a great curve from the river Tees, southward to Birmingham, and round westward and northward to the Mersey. On this great sweep of sandstone are built the important towns of Sunderland, York, Derby, Leicester, Birmingham, Warwick, Worcester, Wolverhampton, Shrewsbury, Stafford, Chester, Liverpool, Manchester, and Stockport." Mr. Rawlinson traces the formation of the deposit of new red sandstone:

Chap. XIII.
1849.
General Sketch of Birmingham.

Geological Formation: the New Red Sandstone.

"Could we have seen the form of country when the diluvium on which Birmingham now stands was being deposited, we should have found the sea-shore forming a boundary probably not unlike the curve of the outcropping lias. The Alps were yet below the salt wave, although the Grampians of Scotland had existed countless centuries, and the hills of Cumberland had passed their state as glaciered mountains. Wales was dry land, and the Cotteswold Hills, in Gloucestershire, and some few parts of central England, were above water. The rocks of Dudley had subsided even before the deposit of the sand-rock began; huge ice-floes and bergs came floating up from some northern continent long since drowned, grinding the imbedded fragments torn from their parent rock, wearing banks and shoals, and

CHAP. XIII.
———
1849.
Mr. Rawlinson's Report: Geological Strata.

ultimately depositing their stony burden in scattered groups over vast areas hereafter to become dry land. The whole site on which Birmingham stands has been subjected to this wearing action, and the present valleys of the rivers Rea and Tame are but the indentations of the old sea-shore; the sand and gravel now dug from beneath the streets was washed and rolled by comparatively shallow water into its present bed; the alternations of clay and marl speak of deeper water, or a more quiet shore. In a section along the bed of the Rea we find, at its junction with the Tame, soil 2 feet, sand and gravel 20 feet, black peat 4 feet, clay 3 feet, and sand and gravel repeated. This peat indicates land at or near the level of the sea. Near Balsall Heath Road, at a higher level, we find soil 2 feet, peat 3 feet. This is a formation distinct from that previously named, and about 30 feet above it, with gravel and sand 12 feet, clay 4 feet, and 14 feet of marl betwixt. On either side of the valley of the Tame we find, first, soil 2 feet, sand and gravel 15 feet, clay 5 feet, resting on sand and gravel; then soil, sand, and gravel 10 feet, and clay 25 feet; and, at another point on the south side, sand and gravel 32 feet, clay 27 feet, gravel mixed with clay 4 feet, resting on running sand; near St. Philip's and St. Paul's churches the sand and gravel is only from 9 to 17 feet deep down to the red sandstone rock. The site of St. Philip's Church is a portion of the highest land in the town; the junction of Anne Street and Newhall Street, Regent's Street and Frederick Street, are on the same level; the waterworks' reservoir is on land 60 feet above these points. The junction of the rivers Rea and Tame is 168 feet below the site of St. Philip's Church. The undulating surface of the land renders the town clean; ventilation is more freely obtained; the surface of the streets is preserved comparatively dry by their general inclination; and the sand and gravel tends to preserve the foundations of the buildings dry."

The Rainfall.

There is, the report proceeds, a marked dryness in the air—"the average fall of rain in Birmingham is about one-third less than in Liverpool or Manchester; and this difference in the amount of rainfall or damp in the atmosphere of Warwickshire and Lancashire is worthy of particular notice, as it must have a sensible effect on the manufactures of the district, as also on the health of the inhabitants. It is said that the damp atmosphere of Lancashire is necessary to the profitable spinning of cotton-yarn, and certainly the drier atmosphere of Warwickshire is equally advantageous to the iron manufacture, to the production of polished steel implements, and the metal-plated wares in general of Birmingham. The elevated and comparatively dry site of the town and dry atmosphere of the district, no doubt contribute to that favourable difference in the health of the people which is known to exist as contrasted with Liverpool and Manchester." The extreme length of the borough, Mr. Rawlinson reports, "is $5\frac{3}{4}$ miles, average breadth 3 miles; it is 21 miles in circumference, and contains 8,420 acres, has 100 miles of streets and 40 miles of suburban roads; it has an average rising gradient of 1 in 108 from east to west, being a rise of 250 feet from the point near the River Tame where the whole of its sewage will be concentrated, to the highest table land of the west; it arises from the south to the north-west (*i.e.*, from Vaughton's Bridge to the Gaol) 122 feet, a gradient of 1 in 121." The mortality of the town was $26\frac{1}{2}$ per 1,000 in 1847, and 30 in 1848; but "it contrasts favourably with most large towns"—though "infant mortality is very considerable."

TRADES OF BIRMINGHAM.

CHAP. XIII.
1849.
Mr. Rawlinson's Report: Variety of Trades.

On the trades of Birmingham Mr. Rawlinson has interesting information to give:

"There are about 520 distinctly classified manufacturers, traders, or dealers, and about twenty separate professions in Birmingham, and each trade may certainly be divided into five branches, which will give 2,600 varieties of occupation; but I have no doubt this is understated, as there are fourteen distinct branches named in the Directory as engaged in the manufacture of guns. The trades carried on in the town are not only numerous, but they are also, in a great measure, distinct and independent of each other in their manufacture and after use. To the knives, swords, and spears of the ancient Britons has been added a splendour of finish and polish unknown to the magical blades of Damascus; and there is a small instrument of skill manufactured in millions, the pen, more powerful in the world at this day than all the swords, spears, and scythe-armed chariots of past ages. The black and dingy 'nayler' of Leland has for his town companion the electro-plate and papier mache manufacturer, by the latter of which the lustre and polish of the precious metals is outshone by the iris-dyes of the pearl.

Distribution of Wealth.

"The variety of trades and occupations exercised is, in many respects, advantageous to the population; it tends to a more equal and general diffusion of wealth amongst the master manufacturers, and the means of acquiring it in moderation amongst the workpeople; there are few, if any, 'millionaires,' connected with trade in or near Birmingham, if we except the Staffordshire ironmasters; there are few who occupy the position of the 'cotton lords' of Manchester, or the 'merchant princes' of Liverpool; but there is a numerous class of master tradesmen whose wealth tends to comfort rather than ostentatious show, and there is a race of workpeople comparatively independent and self-relying. Some observant and intelligent writers have considered the prosperity of the town has arisen from its perfect freedom from the corporate trammels of past ages, or the blind, exclusive guild, which affects to give privileges to a few, by the Chinese plan of stereotyping the initiated; any form of trade or occupation might and may be commenced and carried on without local restriction or interference: the only question to be answered rests with the individual, 'Can he make it pay?'

<small>Chap. XIII.
1849.
Mr. Rawlinson's Report: Trades of the Town.</small>

"The diffusion and variety of occupation gives an elasticity to the trade of Birmingham unknown in towns and districts confined to the manufacture of one article, or one material; and it also gives to the workmen an aptitude which enables them to change their occupation should any form of trade die out, as shoe-buckle making at the beginning of this century, which in 1812 became totally extinct; and the carpenters frequently turn gun-stockers, so that, if required, 10,000 stand of arms could be completed in a week. The variety and independence of labour exercised produces freedom and independence of thought and action, which unfortunately has not always met with the best advisers and directors, so that one or two riotous errors have given to Birmingham a name very undeserved. In no place will there be found more freedom of intercourse between the employer and employed, or more general intelligence and comfort amongst the workpeople, or more forethought and kindness from the employer for the employed."

In connection with the trades, the increase of steam power is recorded. From 1780 to 1836 there were 169 steam engines erected in Birmingham with a total of 2,700 horse-power. In 1839 the horse-power was 3,436, consuming 240 tons of coal daily. In 1849 "the engine power is about 5,400 horse-power, consuming about 377 tons of coals each day, and equal to the labour of 86,400 men."

<small>Steam Power.</small>

One feature of the social arrangements of the town, the inspector notes with concern: the large number of

<small>Public House</small>

CHAP. XIII.
1849.
Mr. Rawlinson's Report:
Social Habits, Clubs, &c.

public houses—564 licensed houses, and 661 beer houses. To these he adds " 54 wine and spirit merchants, 14 ale and porter merchants, 60 tobacconists and snuff dealers, and 10 tobacco pipe makers: in round numbers 1,363 places of business to supply spirituous liquors, ale, porter, tobacco, and pipes to smoke it in." Against this list he sets the allotment gardens—then a great feature of Birmingham [there are, he reports, 250 of these on Lord Calthorpe's Edgbaston estate alone, and many others in various suburbs]. The clubs and friendly societies number 213, of which 159 meet in public houses. The members are about 30,000. The public house clubs are badly managed: it is "false economy to take a shilling to a public house, to give a club threepence to take care of it, and to spend another threepence over the arrangement; and frequently losing principal and interest." The club feasts—then general—are denounced as wasteful. "Once a year, generally in Whitsun week, they marshal themselves into a procession, with bands of music, colours, flags, and banners dispersed along their ranks, and each man or woman is ornamented with sashes and rosettes of ribbons. The wise and otherwise moderate teetotaller errs in this; and it is not too much to say that more money is expended in these processions, in loss of labour and in the attendant expenses of the day, than would pay the rent charge of a full supply of water, and perfect sewage. The dinner and day's enjoyment will not, on an average, cost less than five shillings each individual." This is described as a heavy tax on the wages—though these

Club Feasts and Processions.

range high for the time. "Many of the workmen earn from 30s. to 40s. a week, and women from 10s. to 14s. a week. As trade is brisk or dull, these persons prosper or suffer. Many of the men work in garrets in their own houses, and have several boys under them." The workmen who earn high wages, it is noted, are often drunken and improvident. "The improvidence is said to arise, in many instances, from extreme ignorance on the part of the wives of these people; many of the females, having been bred up from their youth in the workshops, have no knowledge of household management and economy, or any inclination for domestic industry. The habit of a manufacturing life once formed in a female, she generally continues it, and her children are left in comparative neglect, to the care of a neighbour or child. To this may be traced the premature death of many children, and accidents from fire are very frequent. More comfort and happiness is found in families superintended by a careful wife, where the earnings are comparatively small, than in others whose wages are very considerable, but where there is improvident management at home."

The allotment gardens—once a marked feature in Birmingham—are noticed with approval in the report. At the time of Mr. Rawlinson's inspection, and indeed for many years later, these gardens, varying in size from a quarter of a rood up to a quarter of an acre, were commonly found in all the suburbs of the town. Some of them were let to tradesmen, and others, the majority, to workmen, who took great pride in their patches of garden ground, fenced them carefully, grew vegetables for the family use, made them gay with old-fashioned flowers, and besides working in them at all spare hours, occasionally made them the scenes of little family festivals—the rustic arbour constructed on almost every allotment serving as a place for tea-drinking. In Mr. Rawlinson's report it is mentioned that upon Lord Calthorpe's Edgbaston estate alone there are 250 of these gardens, containing from an eighth to a sixteenth of an acre each, and let at the rate of £10 to £15 an acre, according to situation. "These (so Mr. Yates, then Lord Calthorpe's agent, reports) are much sought after, and are found to be highly conducive to the health and morals of the occupiers, who are principally inhabitants of the town, engaged in manufactories or shops." Besides the gardens at Edgbaston, there were others in Bordesley, along the valley of the Rea, and in the direction of Handsworth and Moseley. Very few are now (1878) to be found—the principal group remaining being in Westbourne Road and Chad Valley, in Edgbaston: almost all the rest have been swept away by the extension of the town, and even those just mentioned appear to be doomed to the same fate, as the surrounding land is being rapidly cut up for suburban villas. As indicating the increased value of land, it may be mentioned that Mr. Yates, Lord Calthorpe's agent, states that the Calthorpe estate at Edgbaston includes 2,065 acres, and that the land is let on 99 year leases, "reserving fixed annual rents, generally of 1d. per square yard for the land near the town, but at a distance, where six or more acres have been leased in one lot, the reserved rent is somewhat less than £10 per acre," or about ½d. per square yard. At that date (1849) Mr. Yates says that "probably one-third of Lord Calthorpe's estate has been already leased, the remainder being farming, accommodation, and garden land." The general ground rents of the town in the suburbs are stated by Mr. Rawlinson at from 1d. to 4d. per square yard.

Amongst the miscellaneous information in the report we have some notes on the prices of gas and the quantity made. The Birmingham Gas-light Company at that date (1849) had 244 retorts in use; 10 gas-holders, with a working capacity of 870,000 cubic feet; and in 1848 they made 145,000,000 cubic feet of gas. The Birmingham and Staffordshire Company had 176 retorts, 14 gas-holders, containing in the aggregate 1,000,000 cubic feet, and their largest annual make of gas was 216,000,000 feet. The Birmingham Company supplied 805, and the Staffordshire Company 1,280 public lamps, each lighted nightly through the year, each consuming five cubic feet of gas per hour, and each company charging 70s. per lamp yearly, a price which, after deducting cost of lighting, repair, &c., left the companies a net return of 52s. per lamp yearly, or a fraction more than 2s. 4¼d. per 1,000 feet of gas consumed. The prices charged to the general consumers were much higher than those charged for the public lamps. The following was the scale adopted by both companies, subject in each case to a discount of ten per cent. for quarterly cash payments:

SCALE OF CHARGES FOR QUARTERLY CONSUMPTION.

	s.	d.	
Under 5,000 cubic feet ...	6	8	per 1,000 feet.
5,000 and under 25,000 ...	6	0	,,
25,000 ,, 50,000 ...	5	0	,,
50,000 ,, 100,000 ...	4	9	,,

SCALE OF CHARGES FOR ANNUAL CONSUMPTION.

	s.	d.	
100,000 and under 200,000 ...	4	6	per 1,000 feet.
200,000 ,, 400,000 ...	4	3	,,
400,000 ,, 600,000 ...	4	0	,,
600,000 and upwards ...	3	9	,,

These prices, Mr. Rawlinson justly says, "must be considered excessive," considering the advantage of cheap fuel near Birmingham, and the large consumption in the town; and he further points out that "the two companies at present supplying the town must necessarily increase the expense, as there are two separate establishments, with distinct offices, and two sets of mains. The inconvenience to the inhabitants will also frequently be doubled, as some streets will be twice broken up where once would have served. Unity of works and of management is most desirable for efficiency and economy."

The water supply of the town naturally comes under review in the report. The Inspector notes it as being imperfect, derived from the following sources— "1st, the stratification of the district is full of water, and consequently private wells and pumps are constructed very generally;. 2nd, there are several public wells or pumps in the town, from which the water is obtained by the neighbouring inhabitants [these were Lady Well, Digbeth, Jamaica Row, and Allison Street]; 3rd, many private water-carts traverse the town, from which water is purchased by the cottagers at a halfpenny the can full, or about 3½ gallons; 4th, there is a public Company (the Waterworks Company) supplying portions of the town [about one third] three days in each week, with about one million gallons a day." Commenting upon this condition of affairs, Mr. Rawlinson strongly urged the importance of a better water supply, which it was then thought might be derived from the Lickey Hills. His general observations on the subject are worthy of quotation, as they still apply with justice to the supply from private wells:—

"There may be advantages in a district where the subsoil is porous, as found in the new red sandstone districts generally, and in thinly peopled districts it may be highly desirable to have water easily obtained; but when such a district becomes crowded with inhabitants, streets, middens, cesspools, and graveyards, as all large towns are, then an open subsoil, full of water, is rapidly converted into a dangerous nuisance. The infiltration from every source of impurity passes into the sand and gravel, and all the water drawn from such strata is of necessity impregnated with the offensive matter. Many of the wells now in existence in Birmingham, when first made, yielded comparatively pure water, and it was used for drinking,

CHAP. XIII.
1849.
Mr. Rawlinson's Report:
Extravagant Cost of Well Water.

and all other purposes, but at present this water can only be used for washing and scouring; the supply for cooking and drinking has to be drawn from some other source, namely, the public pump, or water-cart. The public pump yields identically the same water as the private pumps, only it may be drawn from a lower depth, and the 'quick draft' of a more constant pumping does not allow it to stagnate in the well, and this gives it the appearance of greater purity, although in reality it is the same water. The bright appearance of water is no test of its purity, it is the chemical analysis alone which will reveal true results. Dr. Robert Angus Smith, of Manchester, analysed upwards of 90 of the wells in Manchester, and found all more or less impregnated with impurities, some of them, from within the vicinity of the graveyards, most offensively so. The stratification of Manchester and Birmingham are identical. The supply from public pumps and water-carts is most extravagantly expensive, if even the water was pure. One halfpenny for four gallons is 10s. 5d. for 1,000 gallons; a proper scheme of water supply can furnish 1,000 gallons for less than 3d., or 41 times cheaper than the carts; there is also the cost of pots or cans to hold it for use; and not the least disadvantage arising from this mode of supply is, that water kept for a few hours, exposed to the atmosphere of a dwelling-house, imbibes all the deleterious gases of the district, and rapidly becomes unfit for purposes of household use and drinking. The supply from wells and pumps is also most expensive. It was given in evidence that a well and pump would cost about £25 complete, and about 10s. annually to maintain and keep it in repair, or the account would stand as under:—£20 first cost of pump, at 5 per cent., £1 per annum; Repairs, 10s. per annum; or, per annum for one pump, the sum of £1 10s. To this may with fairness be added the labour of pumping and fetching the water, the use and wear of cans and pots to hold it, and we shall have an annual outlay for one pump, of not less than £2. This [cost] would give a constant supply of pure water to eight houses, of 100 gallons a day to each house. The water would be pure, ready at hand, and the supply constant. To have a pure supply ensured is of vast importance, as there is a liability on the part of persons imperfectly supplied, and who have a vitiated source at hand, to make use of it, to the serious injury of the health of themselves and their families. This vitiated water frequently, when used, produces dysentery and death."

The graveyards of the town are also dealt with by the Inspector. They are described as being "full to repletion; almost every square yard of their surface is covered with a stone, or bears evidence of a grave." In the centre of the town, within the compass of a square mile, are six large graveyards—St. Philip's (4 acres); St. Paul's (2½ acres); St. Mary's (3 acres); St. Bartholomew's and Park Street (together about 5 acres); and St. Martin's. Altogether these burial grounds occupied about 15 acres; all of them were full or practically so; "they are situated within the heart of the town, built in on all sides, so that any effluvium or evaporation that arises must inevitably be carried upon and through these dwelling houses." In none of these burial grounds, Mr. Rawlinson observes, "are there any plans kept of the yard, on which to show the progress of interment, and the sexton has no means but the appearance of the surface to ascertain where former burials have taken place; and he consequently uses that revolting implement, the 'boring rod,' and even then, according to the testimony of every sexton examined, graves are frequently disturbed in which half-decayed bodies are exposed." In contrast with these burial grounds the Inspector puts the two cemeteries then existing—the General Cemetery at Key Hill (12 acres) and the Church of England Cemetery adjoining it (11 acres.) In each of these regular plans are kept and followed, the soil is suitable for interments, "the grounds are beautifully laid out, and everything about them is in a clean and neat condition, offering a strong contrast to some of the churchyard burial grounds within the town, where all is neglected and wretched-looking to a degree."

The government and the sanitary condition of the town—the main subjects of enquiry—have now to be considered. The governing bodies within the borough are described in the report as follows:—

1. Birmingham Commissioners of Street Acts, with powers of paving, lighting, cleaning, and regulating streets, markets, &c., in the parish of Birmingham.

2. Deritend and Bordesley Commissioners, with similar powers for those hamlets.

3. Duddeston and Nechells Commissioners.

4. Guardians of the Poor of Birmingham.

5. Municipal Corporation.

6. Deritend Surveyors of Highways.

7. Bordesley Surveyors of Highways.

8. Edgbaston Surveyors of Highways.

Thus, the Inspector observes, "there are eight distinct

borough of Birmingham, and consequently eight separate sets of officers have to be paid to do the work which may be done by one efficient staff. These establishments act in opposition to each other. The Commissioners of Birmingham expend large sums of money to keep the sewage of the town out of the River Rea, and the surveyors of Edgbaston make a sewer to turn their refuse into that river. There is no general plan of the district, and though Nature has combined the whole so as to render one set of sewers imperative, there is no power to levy a common rate, although the benefits must be general. However willing all may be to act in concert for the common good, their present Acts imperatively forbid, or lack the necessary powers to sanction such a measure. The Commissioners of Birmingham have made sewers, but have no power to construct private drains, or to compel parties to construct them, although large sums of money have to be expended to remove and cleanse accumulations of foul, dangerous, and highly offensive matters, which might be more cheaply passed into their sewers." The minor local boards not only thwarted and opposed the Birmingham Commissioners, but they obstructed each other. Deritend, for example, had sufficient drainage to carry off its own water; but the Bordesley Surveyors either would not or could not make sewers communicating with those of Deritend, and so Bordesley, being on higher ground, flooded Deritend, and as Der

the rising of the stream. The common testimony of the surveyors and other witnesses was that improvements necessary to health and convenience could not be carried out for want of the necessary powers, and these difficulties were increased by disputes as to boundaries, which sometimes led to streets becoming impassable, and having to be stopped up, as neither of the conflicting bodies would take them in hand.

Excessive Officers.

While the work of good government and sanitary progress was hindered by this division of the governing bodies, heavy costs were imposed upon the ratepayers by the multiplicity of officers. Thus, as Mr. Rawlinson reports, the governing bodies employed amongst them nine solicitors, four surveyors, thirty-eight collectors, and four clerks and treasurers—altogether fifty-five officers, who collected and managed thirteen distinct rates, and whose duties frequently over-lapped each other. To show this, the Inspector quotes from a report presented by a Ratepayers' organisation in 1842:—

Confusing and irritating Demands.

"The popular jealousy is excited and irritated by the number of unmeaning offices and officers, and the annoyance of so many collectors. Where there are a variety of rates collected at different periods, without concert, some are forgotten at the proper period, and not provided for; and when demanded in rapid succession, they fall with inconvenience, and create the irritation of a new tax. The householder may have just paid the collector of his poor's rates, when the collector of his highway rate calls, and immediately after, the collector of the lamp and scavenger rate, then the collector of the gas rate calls next morning, and the collector of his water rate looks in during the day, and is paid, when with good right he may now think he is done; but no, another collector calls to demand the payment of the Town Hall rate; he pays him in a pet, when up turns another collector, and demands payment of some other rate for the period of a former tenant, and for which he, the present tenant, on whom the demand is levied, receives no apparent advantage. This fairly breaks down his temper; and all rates, taxes, collectors, and improvements, are denounced in the bitterness of confused agony and despair."

In order to illustrate the justice of these remarks, Mr. Rawlinson gives a detailed statement of the rates levied by the several governing bodies within the borough at the period of his enquiry.

"LIST OF RATES WITHIN THE BOROUGH OF BIRMINGHAM.—Birmingham poor-rate during one year ending Lady-day, 1849, 5s. in the £, 81,871l. 3s. 1d.

"*Birmingham Street Commissioners' Rates.*—Highway rate, 1s. 6d. in the £. Lamp rate, 1s. 3d. on 15l. and upwards; 10d. on 10l. and under; 7½d. above 5l. and under 10l. Town Hall rate 4d. in the £ on all assessments of 15l. and upwards.

"*Aston within the Borough—Deritend and Bordesley Commissioners' Rate.*—Assessment under 6l. are rated at 6d. in the £; 6l. and under 10l. at 9d.; 10l. and under 15l. at 1s.; 15l. and under 20l. 1s. 3d.; 20l. and all above, at 1s. 6d. The Bordesley Surveyors levy annually a rate of 5d. in the £. The Deritend Surveyors levy annually a rate of 6d. in the £.

"*Duddeston and Nechells Commissioners' Rate.*—Two rates are levied annually, 9d. in the £ each, together 1s. 6d. in the £.

"The poor rate for the whole parish of Aston is 10d. in the £.

CHAP. XIII.
1849.
Mr. Rawlinson's Report: Rates levied by various Bodies.

"N.B.—Aston has the benefit of belonging to a Union, which has very much reduced the poor rate. The borough rate in that part of Aston parish within the borough is made and levied by overseers appointed for that express purpose by the Council. Birmingham and Edgbaston being wholly situated within the borough, pay the borough rates out of the poor rates.

"In 1848, two borough or district rates were made in that portion of Aston within the borough, one at 10*d.* and one at 11*d.* in the £, together 1*s.* 9*d.* in the £.

"*Edgbaston.*—Poor rate, 1*s.* 10*d.* in the £. Highway rate, 9*d.* in the £. Lighting rate for part of the parish (Hagley Road) 6*d.* in the £.

"N.B.—The borough-rate is 1*s.* in the £ per annum. In Aston the borough rate is higher in consequence of not being collected with the poor rate."

The assessment for 1849 was returned to the Mayor's precept as follows:—

	£	s.	d.
Birmingham parish ...	462,025	1	7
Edgbaston parish ...	46,341	3	6
Aston within the borough	106,846	7	2
Total ..	£615,212	12	3

Comparison of Rating with 1878.

Thus, in the parish of Birmingham the rates levied for local government amounted to 4*s.* 1*d.* in the pound—namely, 3*s.* 1*d.* by the Commissioners, and 1*s.* by the Corporation; and for this amount of rating most inefficient service was rendered in a sanitary point of view—there was no general system of sewerage, the streets were imperfectly made, paved, and lighted, no special attention was paid to the maintenance of the public health, there were no free libraries, or parks, or baths, nor were any considerable town improvements attempted. In the present year (1878), when all the matters then omitted or inadequately carried out are undertaken and are thoroughly performed, under the sole authority of the Corporation, the rating for purely municipal purposes is only 3s. 9d. in the pound; thus giving probably more than double the work and advantages of 1849 with a considerably diminished burden on the ratepayers. Of course, the growth of the town in value has advanced with the amount of population and with the requirements of the municipal service, the assessment or rateable value for 1878 being £1,400,000 as compared with £615,000 in 1849; the yield of the markets has considerably increased, and a handsome contribution of £25,000 is made to the general funds of the Corporation from the profits of the gas department, the direct fruit of the spirited and sound policy which led to the purchase of the gasworks for the public benefit.

CHAP. XIII.
1849.
Mr. Rawlinson's Report: Comparative Rating.

From this abstract of Mr. Rawlinson's report the reader will have gathered much information as to the divided and chaotic state of local government thirty years ago, the cost of it, the hindrances which it interposed in the way of improvement, and the social and commercial state of the population. One feature of this method of government still remains to be noticed—

Sanitary Defects.

the result of divided authority and restricted powers upon the sanitary state of the town. Much evidence was taken by the Inspector on this matter, and when we look at the present state of Birmingham, and compare it with the condition reported in 1849, the contrast seems well-nigh inconceivable, and might be regarded as incredible, if it were not so formally authenticated.

The parochial medical officers presented reports on their several districts for Birmingham parish. The story told by them is uniform—long lists of streets continually or frequently affected by typhus fever, scarlet fever, dysentery, diarrhœa, measles, with occasional visitations of small-pox: diseases (excepting the last named) directly traceable to bad drainage, polluted earth, poisoned air, and contaminated water. Some of the officers report courts "covered with pools of stagnant filth," districts with "no water whatever," ashpits, &c., of indescribable filthiness. One of them describes a court in Sheep Street, which may be taken as a specimen case:—"There are 12 houses in it; one-sixth of its surface is covered with water, this runs into a cistern, from which it is pumped into a well as occasion may require." Another cites a court in Masshouse Lane—"The drainage is very bad; the water, mixed with the ashes and filth from the dust-hole, extends itself up the court to the fronts of the houses, to approach which, to see patients, I have been obliged to walk on bricks placed for the purpose, and the poor have been unable to prevent the filth from running into their houses." Mr. Rawlinson's own inspection confirmed these and other statements of the same kind, capable of being multiplied by the hundred. There are, he says, "about 2,000 close courts undrained, many unpaved, and where privies exist they are a source of nuisance."

Chap. XIII.
1849.
Mr. Rawlinson's Report.

"Many of these places I personally inspected, and found that want of water, of drainage, and of proper pavement to the yards was common. Many of the courts are closed in on all sides, and are entered from the street by a common passage; the privies and cesspools are crowded against the houses, and there is a deficiency of light and ventilation; there are about 336 butchers in the town, most of whom have private slaughter-houses crowded in amongst the cottages."

Appended to the Inspector's report are two statements of special value. They were prepared by Mr. Joseph Hodgson, F.R.S., and by Mr. Russell, two eminent surgeons, who then acted gratuitously as Medical Sanitary Inspectors to the Corporation. The length of these documents renders it impossible to reprint them, and their fulness of detail makes it difficult to present a satisfactory abstract. A few illustrative notes, however, may be grouped together to show the sanitary condition of the town. Mr. Hodgson's report comes first. It speaks very strongly of—

Testimony of Medical Officers.

"The condition of the privies, the mixens, and the surface of the courts. The common practice is that the manure is mixed with ashes and rubbish, and there it lies till the place is full. Disputes occur as to the liability to remove it, till it over-runs the seats, runs into the courts, and gives rise to noxious exhalations." Out of many hundreds of cases visited, no special

Mr. Hodgson's Report.

provision is made for the children; consequently they use conveniences in the houses, or convert the courts into closets. The privies are too few for the houses, they are "generally in a very conspicuous part of the premises, and it rarely happens that there is any door." Women are therefore subjected to gross annoyance—"they are obliged to pass their neighbours' houses, and be subjected to the annoyance of laughing and derision from the men." Ordure is consequently often kept in the houses, and emptied anywhere at nightfall; in other places, such as the Inkleys, and other Irish quarters, "the door is opened, and it is thrown out without the least reference to the spot where it falls, or anything else." Edgbaston, Mr. Hodgson reports, is not much better in some respects than Birmingham. "The public gullies or ditches of the town, in many situations, are made to answer the purposes of cesspools. In the Hagley Road the water-closets of some of the houses absolutely discharge themselves into the road. In the Bristol Road the same thing takes place." The drainage of privies and closets commonly runs into ditches and brooks, which become sewers, and these run into rivers, especially the Rea, which emits the most noxious exhalations. "I have seen it within this last summer, when it has been as black as a pretty strong solution of Indian ink; and it is to be found in that state, flowing as darkly as I tell you, till it arrives at Duddeston Mills, so that the froth of it, instead of being white, is brown." In a bend of the Rea [behind Great Barr Street] Mr. Hodgson finds a sort of sewage lake. "When the Warwick and Birmingham Canal was formed the natural course of the river was diverted for some purpose connected with the canal— they made a sort of loop to avoid going over the work twice; the consequence is that there remains a sort of lake, or inner place, or morass of filth, into which a part of the Deritend sewage is discharged. It is discharged into this Dead Sea, and it has no mode of getting out again; so there it lies to evaporate." Hockley Brook, a stream on the other side of the town, is described as being as bad as the Rea. Where the rivers cannot be easily got at, drains discharge into the canals; this having gone on so long that "the owners of property have acquired a prescriptive right." Mr. Hodgson describes the drainage of the town. "A very large portion of it is without drainage: out of 124 miles of roadway existing in 1848, only 43½ miles had sewage; and this does not include the courts and yards. In many places the old drainage is not of sufficient depth to drain the cellars; and where there are new sewers, properly made, the authorities have no power to compel houseowners to drain into them." Finally, Mr. Hodgson condemns the water supply, the slaughter-houses, the knackers' yards, the over-crowded state of the burial grounds, and the condition of the common lodging-houses.

<small>Chap. XIII.
1849.
Mr. Rawlinson's Report.</small>

Mr. Russell's report corroborated in a striking manner that which was presented by Mr. Hodgson. The defective drainage was very strongly condemned by this witness:—

<small>Mr. Russell's Report.</small>

"In those localities (he wrote) where this has not been provided, we see ditches and open spaces filled with foul, green-coloured, stagnant water, emitting disgusting odours into the adjoining atmosphere. The consequence of this neglect is strikingly conspicuous in the populous and wealthy district of Edgbaston; in the part of the Ryland Road and all along the Bristol Road, where public sewers are not laid down, the contents of water-closets either pass into the open ditch by the side of the road, or into dumb wells. A short time since one of these wells became overcharged, and it was necessary that it should be emptied. Men were engaged to perform this office at a remuneration of two guineas. On commencing their work the stench from the well was so horrid and overpowering that they refused to continue without a further sum of one guinea being paid them, and a pint of brandy allowed them every hour. These terms were acceded to them, but they again withdrew from their work, and could only be induced to renew it by promise of higher pecuniary reward."

<small>Dumb Wells.</small>

Similar nuisances, the writer states, exist in localities crowded with population, and "even close upon a street sewer, where either the cupidity or the obstinacy of individuals prevents the judicious precautions of the Commissioners against such places from being carried into effect." Great numbers of the courts, filled with houses varying from 3s. 6d. to 2s. 6d. per week, are described as being in a deplorable condition:—

"The drainage is very imperfect; often the drains are choked up at their outlet so as to be rendered useless. In some courts there are good drains, but the levels are so bad that the drains are useless. There is a want of good privy accommodation; in some instances there is none at all. The mixen and the ashpit form always one arrangement, the consequence of which is that in a short time the pit becomes full and choked with filth, and, being open to the weather, the liquid stercoraceous filth decomposes the mortar, and penetrates through the walls, and either flows into the adjoining house or shop, or is seen runing down the surface of the yard in streams. The powers of the Commissioners do not extend into these courts, and the occupiers are left to the mercy of the proprietors, who are sometimes too poor or too mercenary to remedy the evil, or are often shamefully indifferent to the comfort of their humble tenants."

Other nuisances are noticed by Mr. Russell: the numerous pigsties in the courts; the accumulation of town refuse, "deposited in large heaps in exposed situations, often in the middle of a dense population," there being no proper depôts for it; and the inefficient water supply. Appended to his report is a long list of streets which are in a hopelessly insanitary state, and are in consequence the abiding homes of fever. Evidence of the same kind is given by other witnesses; but it is needless to accumulate details,

One exception, however, should be made, in order to show the condition of Edgbaston, the wealthiest district, "the Court end of the town," as one witness described it. A number of residents in George Street (now George Road) presented a memorial, in which they stated that "not only the drainage of this street, but of a wide adjacent area finds its way into the Worcester Canal, which runs at the backs of the houses on one side of the street. One important drain actually discharges itself across the towing-path; and the surveyor of highways pleads that 37 years usage have confirmed a title to its use." Unless, the memorialists add, "some competent authority steps in to force sanitary regulations, the comfort and health of the inhabitants will continue to be sacrificed and put in hazard." Mr. R. T. Cadbury, a witness at the enquiry, deposed that "not only that street, but all the streets adjoining, are almost deluged with filth. In the Hagley Road the gutters are receptacles of drains and filth till they become in a most putrid state, reeking with the contents of water-closets in the finest neighbourhood of Birmingham." Several witnesses, Mr. Rawlinson says, "some of them Birmingham Street Commissioners, complained of the utter impossibility of constructing sewers as they were at present situated, and of the nuisances around their own houses." Mr. William Wills described the state of the Bristol Road, one of the most important highways into Birmingham from the south. "The contents of the water-closets are turned into the gutters. The condition of the locality is a disgrace to the borough."

CHAP. XIII.
1849.
Mr. Rawlinson's Report.

The Commissioners had induced Lord Calthorpe to make a sewer from this road into the River Rea; but when it was made, there was no power to compel the house-owners to use it, and so the nuisance continued unabated. Other complaints of want of power, and of the uselessness of conflicting authorities are given. One example may suffice. A Ratepayers' Protection Society issued in 1848 a report on the local government and its defects. Mr. Rawlinson quotes a striking passage, relating to the hamlets of Deritend and Bordesley:—

Deritend and Bordesley.

"The three Boards in Deritend and Bordesley have no powers for promoting the comfort and the health of the inhabitants. Where filth accumulates, there it must remain. The Surveyors of Deritend, the Surveyors of Bordesley, and the Commissioners of Deritend and Bordesley, make, levy, and collect rates. One Board professes to repair and mend the footpaths, and another the horse-roads, neither allowing the other to encroach upon its jurisdiction by even the removal of a stone. The external appearance of the hamlets has not been in the least improved during the last century. The stagnant filth and the putrid accumulations which are allowed year after year to exist in the several parts of Deritend, without any attempt at their removal, or any effort being made on the part of the authorities to relieve the industrious poor from the baneful effects of the atmospheric impurities they engender, are a disgrace to civilisation."

The Inspector's Conclusions.

On the evidence laid before him, and as the result of his own enquiries, Mr. Rawlinson reported the following recommendations to the Government:—

"Having fully examined the town and suburbs of Birmingham, I beg respectfully to recommend that the Public

Health Act be put in force; that the local power so necessary to cheap and efficient government may be consolidated, and that the whole sanitary work of the borough may be placed under one establishment.

"I beg respectfully to lay the following summary before the General Board of Health for their consideration:

"1. That the borough of Birmingham is not so healthy as it may be, on account of unpaved streets, confined courts, open middens and cesspools, and stagnant ditches.

"2. That excess of disease may be distinctly traced to crowded lodging-houses and want of ventilation in confined courts, and to the want of drains generally.

"3. That the present church and chapel yards within the town which are used as burial grounds should be closed.

"4. That a better supply of water should be provided, and that a perfect system of sewers and drains should be laid down.

"5. That public parks and pleasure grounds would be very beneficial to the working classes and their families.

"6. That a consolidation of the conflicting powers exercised within the borough would produce great economy.

"7. That the health of the inhabitants would be improved, their comforts increased, and their moral condition raised—1. By a perfect system of street, court, yard, and house drainage. 2. By a constant and cheap supply of pure water under pressure, laid on to every house and yard, to the entire superseding of all local wells and pumps, the water of which is impure. 3. By the substitution of water-closets or soil-pan apparatus (for the more expensive existing privies and cesspools), with proper drains to carry away all surface-water and refuse from the roofs, streets, yards, and water-closets. 4. By properly paved courts and passages, and by a regular system of washing and cleansing all courts, passages, footpaths, and surface channels.

"8. That these improvements may be realised, independently of any advantage to be derived from the application of town refuse to agricultural purposes, at the rates per week for each house and labourer's cottage here stated:—1. A full and complete system of house and yard drains, with a water-closet and soil-pan, and yard drain to each house, three halfpence per week. 2. A constant high-pressure supply of pure water laid on in each house, with a water-tap and waste-water sink to each house complete, for three halfpence a week. 3. Complete and perfect pavement to all yards and courts, with proper surface channels and grates, at one farthing a week each house. 4. Washing, cleansing, and watering streets, courts, foot-walks, and surface channels, at one farthing a week each house.

"9. That from the character of the soil in the neighbourhood of the town, sewage manure may be applied to the agricultural land by irrigation, with singular advantage, so as to increase its value to the farmer, and yield an income for the benefit and improvement of the town.

"10. That these improvements will increase the health and comfort of all classes, and reduce the amount of poor's rates.

"11. That the direct charges stated will be the means of a direct and indirect saving to the inhabitants generally, but to the labouring man especially, of many times the amount to be paid.

"12. That the outlay will not be burthensome or oppressive to any class of the community, as the capital required may be raised by loan, and the interest upon it reduced to an annual or weekly rent-charge.

"13. That the Public Health Act is not only necessary, but will be of the greatest advantage to the ratepayers generally, as it will render their public officers responsible, and make an annual published account imperative."

Acting upon Mr. Rawlinson's report, the Government, on their own motion, at once included Birmingham in the schedule of a bill applying the Public Health Act to a number of places; but a protest was immediately raised against this inclusion, and the name of the town was consequently dropped from the list. This was only reasonable, for a lively opposition sprang up in the town. Mr. Rawlinson's report was vigorously and even bitterly criticised, many of its conclusions were disputed, and its recommendations were contested with a vehemence which seems very strange when looked back upon from this distance of time. The controversy was general—in the privileged governing bodies, in the Town Council, at public meetings, in the newspapers. Opposition memorials were sent up to the central authorities from all the local bodies excepting the Town Council, from landowners and companies who thought themselves aggrieved, and from private persons who had interests to preserve or theories to advocate. It would be a wearisome and a profitless task to recount in detail all the movements and counter-movements which now took place. For more than twelve months there was incessant conflict between the Town Council and the Commissioners of the Birmingham Street Act—the other local bodies practically standing aside, and allowing these two to conduct the attack and the opposition respectively. The Town Council began (July, 1849) by referring Mr. Rawlinson's report to their General Purposes Com-

The Commissioners prepare another Bill.

mittee, with the view of taking measures to obtain a provisional order under the Public Health Act. This movement was followed by one on the part of the Commissioners, who (August, 1849) passed a resolution declaring that they recognised "the necessity of additional sanitary and other powers and regulations in the town, and hamlets, and places adjacent, with a view to the preservation of the public health." In conformity with this resolution, the Commissioners appointed a committee of their body to consider "the best means of carrying out these objects, keeping in view the natural drainage area and the principle of local self-government," and this committee was directed to confer "with other public bodies which may be comprehended in, or affected by, such improvements, powers, and regulations," in order to ascertain "whether these objects can be best effected, with a due regard to efficiency and economy, by a consolidation of the powers and authorities of the existing governing bodies." The interference of the Commissioners was not favourably regarded. The Duddeston and Nechells Commissioners made no reply at all to their invitations. The Deritend and Bordesley Commissioners declined to appoint a deputation to confer with them, on the ground that all necessary powers might be obtained under the Public Health Act. The Town Council passed a resolution affirming the desirability of obtaining a provisional order under the Public Health Act, and authorising the General Purposes Committee to confer with the Commissioners' Committee "with a view of providing, so far as may be possible, in the provisional

Resistance by the Town Council.

order to be laid before Parliament, and in the Act of Parliament for confirming the said order, for all matters calculated to improve the sanitary condition and amend the general government of the borough." The conference, thus limited, was not to the taste of the Commissioners, who immediately gave notice of their intention to introduce a bill into Parliament early in the following session. In this bill they proposed to make provision for the following objects— 1, to constitute the Town Council the sole governing body for municipal purposes, and to transfer their own powers and property to it; 2, to constitute, for drainage and other sanitary purposes, a district extending beyond the limits of the borough, and including parts of Aston, of King's Norton, and of Handsworth, defined by them as "the natural drainage area;" and for these districts they proposed to add to the Town Council (solely for sanitary purposes) members elected to represent the non-corporate parts of the borough; 3, to alter and amend the system of rating. By this measure the object of having one governing body within the borough would have been at best imperfectly effected, and confusion and difficulty would have been caused by the creation of a sanitary board in addition to the municipal Corporation. The Town Council, on their part, met the Commissioners by approving of a draft order for the introduction of the Public Health Act, and the consequent consolidation of all the governing powers in their own hands. The application was entertained by the Board of Health, and the provisional order was made,

CHAP. XIII.
1850.
The Commissioners' Bill thrown out.

and was laid before Parliament in a confirming bill, in the session of 1850. The Commissioners' Bill was also prosecuted in the same session; but it failed, a House of Commons' Committee reporting that the standing orders of the House had not been duly complied with. The Commissioners' Bill being thus disposed of, the Town Council now endeavoured to induce the Commissioners to support the application of the Public Health Act, as the only way of consolidating the governing powers, and of thus finally settling a question which had been in debate for so many years. The Commissioners met the proposal with a blank refusal. They were irritated because the Council declined to adopt their scheme of an extension of the borough boundaries so as to include "the natural drainage area," and they further resisted the Public Health Act on the ground that it was hostile to the principle of local self-government, because it conferred upon the Central Board the right of interference with the appointment of a surveyor and of a medical officer of health under the Act. The Commissioners not only refused concurrence in the application of the Town Council, but also entered upon active measures of hostility. They issued an address (drawn up by the late Mr. Toulmin Smith, one of their counsel) with the view of "showing that [on the grounds above stated, and others] the introduction of the Public Health Act into Birmingham would be unconstitutional, inefficient, and mischievous." They also took measures to oppose the provisional order in Parliament; and, to give effect to this opposition,

Commissioners oppose Public Health Act.

they induced Mr. Newdegate and Mr. Spooner, the Conservative members for the county of Warwick, to bring pressure to bear upon the Government. Once more in the history of Birmingham there was now repeated the discreditable spectacle which had been witnessed before the Charter of Incorporation was granted—the conflict of opposing parties, the adoption of legal measures to hinder each other, the employment of personal and political influence on both sides, and the despatch of rival deputations, which met and, so to speak, almost fought in the ante-chambers of the Government offices and the lobbies of the House of Commons. Ultimately, the Commissioners triumphed. The Government yielded to private pressure, or despaired of carrying through their measure in the face of a powerful opposition; and, without obtaining or even asking the concurrence of the Town Council, the provisional order applying the Public Health Act to Birmingham was withdrawn from Parliament. This resolution aroused the bitterest indignation on the part of the Town Council, by whom the conduct of the Government was vehemently condemned. The strength of the feeling excited may be inferred from the language used by Mr. Martineau, a leading member of the Council, and one who was remarkable for sobriety of judgment and moderation of tone. "The manner (he said) in which the Council had been treated by the Board of Health was most contumelious. He had never seen so much bad faith, positive duplicity, and pusillanimity displayed in any public body as had been exhibited in

Chap. XIII.
1850.
Contests in Parliament.

Council defeated.

CHAP. XIII.
1850.
Council Bill to amalgamate Governing Bodies.

the proceedings of the General Board of Health." This declaration, strong as it was, received the testimony of general concurrence in the Council.

Perhaps, however, though the failure was extremely irritating at the moment, it was the best thing that could have happened for Birmingham, since it led to the passing of a local Act which effected completely, and with many useful additions, the purposes contemplated by the Public Health Act, and which, at the same time, effectually excluded the control of a Central Board. This important work was mainly directed by the late Mr. Henry Smith, a man whose name, from the eminent services he rendered to local government, in promoting, and afterwards, as Mayor, in executing the Improvement Act, deserves to be held in honourable remembrance by the citizens of Birmingham. Under his influence the Council now (August 1850) resolved themselves to grapple with the chaos of conflicting misgovernment by preparing a bill to consolidate the governing bodies of the borough. Notice to this effect was given to the Commissioners, who thereupon appointed a committee to confer with the Town Council on the proposed measure; and the two bodies agreed upon a draft scheme. The Commissioners fought hard for the drainage area, for separate representatives from outside districts, and for other points which had been included in their own bill; but in each respect they failed—the boundaries of the borough being retained intact, and the whole of the

The Commissioners practically concur.

governing powers within the area being concentrated in the hands of the Corporation. The idea of central interference, however, still haunted the Commissioners, and in order to avert it they took powers to oppose the Improvement Bill before Parliament, and this enabled them in some degree to harass the Corporation by proposed amendments in Committee, a few of which were accepted, and others were rejected. In one instance the Town Council and the Commissioners acted cordially together, by uniting to oppose and to prevent the action of the Government, which desired to introduce into the Improvement Bill clauses which would have given a Central Board authority over certain corporate local officers. Into the details of the opposition, locally and in Parliament, it is needless to enter—the controversies of that day, not always intelligible even at the moment, have now lost all interest; the personal jealousies may well be left undisturbed. We are concerned only with the results, and this, thanks to the fidelity and the perseverance of the Town Council —the elected representatives of the burgesses—was the passing of the Improvement Act. The measure was introduced in the House of Commons in March 1851, and was at first threatened with a formidable opposition, from the Street Commissioners, the Duddeston Commissioners, the Governors of the Grammar School, the Gas and Water Companies, and the representatives of other public and private interests which were supposed to be affected by the provisions of the bill. By degrees, however, the opposition was conciliated, defeated,

CHAP. XIII.
1851.
Establishment of United Local Government.

or withdrawn, and on the 24th of July the Improvement Bill was converted into an Act of Parliament by receiving the Royal assent. Thus, after thirteen years of almost incessant conflict, the triumph of the representative principle was finally and firmly achieved; and there was established in Birmingham an united, complete, and unfettered system of local government, based upon the will of the inhabitants themselves, and adequate to all the purposes of public improvement, sanitary reform, and general administration. "The event (says the *Journal* of July 26) is an important one in our local annals, and though of late we have become familiarised with the idea of its speedy accomplishment, we have only to glance back at our position six years ago, when we were hopelessly working in favour of amalgamation, to measure the vast advance we have made in the application of the principle of responsible local government, and of a consolidated form of management, which, if prudently, economically, and fairly carried out, will assuredly tend to the mutual advantage of a community whose interests are in reality one and indivisible." Congratulations of a similar tenour were offered in the Town Council and in the Commissioners' body, and even those who had most stoutly opposed the passing of the Act now appeared to be satisfied with a measure which may justly be described as the second Charter of the town.

Causes of Success.

The comparative ease with which this great result was finally accomplished was due to various causes, but mainly to the growing conviction, which even those most opposed to the Corporation were unable to resist, that the divided state of government in the town rendered efficient administration impossible. The Commissioners of the Street Act—the principal governing body independently of the Town Council—had unquestionably exercised their powers with zeal and discretion, and with the strongest desire to promote the interests of the town; but their means and their authority were restricted, and, by the growth of public opinion, the principle of close election, the leading feature of their constitution, had become discredited. This was indicated very clearly by the changes of attitude which had occurred in the course of the twelve years which had elapsed since the grant of the Charter. The first Council, elected in 1839, included very few members of the Commissioners' body, and these were looked upon with great disfavour by their fellow Commissioners, and were, indeed, regarded as adversaries rather than as colleagues. By degrees, however, many leading Commissioners—notably Mr. Henry Smith, Mr. William James, and Mr. David Malins—became members of the Town Council, and their efforts exerted a powerful influence upon the movement for the transfer of the powers of the various local bodies to the Corporation; Mr. Smith and Mr. James becoming, in fact, the most strenuous advocates for amalgamation, and rendering important services in the preparation and promotion of the Improvement Act of 1851. The general body of the Commissioners followed the lead of the members just

Chap. XIII.

1851.

Gradual Decay of Opposition.

Conversion of leading Commissioners.

mentioned, and prepared with a good grace to surrender authority which they felt could no longer be separately exercised to the public advantage. A few of the Commissioners—headed by Mr. R. T. Cadbury, Mr. Arthur Ryland, and Mr. H. M. Griffiths—still held out to the last: accepting the transfer in principle, but seeking to incorporate in the Act their own peculiar views with reference to detail, and influenced, to the close of the proceedings, by vague alarms lest the interference of a Central Government Board should become possible through the provisions of the measure. Even the Duddeston Commissioners, represented chiefly by Mr. Henry Hawkes, were little more than half-hearted in their opposition—their efforts being directed chiefly to amendments in clauses, especially those affecting rating, and Mr. Hawkes, as a member of the Council, giving a general support to the Improvement Bill. This change of attitude on the part of the Duddeston Commissioners marked very clearly the advance of public opinion in favour of amalgamation, for in the notices for their own latest Act (obtained in 1845, notwithstanding the opposition of the Corporation) they actually proposed to repeal the Charter of Incorporation so far as the hamlets of Duddeston and Nechells were concerned! This attempt, of course, had to be abandoned, but the fact that it was made sufficiently indicates the feeling of hostility which then prevailed. It should be mentioned, however, to the credit of the Duddeston Commissioners, that, under the influence of Mr. Hawkes, they embodied the principle of popular representation in their Act of 1845, by abolishing the previous system of self-election, and substituting that of election by the ratepayers. Such a reform was greatly needed, for the government of these hamlets was in a deplorable state, and their sanitary arrangements, like those of the other outlying districts, were of the most primitive kind. A significant indication of this condition was afforded by the evidence given before the Parliamentary Committee in 1845, by a witness who described himself as the acting surveyor of the hamlets of Duddeston and Nechells. He was a saddler and beerseller by trade, he had received no training of any kind as a surveyor, but, for a salary of £30 a year, he boldly undertook the management of the drainage of the district, his qualification for this function being, to use his own phrase, that he was a kind of "universal genius." In his case, however, genius failed to supply the place of science. Amidst roars of laughter from Committee and counsel, he declared that "he never could see that there was any art in laying down sewers," that "he never had no instruction," that he knew nothing of the use of a spirit level, and that he "took levels (for sewers and roads) by three sticks: crow-sticks." After such an admission, it is not surprising to read in Mr. Rawlinson's report (1849) that the drainage of Duddeston was unsatisfactory—that "an expensive culvert of little or no use to the hamlets had been made, as one part is too low and other parts are too high, and that no side or cross street drains had been laid in." Obviously,

CHAP. XIII.
1851.

it was quite time to replace the "crow-sticks" regime by a system of a more intelligent kind; and this, as even Duddeston at last confessed, could be done only by establishing one authority throughout the borough.

General Sketch of Act.

Into the details of the Improvement Act of 1851 it is not necessary to enter. Generally speaking, the Act transferred to the Corporation all the powers exercised by the previously existing local governing bodies; and to these powers it added others which gave the Town Council complete authority over the roads, sewers, lighting, and sanitary arrangements of Birmingham, and also over the public buildings and other properties, such as the Town Hall, the Market Hall, and the market tolls and rights, acquired or constructed by the Street Commissioners. It also gave power for street improvements, for the removal of turnpike gates from within the borough, and for the purchase of the Waterworks (a clause which was allowed to lapse). The rating for the purposes of the Act was fixed at an Improvement Rate, for general purposes, not exceeding two shillings in the pound; and a Street Improvement Rate, for the purchase of scheduled properties, not exceeding sixpence in the pound. The formal transfer of the Commissioners' powers and property took place in December, 1851, and a report from the Final Arrangements Committee was forwarded to the Town Council, with an account of the Commissioners' property, &c., accompanied by a friendly letter from their Chairman,

Rating Clauses.

Final Transfer of Powers.

Mr. R. T. Cadbury, expressing the desire of himself and his colleagues that "the body to whom the great and extended powers are now confided may with united energy and patriotism carry out the important trusts reposed in them for the benefit of the community at large." A formal resolution of the Commissioners assured the Town Council of the "cordial good wishes" of the expiring body, and offered them all "the information which the experience of the Commissioners enabled them to give" in making their new arrangements.

These arrangements involved the general reorganisation of the work of the Corporation, and its division into departments, each under the charge of a special Committee. First, however, a deserved compliment was paid, on the 9th of November, 1851, to Mr. Henry Smith, the Chairman of the Improvement Bill Committee, by his unanimous election as Mayor, in place of Mr. William Lucy, who had also rendered efficient service in the promotion of the measure. This just and honourable tribute rendered, the Council proceeded to arrange its Committees for the transaction of the extended business entrusted to it by the Improvement Act. These Committees were settled, and their duties defined as follows:—

Finance (8 members) — to prepare and submit estimates of expenditure, and generally to have charge of the financial department of the borough.

Assessment, Rate, and Appeal (8 members)—to prepare and collect rates, and to hear appeals.

Estates and Public Buildings (8 members)—to take charge of all estates and public buildings belonging to the Corporation, and to manage the purchase of all lands required for public improvements.

Watch Committee (12 members) — to have charge of all matters relating to the Police Force.

Public Works (12 members)—to take charge of roads, sewers, paving, watering, lighting, and scavenging.

Markets and Fairs (8 members) — to have charge of the markets, fairs, and wakes; to regulate slaughter-houses, weights and measures, and to prevent the sale of unwholesome food.

Lunatic Asylum (8 members)—to carry out the provisions of the Lunatic Asylum Acts.

Baths and Wash-houses (8 members) — to superintend the baths and wash-houses.

General Purposes (8 members)—to take charge of all business and matters of a general character referred to it by the Council, not entrusted to the various other Committees; and to suggest to the Council, from time to time, any new business which, in its opinion, is important to the public interest.

The members of these several Committees were named by a Committee of Selection, but changes were made in them on the names being submitted to the Council. As finally settled, they elected the under-mentioned members as Chairmen, or, practically, as heads of the various departments under the new order of borough government:—

Finance: Alderman Van Wart.
Assessment, Rate, and Appeal: Alderman Hawkes.
Estates and Buildings: Alderman Muntz.
Watch: Alderman Martineau.

Markets and Fairs: Alderman Phillips.
Public Works: Alderman James James.
Baths and Wash-houses: Alderman J. H. Cutler.
Lunatic Asylum: Alderman Smith (Mayor).
General Purposes: Alderman Smith (Mayor).

Mr. J. Pigott Smith, formerly surveyor to the Commissioners, was appointed Borough Surveyor, at a salary of £600 a year (with the keep of two horses), and with Mr. John Heminsley and Mr. W. S. Till as his assistants, at salaries respectively of £100 and £80 a year. Mr. James Bliss was appointed Inspector of Nuisances, at a salary of £150 a year; and Mr. T. H. Fiddian was appointed Superintendent of the Rate Department, at a salary of £160 a year.

These nominations and appointments completed the arrangements required by the amalgamation of governing powers; and with this record it will be convenient to close the first period of the history of the Corporation, leaving to the second volume a general statement of the work undertaken by the Corporation since 1851, and a detailed examination of the progress made in the several departments of public business in the borough from the date just mentioned until the close of the present year.

CHAPTER XIV.

SUMMARY AND REVIEW.

<small>Chap. XIV.

Early Objections to the Representative Principle.</small>

The accomplishment of the work just described—the union with general consent of the governing powers of the town in the hands of a representative body—marks, in a most significant manner, the advance of public opinion towards the true principles of local government. The record of the earlier history of the Corporation shows that the Town Council, as the embodiment of the representative principle, was regarded at the outset with strong dislike and suspicion by an important minority, and was met with violent and persistent opposition. This was no merely local feeling; but is rather to be considered as an incident of the battle between privilege and popular control which was then being fought throughout the country, both in political and municipal institutions. The great wave of agitation which preceded and accompanied Parliamentary reform had scarcely begun to subside when the reform of the Municipal Corporations was undertaken by the Liberal Ministry then in power. The new movement was not less alarming, and was perhaps even more distasteful to the advocates of privilege and restriction than the more striking and general political measure

<small>Reform of Municipal Corporations.</small>

which had been passed in 1832. Vital as it was, and extensive and radical as were the changes it introduced, the Reform Act failed to come so closely home to the privileged class as did the Municipal Corporations Act, for while the former affected them chiefly as citizens of the State, the latter struck at once and completely at their local predominance, their social superiority, their personal authority, and their long-established power of dealing at pleasure with the rates and the property of towns governed either by self-elected bodies or by narrowly restricted franchises. The conflict thus initiated was conducted with considerable disadvantage on the popular side. The advocates of the new Corporations were not quite sure of their ground—the principles of local government, in a popular sense, were not then so well understood, so thoroughly appreciated, or so easily applied, as they are now. Traditional usage involved a certain sense of social inferiority as regarded their members. The localities which were benefited by the reformed Corporations, or by new Corporations established under the Act, were indisposed to submit to the additional burdens imposed upon them. An increasing rate shook the popularity of the recently created governing bodies. The electors grew apathetic, or in some instances even hostile, on discovering that their representatives enjoyed only divided authority and restricted powers. The Government which had passed the Municipal Corporations Act encouraged the difficulties of putting their measure into operation by neglecting or refusing to support those who, in their several

CHAP. XIV.
Difficulties of Pioneers of Local Government.

localities, were engaged in administering it. Evidence of this indifference is afforded by the course adopted by Lord Melbourne's Government with regard to the Charters of Birmingham, Manchester, and Bolton, and also with regard to the Birmingham Police Act. Ministers, indeed, seemed to take pleasure in discrediting their own work, and in favouring the policy of resistance adopted by its local and political opponents. Manchester, for example, was compelled to fight a long and costly battle in the law courts to maintain the right of corporate representative government bestowed upon it by Royal Charter. Birmingham saw its Charter questioned, its sessions suspended, its magistracy discredited, and its police force placed under a Government officer—and all this in consequence of the supineness or of the secret hostility of the very Ministers who had made local representative government one of the leading features of their policy. To us who, after the lapse of a generation, see municipal institutions powerful and accepted throughout the country, cherished in their various localities by universal consent, potential in Government departments, influential in Parliament, unchallenged in authority, and increasingly vigorous in operation, it seems hardly possible to conceive a period such as that above described, or to realise the difficulties encountered by the pioneers of local government, in the days when they had literally to fight for existence.

Special Conflict in Birmingham.

The conditions above indicated affected Birmingham as strongly, perhaps indeed more strongly, than any place in the kingdom, for local and personal considerations were brought out with marked force by the political characteristics of the borough, and by the antagonism between Liberal and Tory, and Nonconformist and Churchman, which had never wholly ceased since the Civil Wars, when Birmingham was mainly Puritan and anti-Royalist. This antagonism had again been exhibited with memorable fury in the Church and King Riots of 1791, when Priestley, burned out of house and home, chapel and laboratory, was driven to seek in the United States the safety denied to him in the town of his adoption and in the country of his birth. Still later, in the great agitation which preceded and compelled Parliamentary reform, the Birmingham Political Union, by the leading part it played in the conflict, had once more brought into high relief the local as well as the national strife of parties. To understand the dislike and distrust, amounting to hatred, with which the grant of a Royal Charter of Incorporation was received in Birmingham by the leaders of the anti-popular political parties we must go back to the conditions of that period, and recall to mind the fact that the new Corporation was the work of the most advanced politicians of the most advanced school, and that it was conceded to them by a Ministry hateful to the Tories, and doubted by many of the Whigs, as being in their view a Ministry influenced by democratic ideas and aiming at revolutionary designs.

It is creditable to Birmingham that under such circumstances, and in despite of the existence of such

CHAP. XIV.

Support received from leading Citizens.

a feeling, the new Corporation from the first attracted to itself the support and the services of some of the ablest and foremost citizens belonging to the Whig as well as to the Radical political sections. The names of Scholefield, Muntz, Beale, and others of the same stamp in the earliest lists of the Town Council, sufficiently indicate to Birmingham men the significance of these adhesions. It is creditable, too, that from that period to the present date—of course with the exceptions inevitable in a generation—the succession of such men has been maintained in the representative body of the municipality: that at all times, many of the burgesses foremost in ability, in means, and in public estimation have been willing to render long, and arduous, and self-sacrificing services for the promotion of the interests of the town, by taking a full share of its local government. It would be invidious, perhaps, to introduce names into a record of a semi-official character; but the fact is proved by the large proportion of magistrates who have passed through the Town Council or still remain members of it, and by the circumstance, honourable alike to the persons concerned and to the constituency, that of the nine representatives who have from 1832 been sent to Parliament by the borough, four of them—Mr. William Scholefield, Mr. P. H. Muntz, Mr. George Dixon, and Mr. Joseph Chamberlain—earned the confidence of the electors by important municipal work, all of them having filled the office of chief magistrate; while in the case of other members of the Council—Mr. Geach and

Members of Parliament and Magistrates in the Council.

Mr. Samuel Beale—the training received in our municipal work rendered them acceptable to the constituencies of Coventry and Derby respectively. Indeed, from the outset, the Town Council of Birmingham, always instinct with vigorous life, has proved a training school for public work; and through the operation of this educative influence we have reached a period so wholly unlike that which existed forty years ago as to render it difficult to recall, and impossible to realise, the conditions which then prevailed. Instead of a local government divided, exposed to fierce assault, discredited in its authority, restricted in its powers, and weakened by incessant conflict with rival bodies, we now have a representative Authority united, active, and powerful, linking together parties, sects, and classes in one interest and in a common pride in municipal institutions; an Authority which is thus enabled to undertake public works such as compare not unfavourably with the memorials of municipalities of historic renown; an adequate Representation of a community great in numbers, intelligence, and wealth, caring for and promoting all that concerns its good and orderly government, its health, its intellectual culture, its material progress, and its due place and influence in the affairs alike of the locality and of the nation.

The progress made in the development of a vigorous corporate life in the town has not, as the preceding pages may serve to show, been accomplished without laborious and long-sustained effort — nor without

CHAP. XIV.
First Period:
Conflict.

alternations of energy and of lassitude; of well-understood and firmly-directed purpose and of hesitating and divided counsels; of bold and lofty aims and of the ascendancy of a merely parochial spirit. Three periods may be broadly traced in the history of the Corporation. First in order came the struggles attendant upon the establishment of representative government—the recognition in local affairs of the true constitutional principle—ending in 1851, after a contest of thirteen years' duration, in the union of governing authority in one representative body: the crown and completion of a system which placed the administration of the borough under the guarantee of the consent and the

Second Period: Administration.

control of a self-governing community. Next came a lengthened and active period of administrative vigour— the construction of public works conducive to the health, the comfort, and the dignity of the municipality; this being accompanied and followed by the consolidation of corporate influence, and the gradual effacement of the active causes of hostility and conflict which marked the earliest period: an effacement so complete that even the memories of those days are recalled only in the record of the historian. By what was perhaps a natural change, the tension of this period of activity slackened, public interest became enfeebled, smaller aims occupied the attention of the Corporate body, personal rivalries and petty jealousies asserted sway, and many of the ablest and most influential citizens shrank from

Third Period: Revival.

taking their just share in local government. Happily for Birmingham, the third and healthiest period of its municipal history succeeded. The principle of abstention, always dangerous and often fatal, was abandoned. A higher standard of public duty was developed. Men who had made fortunes in the town, and had acquired leisure, began to feel that they owed to the community a debt of service, and that in doing work for others they were acquiring for themselves the reward of a loftier and nobler benefit than could result from the mere enjoyment of personal ease. For some years past the town has reaped the advantage of this truer view of the responsibility and the duty of individual members of a common society. To this revival Birmingham owes in a large degree its later and more vigorous progress in the development of municipal government—the keener interest taken in it by the burgesses—the more zealous, devoted, and unselfish labours of the representative body. Humble as such things may seem when placed beside events of national importance, it is no slight advance for a town to have entered upon three such undertakings as those which distinguished the mayoralty of Mr. Chamberlain: the acquisition of the gas and water works—thus extinguishing monopoly for the common benefit; and the prosecution of a great improvement scheme—thus recognising the duty of providing healthier dwellings and purer surroundings for the poorer classes. Nor is it an ordinary matter to have grappled with and solved one of the most perplexing problem of great communities, the disposal of sewage: a work with which the name and the labours of Mr. Avery are honourably associated.

CHAP. XIV.

Contrast of 1878 with 1888.

To look back over the period of forty years—from the development of corporate life in Birmingham as it now exists, to the feeble beginning of it in 1838—is like a feat of the imagination, so vast is the progress, so marvellous the contrast. When the Corporation first came into being Birmingham was a town of about 180,000 inhabitants, with an annual property (rateable value) of something over £400,000. Now it has a population of nearly 400,000, with a rateable value of more than £1,400,000. Then the total number of burgesses was under 6,000, qualified by a £10 rental; now the division of a single ward equals this number, and the total, under the qualification of household suffrage, rises to 60,000. There were then numerous independent governing bodies, each possessing restricted powers and limited jurisdiction, exercised with timidity, and derived from the unpopular source of self-election; now there is but one, invested with ample authority, acting with intelligent resolution, and based upon household franchise. There were then few public works of magnitude or public buildings of importance, streets were imperfectly made, sparingly lighted, inadequately watched, and partially drained; no provision was made for the recreation, the cleanliness, the health, or the culture of the artisan classes; the supplies of gas and water were monopolies worked for private profit; there was no local magistracy or superior administration of justice, no community of opinion or interest, no common bond of union in public life. Forty years of steadily growing municipal government have changed all this: supplied omissions, remedied defects, created public spirit, and given form and purpose alike to individual and corporate action. Much, doubtless, remains to be done; for the necessities of a great community are ever increasing, and successive years bring new demands, stimulate fresh efforts at reform, and open unexpected fields of administrative labour. But upon the progress actually made, and the spirit which has guided and animated it, Birmingham may look back with honest pride. The government of the town is in its own hands, free, unfettered, and complete. We have public edifices not unworthy of the place. Our streets are well kept, lighted, drained, and watched. We have means for the administration of justice by our own magistrates and in our own courts. The monopolies of gas and water have ceased to exist: these undertakings have passed into the hands of the community. The health of the population is cared for by an efficient system of sanitary measures; the means of cleanliness are afforded by baths and wash-houses; recreation is provided by parks and pleasure-grounds (some of them the gifts of public benefactors); and the opportunities of culture are offered to all classes in free libraries and museums of art. These benefits result directly from the institution of corporate government, for by such an agency alone could the force and the means of the community be directed to purposes of general advantage, or could there be evoked and sustained the true communal spirit necessary to the prosecution of common objects. The machinery by

CHAP. XIV.
Concluding Remarks.

which these results have been attained will be exhibited in its various departments, with some degree of detail, in a succeeding volume. Here it is possible only to sketch the work in its broadest features; and to say, in conclusion, that results such as those indicated have not been attained without long and patient labour, guided by no mere spirit of vestry politics, but with something of the statesmanship which must always enter into the right government of our great English municipal communities; a government directly tending to produce a real communal life, in all its freshness and variety, its freedom, the frank expression of its opinion, the opportunities offered to individual effort, and the force and vitality derived from union in a single purpose and a common interest. It is thus that municipal institutions, as we have them in England, not only fulfil the immediate objects of local government, but confer incalculable benefit upon the country, by training the citizens who serve in them to take their places in the wider field of national politics, and to share in the more conspicuous though scarcely severer labour of the administration of the State.

END OF THE FIRST VOLUME.

APPENDIX.

APPENDIX I.

CHARTER OF INCORPORATION

OF THE

BOROUGH OF BIRMINGHAM,

1838.

VICTORIA, by the grace of God, of the United Kingdom of Great Britain and Ireland, Queen, Defender of the Faith:—To all to whom those Presents shall come greeting.—Whereas, by an act passed in the first year of our reign, intituled, "An Act to amend an Act for the Regulation of Municipal Corporations in England and Wales," it was enacted—That if the inhabitant householders of any town or borough in England or Wales should petition his Majesty to grant to them a Charter of Incorporation, it should be lawful for his Majesty by any such charter, if he should think fit, by the advice of his Privy Council, to grant the same, to extend to the inhabitants of any such town or borough within the district to be set forth in such charter, all the powers and provisions of an act passed in the fifth and sixth years of the reign of his late Majesty King William the Fourth, intituled, "An Act to provide for the regulation of Municipal Corporations in England and Wales, whether such town or borough should or should not be a corporate town or borough, or should or should not be named in either of the schedules to the said Act for regulating Corporations in England and Wales," provided, nevertheless, that notice of every such petition, and of the time when it should please his Majesty to order that the same may be taken into consideration by his Privy Council, should be published in the *London Gazette* one month at least before such petition should be so considered, but such publication should not need to be by royal proclamation. And whereas, the inhabitant householders of the borough of Birmingham, in our county of Warwick, comprising the parishes of Birmingham and Edgbaston, and townships of Bordesley, Deritend, and Duddeston *cum* Nechells, in our said county of Warwick, did petition us to grant to them, the said inhabitants, a Charter of Incorporation, and notice of such petition, and of the time when the same was ordered to be taken into consideration by our Privy Council, was accordingly published in the *London Gazette*, one month at least before such petition was so considered. And whereas, afterwards, to wit, on the sixth day of October, in the year of our Lord one thousand eight hundred and thirty-eight, our Privy Council, after maturely considering the said petition, did then advise us to grant a Charter of Incorporation for the district comprised within the boundaries of the borough of Birmingham, in our said county of Warwick, as the same were settled and determined by an act passed in the second and third years of his late Majesty's reign, intituled, "An Act to settle and describe the divisions of counties, and the limits of cities and boroughs in England and Wales, in so far as respects the election of members to serve in Parliament." We, therefore, as well by virtue of the powers and authorities vested in us, as by virtue of the powers and authorities given to us by the said recited act, made and passed in the first year of our reign, do hereby grant and declare that the inhabitants of the said borough of Birmingham, comprised within the district hereinbefore described, and their successors, shall be for ever hereafter one body politic and corporate, in deed, fact, and name. And that the said body corporate shall be called, "The Mayor, Aldermen, and Burgesses of the borough of Birmingham, in the county of Warwick," and them by the name of the Mayor, Aldermen, and Burgesses, of the borough of Birmingham, in the county of Warwick, into one body corporate and politic, in deed, fact, and name, do for us, our heirs and successors, erect and constitute by these presents; and we do grant to the said body corporate that by the same name they shall have perpetual succession, and be for ever hereafter persons able and capable in law to have and exercise all the powers, authorities, immunities, and privileges, which are now held and enjoyed by the several boroughs named in the said Act for regulating Municipal Corporations in England and Wales, in the like manner, and subject to the same provisions as fully and as amply to all intents and purposes whatsoever, as if the said borough of Birmingham had been included in the schedule to that act annexed. And that the said Mayor, Aldermen, and Burgesses of the said borough of Birmingham, and their successors, shall and may for ever hereafter have a common seal to serve them in transacting their business from time to time arising within the said borough. And we further will, grant, and declare that the said Mayor, Aldermen, and Burgesses shall be able and capable in law to purchase, take, and acquire lands, tenements, hereditaments, and all other possessions whatsoever, to any value, situate, lying, or being, within the said borough : and also to purchase, take, and acquire lands, tenements, hereditaments, and all other possessions elsewhere, out of the said borough, not exceeding the sum of ten thousand pounds by the year; to have and to hold the said lands, tenements, and hereditaments, to the said Mayor, Aldermen, and Burgesses, and their successors, for ever. And we further will, grant, and declare that the council of the borough shall consist of a Mayor, sixteen Aldermen, and forty-eight Councillors, to be respectively elected at such times and places, and in such manner, as the Mayor, Aldermen, and Councillors for the said borough, named in the schedules to the said act for the regulation of Municipal Corporations in England and Wales, except that the first Mayor, Aldermen, and Councillors, for the said borough shall be respectively elected at such times and places, and in such manner, as hereinafter mentioned; and that the said Mayor, Aldermen, and Councillors, so to be elected for the said borough of Birmingham, shall respectively have, exercise, and enjoy, all the powers, immunities, and privileges, and be subject to the same duties, penalities, liabilities, and disqualifications, as the Mayor, Aldermen, and Councillors, of the several boroughs enumerated in the said act for the regulation of Municipal Corporations in England and Wales, so far as the same are applicable to the said borough of Birmingham. And we further will, grant, and declare, that the said borough, comprised within the district hereinbefore described, shall be divided into thirteen wards, to be respectively called Lady Wood Ward,

APPENDIX.

All Saints' Ward, Hampton Ward, Saint George's Ward, Saint Mary's Ward, Saint Paul's Ward, Market Hall Ward, Saint Peter's Ward, Saint Martin's Ward, Saint Thomas's Ward, Edgbaston Ward, Deritend and Bordesley Ward, and Duddeston *cum* Nechells Ward. And that the said Wards shall henceforth be respectively bounded and described as follows, that is to say—

LADY WOOD WARD

Shall be and include all that part of the town and parish of Birmingham, following:— that is to say, from the point at which the Dudley road crosses the boundary of the parish of Birmingham, eastward along the Dudley road, to the point at which the same meets Summer-hill road, thence along Summer-hill road, to the point at which the same meets the Parade, thence along the Parade, to the point at which the same meets Summer-row, thence along Summer-row to the point at which the same meets Great Charles-street, thence westward along Great Charles-street, to the point at which the same meets Easy-row, thence along Easy-row, to the point at which the same meets Broad-street, thence along Broad-street, to the point at which the same meets Islington, thence along Islington, to the point at which the same meets the boundary of the parish of Birmingham; thence westward along the boundary of the parish of Birmingham to the point first described. And that

ALL SAINTS' WARD

Shall be and include all that part of the town and parish of Birmingham, following:— that is to say, from the point at which the Dudley road crosses the boundary of the parish of Birmingham, eastward along the Dudley road, to the point at which the same meets Summer-hill road, thence along Summer-hill road, to the point at which the same meets George-street, thence eastward along George-street, to the point at which the same meets Brook-street, thence along Brook-street, to the point at which the same meets St. Paul's-square, thence along the northern side of St. Paul's-square, to the point at which the same meets Cock-street, thence along Cock-street, to the point at which the same meets Livery-street, thence northward along Livery-street, to the point at which the same meets Great Hampton-street, thence along Great Hampton-street, to the point at which the same meets Hockley-hill, thence along Hockley-hill, to the point at which the same meets the Shrewsbury road, thence along the Shrewsbury road, to the point at which the same crosses the boundary of the parish of Birmingham, thence westward along the boundary of the parish of Birmingham, to the point first described. And that

HAMPTON WARD

Shall be and include all that part of the town and parish of Birmingham, following:— that is to say, from the point at which the Shrewsbury road crosses the boundary of the parish of Birmingham, eastward along the Shrewsbury road, to the point at which the same meets Hockley-hill, thence along Hockley-hill, to the point at which the same meets Great Hampton-street, thence along Great Hampton-street, to the point at which the same meets Cock-street, thence along Cock-street, to the point at which the same meets St. Paul's-square, thence along the eastern side of St. Paul's-square, to the point at which the same meets the southern side of St. Paul's-square, thence along the southern side of St. Paul's-square, to the point at which Ludgate-hill meets

St. Paul's-square, thence along Ludgate-hill, to the point at which the same meets Church-street, thence along Church-street, to the point at which the same meets Colmore-row, thence eastward along Colmore-row, to the point at which the same meets Monmouth-street, thence along Monmouth-street, to the point at which the same meets Snow-hill, thence along Snow-hill, to the point at which the same meets Summer-lane, thence along Summer-lane, to the point at which the same meets Little Hampton-street, thence along Little Hampton-street, to the point at which the same meets Tower-street, thence westward along Tower-street, to the point at which the same meets Great Hampton-row, thence northward along Great Hampton-row, to the point at which the same meets Wheeler-street, thence along Wheeler-street, to the point at which the same crosses the boundary of the parish of Birmingham, thence westward along the boundary of the parish of Birmingham, to the point first described. And that

SAINT GEORGE'S WARD

Shall be and include all that part of the town and parish of Birmingham, following:— that is to say, from the point at which Wheeler-street crosses the boundary of the parish of Birmingham, southward along Wheeler-street, to the point at which the same meets Great Hampton-row, thence along Great Hampton-row, to the point at which the same meets Tower-street, thence along Tower-street, to the point at which the same meets Little Hampton-street, thence along Little Hampton-street, to the point at which the same meets Summer-lane, thence westward along Summer-lane, to the point at which the same meets Snow-hill, thence along Snow-hill, to the point at which the same meets Bull-street, thence along Bull-street, to the point at which the same meets the Upper Minories, thence along the Upper Minories, to the point at which the same meets Old-square, thence in a straight line, to the point at which Lichfield-street meets Old-square, thence along Lichfield-street, to the point at which the same meets Newton-street, thence along Newton-street, to the point at which the same meets Steelhouse-lane, thence eastward along Steelhouse-lane, to the point at which the same meets Whittall-street, thence along Whittall-street, to the point at which the same meets St. Mary's-row, thence along St. Mary's row, to the point at which the same meets Loveday-street, thence northward along Loveday-street, to the point at which the same meets Price-street, thence along Price-street, to the point at which the same meets Lancaster-street, thence northward along Lancaster-street, to the point at which the same meets New Town-row, thence along New Town-row, to the point at which the same meets Walmer-lane, thence along Walmer-lane, to the point at which the same crosses the boundary of the Parish of Birmingham, thence northward along the boundary of the parish of Birmingham, to the point first described. And that

SAINT MARY'S WARD

Shall be and include all that part of the town and parish of Birmingham, following:— that is to say, from the point at which Walmer-lane crosses the boundary of the parish of Birmingham, southward along Walmer-lane, to the point at which the same meets New Town-row, thence along New Town-row, to the point at which the same meets Lancaster-street, thence along Lancaster-street, to the point at which the same meets Price-street, thence along Price-street, to the point at which the same meets Loveday-street, thence southward along Loveday-street, to the point at which the same meets St. Mary's-row, thence along St. Mary's-row, to the point at which the same meets Whittall-street, thence southward along Whittall-street, to the point at which the same meets Steelhouse-lane, thence westward along Steelhouse-lane, to the point at which the same meets Newton-street, thence along Newton-street, to the point at which the same meets Lichfield-street, thence westward along Lichfield-street, to the point at which the same meets Old-square, thence in a straight line, to the point at which Upper Minories meets Old-square, thence along Upper Minories, to the point at which the same meets Bull-street, thence southward along Bull-street, to the point at which the same meets Dale-end, thence along Dale-end, to the point at which the same meets Stafford-street, thence along Stafford-street, to the point at which the same meets Aston-street, thence along Aston-street, to the point at which the same meets Gosta-green, thence along the western side of Gosta-green, to the point at which the same crosses the boundary of the parish of Birmingham, thence northward along the boundary of the parish of Birmingham, to the point first described. And that

SAINT PAUL'S WARD

Shall be and include all that part of the town and parish of Birmingham, following:—that is to say, from the point at which Church-street meets Colmore-row, westward along Colmore-row, to the point at which the same meets Ann-street, thence along Ann-street, to the point at which the same meets Paradise-street, thence along Paradise-street, to the point at which the same meets Easy-row, thence along Easy-row, to the point at which the same meets Great Charles-street, thence along Great Charles-street, to the point at which the same meets Summer-row, thence along Summer-row, to the point at which the same meets the Parade, thence along the Parade, to the point at which the same meets George-street, thence eastward along George-street, to the point at which the same meets Brook-street, thence along Brook-street, to the point at which the same meets St. Paul's-square, thence along the northern side of St. Paul's-square, to the point at which the same meets the eastern side of St. Paul's-square, thence along the eastern side of St. Paul's-square, to the point at which the same meets the southern side of St. Paul's-square, thence along the southern side of St. Paul's-square, to the point at which Ludgate-hill meets St. Paul's-square, thence along Ludgate-hill, to the point at which the same meets Church-street, thence along Church-street, to the point first described. And that

MARKET HALL WARD

Shall be and include all that part of the town and parish of Birmingham, following:—that is to say, from the point at which New-street meets High-street, southward along High-street, to Nelson's Monument, thence along Spiceal-street, to the point at which the same meets Jamaica-row, thence along Jamaica-row, to the point at which the same meets Bromsgrove-street, thence along Bromsgrove-street, to the point at which the same meets Hurst-street, thence along Hurst-street, to the point at which the same meets Smallbrook-street, thence westward along Smallbrook-street, to the point at which the same meets Suffolk-street, thence along Suffolk-street, to the point at which the same meets Paradise-streeet, thence along Paradise-street, to the point at which the same meets New-street, thence along New-street, to the point first described. And that

SAINT PETER'S WARD

Shall be and include all that part of the town and parish of Birmingham, following:—that is to say, from the point at which New-street meets High-street, southward along High-street, to Nelson's Monument, thence along the eastern side of the Bull-ring, to the point at which the same meets Digbeth, High-street, thence along Digbeth, High-street, to the point at which the same meets Park-street, thence along Park-street, to the point at which the same meets Bordesley-street, thence along Bordesley-street, to the point at which the same meets Ann-street, thence along Ann-street, to the point of which the same meets the boundary of the parish of Birmingham, thence northward along the boundary of the parish of Birmingham, to the point at which the same crosses the western side of Gosta-green, thence southward along the western side of Gosta-green, to the point at which the same meets Aston-street, thence along Aston-street, to the point at which the same meets Stafford-street, thence along Stafford street, to the point at which the same meets Dale-end, thence along Dale-end, to the point at which the same meets Bull-street, thence along Bull-street, to the point at which the same meets Monmouth-street, thence along Monmouth-street, to the point at which the same meets Colmore-row, thence along Colmore-row, to the point at which the same meets Ann-street, thence along Ann-street, to the point at which the same meets New-street, thence along New-street, to the point first described. And that

SAINT MARTIN'S WARD.

Shall be and include all that part of the town and parish of Birmingham, following:—that is to say, from the point at which Bristol-street crosses the boundary of the parish of Birmingham, northward along Bristol-street, to a point at which the same meets Bromsgrove-street, thence along Bromsgrove-street, to the point at which the same meets Jamaica-row, thence along Jamaica-row, to the point at which the same meets Spiceal-street, thence along Spiceal-street to Nelson's Monument, thence along the eastern side of the Bull-ring, to the point at which the same meets Digbeth, High-street, thence along Digbeth, High-street, to the point at which the same meets Park-street, thence along Park-street, to the point at which the same meets Bordesley-street, thence along Bordesley-street, to the point at which the same meets Ann-street, thence along Ann-street, to the point at which the same meets the boundary of the parish of Birmingham, thence southward along the boundary of the parish of Birmingham, to the point first described. And that

SAINT THOMAS'S WARD

Shall be and include all that part of the town and parish of Birmingham, following:—that is to say, from the point at which Bristol-street crosses the boundary of the parish of Birmingham, northward along Bristol-street, to the point at which the same meets Bromsgrove-street, thence along Bromsgrove-street, to the point at which the same meets Hurst-street, thence along Hurst-street, to the point at which the same meets Smallbrook-street, thence westward along Smallbrook-street, to the point at which the same meets Suffolk-street, thence along Suffolk-street, to the point at which the same meets Easy-row, thence along Easy-row, to the point at which the same meets Broad-street, thence along Broad-street, to the point at which the same meets Islington, thence along Islington, to the point at which the same meets the boundary of the parish of Birmingham, thence eastward along the boundary of the parish of Birmingham, to the point first described. And that

EDGBASTON WARD

Shall be and include all that part of the borough of Birmingham that is comprised in the parish of Edgbaston, in our said county of Warwick. And that

DERITEND AND BORDESLEY WARD

Shall be and include all that portion of the borough of Birmingham that is comprised in the hamlets of Deritend and Bordesley, in our said county of Warwick. And that

DUDDESTON cum NECHELLS WARD

Shall be and include all that part of the borough of Birmingham that is incorporated in the hamlet of Duddeston cum Nechells, in our said county of Warwick.

And that Lady Wood, All Saints', Hampton, St. George's, St. Mary's, St. Paul's, Market Hall, St. Martin's, St. Thomas's, and Edgdaston Wards, shall return three Councillors each respectively. And that St. Peter's, Deritend and Bordesley, and Duddeston cum Nechells Wards shall return six Councillors each respectively.

And we will further grant, and declare, that our trusty and well-beloved William Scholefield, Esq., do, on the tenth day of November, in the present year, make out an alphabetical list, (to be called the Burgess List,) of the inhabitant householders within the said borough, who shall possess the qualification required by the said act for the regulation of Municipal Corporations in England and Wales, to be possessed by Burgesses of any of the boroughs enumerated in the said act. And shall cause a copy of such Burgess List to be fixed in some public or conspicuous situation within the said borough, during eight days before the twentieth day of November, in this present year; and that every inhabitant householder so possessed as aforesaid, whose name shall have been omitted in such Burgess List, and who shall claim to have his name inserted therein, shall, on or before the said twentieth day of November, in the present year, give notice thereof to the said William Scholefield; and that every person whose name shall have been inserted in such Burgess List may object to any other person as not being entitled to have his name retained on the Burgess List; and every person so objecting shall, on or before the day and year last aforesaid, give to the said William Scholefield, and also give to the person so objected to, or leave on the premises for which he shall appear to be rated in such Burgess List, notice thereof in writing, which said notice shall specify the name of such person, the nature of the property for which he is rated, and the street or other place in the said borough where the said property is situated; and the said William Scholefield shall include the names of all persons so claiming to be inserted on the said Burgess List, in a list, and shall also include the names of all persons so objected to as not entitled to be retained on the said Burgess List, in a list; and shall cause copies of such several lists to be fixed in some public or conspicuous situation within the said borough, during eight days of December in this present year. And we do hereby appoint our trusty and well-beloved Horatio Waddington, Esq., barrister-at-law, to revise the said Burgess List, as well as the list of claimants and objections, on the eleventh day of December in the present year, in the manner directed in the said act for regulating Municipal Corporations in England and Wales.

And we further will, grant and declare, that the first election of Mayor, Aldermen, and Councillors for the said borough, shall be respectively holden as follows :—that is to say, that the first election of Councillors for the said borough shall be holden on the twenty-sixth day of December in this present year; and that the Aldermen of the said borough shall be elected and assigned to the respective wards on the twenty-seventh day of December in the present year, and that the Mayor of the said borough shall be elected on the twenty-seventh day of December in this present year. And we do hereby appoint our trusty and well-beloved William Scholefield to act as returning officer at such first election of Councillors of the said borough, with the same powers as by the said act for regulating Municipal Corporations in England and Wales are given to the Mayor and Assessors at elections of Councillors for the boroughs in the said act enumerated.

And further we will, and of our special grace have granted, and by these presents for us, our heirs and successors, do grant to the said Mayor, Aldermen, and Burgesses, and their successors, that they and their successors from henceforth for ever, may have and hold within the borough aforesaid, a Court of Record for the trial of civil actions, before the Mayor of the said borough for the time being, in any convenient place within the said borough, on the third day in every week, which court shall have authority to try actions of assumpsit, covenant and debt, whether the debt be by specialty or on simple contract, and all actions of trespass or trover, for taking goods and chattels, provided the sum or damages sought to be recovered shall not exceed twenty pounds; and all actions of ejectment between landlord and tenant, wherein the annual rent of the premises of which possession is sought to be recovered shall not exceed twenty pounds, and upon which no fine shall have been reserved or made payable.

Provided also, that every presiding judge of such court respectively, from time to time, may make rules for regulating the practice of such court over which he presides, but so that no such rules shall be of force until they shall have been allowed and confirmed by three or more judges of the superior courts of common law at Westminster.

Provided also, that no action shall be tried by any judge of any such court of record within the said borough, wherein the title to land, whether freehold, copyhold, or leasehold, or other tenure whatsoever, or to any tithe, toll, market, fair, or other franchise shall be in question in any action; and in case it shall appear in the course of any action in the said court, or shall be made to appear upon oath to the said court, that any such title as last aforesaid is in question in such action, that the jurisdiction of the said court in the matter of such action shall cease; and it shall be in the discretion of the said court to award costs against the party commencing the same.

Provided also, and it is our will and pleasure, that if a Recorder shall be hereafter appointed for the said borough, no issue, either in law or in fact, shall be tried and determined in the said court in the absence of such Recorder.

In witness whereof we have caused these our letters to be made patent. Witness ourself at our Palace at Westminster, this thirty-first day of October, in the second year of our reign.

By writ of Privy Seal,

EDMUNDS.

APPENDIX II.

ACT CONFIRMING THE CHARTER, 1842.
5 & 6 VICTORIA, CAP. 111.

An Act to confirm the incorporation of certain Boroughs, and to indemnify such persons as have sustained loss thereby. [12th August, 1842.]

WHEREAS, since the passing of an Act passed in the sixth year of the reign of his late Majesty, intituled an Act to provide for the Regulation of Municipal Corporations in England and Wales, Charters of Incorporation have been granted to certain Boroughs in England, in pursuance of the provisions of the said Act, and of the Acts afterwards passed for amending the said Act: And whereas doubts have arisen respecting the validity of the said Charters, and it is expedient that such doubts be removed: Be it declared and enacted by the Queen's most excellent Majesty, by and with the advice and consent of the Lords spiritual and temporal and Commons, in this present Parliament assembled, and by the authority of the same, that the said several Charters of Incorporation, and also all grants of separate courts of sessions of the peace, issued or granted to any of the said boroughs, and all acts or proceedings done or had in pursuance thereof respectively before the passing of this Act, shall be deemed good and lawful from the time of such several grants, acts, and proceedings respectively.

II.—And be it enacted, that every officer of any such borough, or of any county in which any such borough is situated, who was in any office of profit at the time of the granting of any such Charter of Incorporation, or of any grant afterwards made by his late Majesty or by her Majesty before the passing of this Act, whose office shall have been abolished, or who shall have been removed from his office, or who shall have been deprived of any part of the fees and emoluments of his office, in consequence of any such grant, shall be entitled to have an adequate compensation, to be assessed by the Council and paid out of the borough fund, for the salary, fees, and emoluments of the office which he shall so cease to hold, or for such part thereof as he shall have been so deprived of, regard being had to the manner of his appointment to the said office and his term or interest therein, and all other circumstances of the case; and all the provisions of the first-recited Act relating to the claim of any corporate officer for compensation, and to the manner of determining and securing the amount of such compensation, shall apply severally to the officers hereby indemnified: Provided always, that the statement to be delivered to the Town Clerks of the said several boroughs by the said officers shall set forth the fees and emoluments in respect whereof they shall claim compensation during five years next before the several times when the profits of their several offices were first affected by any of the said grants respectively.

THE "JOURNAL" PRINTING OFFICES, NEW STREET, BIRMINGHAM.

Lightning Source UK Ltd.
Milton Keynes UK
UKOW041502200212

187624UK00006B/180/P